'Volunteering is so important to our society but is so often misunderstood and misinterpreted. John Mohan brings together all the evidence in a compelling way to tell the real story of UK volunteering, and does a great service to academia, charities, policy makers and government. It's a book that has been needed for a long time.'
Dan Corry, Chief Executive, New Philanthropy Capital

'This long-overdue analysis is a welcome contribution to our understanding of the scope and impact of volunteering. Based upon a wide-ranging review of post-war trends, policies and practice, this thought-provoking critical analysis challenges widely held views on volunteering. It ultimately questions why policy makers and practitioners alike are interested in volunteering – and provides insights into how we might support it in the future. Volunteering shouldn't be taken for granted – and this analysis should inform volunteering policy and practice over the coming decade.'
Karl Wilding, University of Kent

'Volunteering is as old as time – both universal and politically highly contested. In this insightful panoramic view, John Mohan skilfully both interrogates the debate about volunteering and at the same time promotes its real and eternal value.'
Julia Unwin, Chair of Civil Society Futures Inquiry 2017–19

'This wide-ranging review of the data on volunteering will be valuable for anyone with an interest in this topic. For those working with and leading volunteers, it offers an accessible route into engaging with the breadth of academic data on volunteering, and to understanding the changing policy context within which it has been operating in recent years.'
Helen Timbrell, Centre for Charity Effectiveness

Volunteering in the United Kingdom

Manchester University Press

VOLUNTEERING IN THE UNITED KINGDOM

The spirit of service

John Mohan

MANCHESTER UNIVERSITY PRESS

Copyright © John Mohan 2024

The right of John Mohan to be identified as the author of this work has been asserted in accordance with the Copyright, Designs and Patents Act 1988.

Published by Manchester University Press
Oxford Road, Manchester, M13 9PL

www.manchesteruniversitypress.co.uk

British Library Cataloguing-in-Publication Data
A catalogue record for this book is available from the British Library

ISBN   978 1 5261 4551 2   hardback
ISBN   978 1 5261 4552 9   paperback

First published 2024

The publisher has no responsibility for the persistence or accuracy of URLs for any external or third-party internet websites referred to in this book, and does not guarantee that any content on such websites is, or will remain, accurate or appropriate.

Typeset
by New Best-set Typesetters Ltd

Contents

List of figures and tables — vii
Acknowledgements — ix

Introduction — 1

Part I Frameworks
1 Concepts and definitions: hunting Snarks and 'mapping volunteerland' — 15
2 Trends in voluntary action — 34

Part II Contours
Introduction to Part II — 53
3 Diversity and inequality in voluntary action — 55
4 Core and periphery — 75
5 Community-level variations in voluntary action: places don't volunteer, people do — 93
6 Circumstances, habits and trajectories: journeys into and through volunteering — 111

Part III Impacts
Introduction to Part III — 133
7 Do not expect miracles: the impacts of voluntary action — 136
8 Volunteering, employability and policy — 145
9 Volunteering, health and well-being — 162
10 Volunteering and civic engagement — 176

Part IV Changing contexts
Introduction to Part IV — 195
11 Demographic change, economic circumstances and attitudes to volunteering — 198

| 12 | Cultivating and conserving the spirit of service | 216 |
| 13 | COVID-19 and voluntary action | 231 |

Conclusions: Beveridge and the spirit of service 247

References 257
Index 286

Figures and tables

Figures

2.1	Trends in volunteering, 2001–23	38
3.1	Gender breakdown of roles in the voluntary sector	70
4.1	Civic core by qualifications, age and sex	82
4.2	Age, education and non-engagement, ages 18–69	86
5.1	Unpaid help (volunteering) and Townsend Index of Deprivation, English local authorities, 2008	98
5.2	Volunteering and male unemployment rates, Super Output Areas, Northern Ireland, 2011	100
5.3	Formal volunteering rates for percentiles of the distribution of a cross-classification of areas by region and deprivation, 2005–22	102
5.4	Formal and informal volunteering by quintile of deprivation, England, 2007–22	103
6.1	Sample of short-term volunteers' trajectories of volunteering, 1996–2011	116
9.1	Trajectories in GHQ scores by volunteering status and age, BHPS, 1996–2008	170
10.1	Predicted probability of voting at age 50, accounting for social class and volunteering at age 23	183
11.1	Comparisons of the enjoyment of activities in the UK, 1986 and 2014–15, for men and women aged 16–65.	206
13.1	Quarterly trends in volunteering, England, 2016–22	235

Tables

3.1	Analysis of characteristics of formal and informal volunteers, and non-volunteers, England, 2017–22	61

3.2	Analysis of characteristics of people occupying illustrative types of volunteer roles, England, 2017–22	72
4.1	Contributions of groups to voluntary effort, England, 2016–17	79
4.2	Characteristics of the civic core and those who are not engaged in volunteering or charitable giving	80–81
10.1	Relationship between volunteering and membership of groups and aspects of political engagement and interest	187

Acknowledgements

This project draws on experience and learning gained in the course of my work in the Third Sector Research Centre (TSRC), while holding posts at the Universities of Southampton and Birmingham. I begin by acknowledging the support of the core funders of that centre in its initial phases (Economic and Social Research Council (ESRC), the then Office of the Third Sector and the Barrow Cadbury Trust) and beyond (the Barrow Cadbury Trust), as well as the funders of numerous projects which in some way or other enabled the development of our work on volunteering: ESRC, the EU's FP7 programme, the Leverhulme Trust and the National Institute for Health and Care Research. I am also grateful to the University of Auckland for generously inviting me to the university as a Seelye Fellow (2020), which provided an opportunity to think about and present early versions of some elements of the book; in particular I would like to thank Alice Mills (Department of Sociology) for hosting me while there.

Anyone working on this topic in the UK has reason to be grateful for the funding provided from ESRC for the country's longitudinal resources (the birth cohort studies, such as the National Child Development Study (NCDS) and the British Household Panel Study and its successor, the UK Household Longitudinal Study). As well as the projects acknowledged here, the large number of references that are based on these data resources indicate their importance to longitudinal work by many scholars on the patterns and impacts of volunteering.

A great deal of what I have learned about the academic study of this topic is because I've had the pleasure of working with many people in TSRC and elsewhere on volunteering or related topics. I'd particularly like to acknowledge Matt Bennett, Vicki Bolton, Katherine Brookfield, Sarah Bulloch, David Clifford, Angela Ellis Paine, Naomi Harflett, Daiga Kamerade, Rose Lindsey and Andrew McCulloch. Over many years, I've been grateful for the advice of Karl

Wilding, who has been a constant source of ideas not just about changes in volunteering but also about the changing policy environment for voluntary action; he has also kindly commented on versions of this work and much else besides, often at short notice.

The bulk of the book is original to this volume in its present form but there are sections that draw on previous publications. Specific projects on which I have drawn in this book include extensive work sparked off by a collaboration with the Mass Observation Project; much of this was reported in an earlier volume (Rose Lindsey and John Mohan (2018) *Continuity and Change in Voluntary Action*, Bristol: Policy Press). In the present volume, Chapters 4 and 6 draw on that work and, in addition to Rose Lindsey, I would also like to acknowledge the contributions of Sarah Bulloch and Elizabeth Metcalfe. Longitudinal change in voluntary action was also the subject of a collaboration with the Centre for Longitudinal Studies, analysing the resources of the UK's 1958 NCDS in collaboration with Jane Elliott and Sam Parsons. That work led to publications by Vicki Bolton, Katherine Brookfield and Jane Parry which are discussed in Chapters 4 and 6. I have updated earlier work with Sarah Bulloch on the idea of a 'civic core' for this volume, which would not have been possible without Sarah's meticulous earlier research, for which I am very grateful. Sections of Chapters 8–10 draw in part on publications or theses by TSRC colleagues on volunteering and employability (Angela Ellis Paine, Daiga Kamerade, Steve McKay and Domenico Moro), volunteering and self-reported mental health (Faisa Tabassum, Peter Smith) and volunteering and political engagement (where I would like to express particular thanks to Vicki Bolton).

I would also like to acknowledge numerous other researchers, doctoral students and academic colleagues whose work has influenced the development of the ideas herein or contributed to individual pieces of research: Anjelica Finnegan, James Laurence, Pauline Leonard, Silke Roth, Peter Smith, Emma Taylor Collins, Arjen de Wit, Elisabet Doodeman, Paige Wilson, Paul Norman and Ellie Munro.

The majority of illustrations in this book are original to this volume, with the following exceptions. Figure 6.1 originally appeared in Rose Lindsey and John Mohan (2018) *Continuity and Change in Voluntary Action*, Bristol: Policy Press, and I am grateful to Policy Press for permission to reproduce it here. I acknowledge that Figure 9.1 was originally published in *BMJ Open* (2016) under a CC BY licence, in an article co-authored with Faisa Tabassum and Peter Smith. Figure 10.1 is an illustration from Vicki Bolton's doctoral thesis (University of Southampton, 2016) and I am grateful to Vicki for permission to reproduce it here. A version of figure 11.1 originally appeared in

Jonathan Gershuny and Oriel Sullivan's (2019) *What We Really Do All Day: Insights from the Centre for Time Use Research*, London: Penguin. I am grateful to the authors both for permission to reproduce this and for granting access to the data to redraw the illustration.

Much of the work was presented in various forms at conferences of the International Society for Third Sector Research, the Association for Research on Nonprofit Organisations and Voluntary Action, the Australian and New Zealand Society for Third Sector Research, the European Research Network on Philanthropy and the Voluntary Sector Studies Network. I'm grateful to participants in those generous and supportive networks for their feedback and tolerance.

Finally, I am enormously grateful, as ever, for the literary, editorial and emotional support of Ellie, Jenny and Clare.

John Mohan

[M]any were just volunteers trying to do the right thing, and then to do it again and again and again, without expecting pay, let-up, or thanks. If you take one thing away from this story, make it the wonderful web of mycorrhizal strands of human inspiration and effort that is being made every minute of every day, often unpaid, unseen and unheard, on behalf of your nature. (Roger Morgan Grenville, *Across a Waking Land*)

I think it would surprise even the Prime Minister if a register were to be made of everything done voluntarily in this country. (Anonymous writer for the Mass Observation Project, quoted in Lindsey and Mohan, *Continuity and Change in Voluntary Action*)

If one thing above all refutes the suggestion that Britain is broken, it is the strength of our Third Sector. It demonstrates, in essence, the very existence and resilience of civil society. Where that resilience or social glue has been washed away, families lack support, communities become fractured, and it is the job of the Government to support and help their renewal. (David Blunkett, *Mutual Action, Common Purpose*)

Introduction

In her film *From Kindness*, Michele Allen (2018) invites us to closely observe the activities of a group of people engaged in the restoration of old books. The film directs our attention to the care and deliberation with which these individuals approach this task. The setting is a library in a large English city which was established by public subscription some 200 years ago. A particular challenge for the library is that of maintaining its stock of books, many of which are very old. The library's response has been to fund the training of volunteers in bookbinding skills. A group of people meets regularly and, with materials supplied by the library, they are repairing books so they can be returned to the shelves. Only the hands of the individual bookbinders are visible, from which (as far as is possible to do so) we can judge that this is a mixed group, mostly white, and most likely (though not in all cases) beyond retirement age.

Advocates of voluntary action often refer to its value in bringing communities together; witness the view of former Home Secretary David Blunkett, who was concerned about the fracturing of communities (see this chapter's epigraph) and stated that active engagement in voluntary service would 'restore the glue of society' (Blunkett (2008), reported in BBC News, 2008). Glue holds books together, but the vital glue that makes the library's initiative work is the voluntary time and commitment of these bookbinders. Why do they carry out this activity for no financial reward, in a world in which, we are told, a neoliberal calculus pervades all aspects of social life?

Here are some possibilities. They appreciate the chance to use skills they themselves have developed and they find the task intrinsically worthwhile. They may wish to develop new skills, either for their own personal satisfaction or because it may help them in their search for employment. They have an interest in preservation generally, and perhaps a particular appreciation for old books, their aesthetic value and the skills embodied in them. They value what the library offers and perhaps wish to help secure the maintenance of this valuable resource for future generations of readers. They may just have a generalised desire to give something back to the community or have time on their hands and want to occupy it productively. They appreciate the companionship and conviviality of the activity, perhaps because it partly replicates the structure and social networks of the workplace.

How do we understand this activity? Would we describe it as unpaid work or unpaid help? If we were presented with nothing more than a picture of the activity we might say that it appears to resemble work: people are combining materials and skills in a purposeful fashion, with the intention of restoring an artefact. But what matters to classification here, adapting an illustration given by Pahl, are the social relationships within which the activity is embedded (Pahl, 1988). The bookbinders could do this activity for themselves at home, given the availability of tools, materials and a workspace; the beneficiary here would simply be the individual bookbinder, and he or she would be doing it alone. A picture or film of the activity wouldn't tell us whether the people involved were being paid for bookbinding or whether it was something they were doing purely for themselves. The bookbinders could also be paid employees of an antiquarian bookseller, restoring books for sale at a profit, or of a library service; if so, the core motivation might simply be one of earning a living. What differentiates our library from these examples is that the activity is unpaid, although travel and other expenses may be covered; no formal contract binds the volunteers to the library and no compulsion is involved in the relationship. Moreover, the ultimate aim is the long-term goal of preserving this important collection of books; there is no expectation of monetary gain for the library, which itself is a non-profit organisation, run by a volunteer governing body whose members also give their time unpaid. In that sense the activity is for a public purpose, rather than for the profits of a company or the private gain of an individual.

I don't know whether the participants would use the term volunteering at all to characterise what they do. In fact, individuals presented with open-ended opportunities to describe what they do in their spare time rarely seem to use the word volunteering. One example discussed in Chapter 11 is a study of how people aged 50 (chosen because they were participants in a longitudinal study of individuals) were asked to write about how they imagined what their life would be like 10 years later and how they would be spending their time. When individuals envisaged activities undertaken for the benefit of someone outside their own household, a widely used term was 'charity work'. This term doesn't feature, to my knowledge, in the ways questions are posed about voluntary action in British social surveys. But as we will see (Chapters 1 and 2), terminology makes a difference to how we ask people to report certain kinds of activity: if asked whether they give unpaid *help* versus whether they do unpaid *work*, the proportions assenting seem to vary even for activities that are broadly similar. In this field, 'methodology is destiny': how questions are phrased matters to the answers that are received, and therefore to the estimates generated of the prevalence and amount of voluntary action (Rooney et al., 2004; Dean and Verrier, 2022).

The potential motivations I've listed here do not exhaust the range of possibilities, and many of them appear in standard questionnaires about the reasons why individuals become engaged in voluntary action. Typically, these are a combination of perception of need, availability of time, wanting to meet new people and using existing skills or developing new ones. These are very generic categories of motivation which in practice may not correspond very well to a complex and overlapping set of reasons. Each member of the group will have a different biographical narrative about why they come together in this way. The same is also true of voluntary organisations, all of which could produce accounts of a large range of routine activities which justifiably can be said to constitute a 'kaleidoscope' of social action (Cameron, 2006). So this is a complex social phenomenon, but we ought not to forget that it is also one made up of the private actions of individuals. In view of this, should we measure it, and should volunteering become the object of political contestation? The quote from the unnamed writer for Mass Observation about the sheer scale of voluntary action suggests that any attempts at estimating its extent would reveal action on an enormous scale. Substantial resources have been devoted to attempts at quantification, and influential voices continue to call for the repetition and extension of such efforts. However, in the process, is there a risk of neglecting the ways in which voluntary action is woven into the social fabric of the entire country, in ways which are – as Roger Morgan Grenville suggests in the epigraph to this book – as invisible as the mycorrhizae which carry nutrients between plant roots and fungi, sustaining life as they do so?

No book of this kind can capture the diversity of voluntary action. We could all, no doubt, think of ways in which the contribution of volunteers touches our own lives, whether that be through supporting friends and neighbours, campaigning for social change or (as in Morgan Grenville's illustration) sustaining and improving the environment. Rather, this book is about the claims made for voluntary action and the expectations placed on it. To begin, I consider the attempts that have been made to measure and analyse volunteering.

4 Introduction

And I look at the ways in which the level of voluntary action has become a contested topic.

Measurement and politics

Measurement of what individual volunteers and voluntary organisations do inevitably runs the risk of, at best, comparing apples with pears and imposing homogeneity on diversity. At worst, it could squeeze out the essence of voluntary action which, for some, lies precisely in its intangible nature. But the figures are nevertheless impressive. Significant efforts have gone into measurement, with a perhaps idealistically high bar being set by the United Nations and the International Labour Organization's efforts to develop a unified methodology for the assessment of the contribution of unpaid work, including voluntary action by individuals, to the national accounts (ILO, 2011). Few countries have adopted that framework in its entirety. Some academic critics would consciously eschew such enumeration on the grounds that it is not the state's business to quantify the private actions of individuals, even if they are contributing to the solution of public problems, and that accumulation of such data is a prelude to efforts to bend voluntary action to the state's purposes (Rochester, 2013; Eikenberry and Nickel, 2016; Aiken and Taylor, 2019). But current high-profile commentators, such as Andy Haldane (formerly of the Bank of England), are convinced that British society is systematically underestimating the economic benefits of voluntary action; if only these benefits were more widely appreciated, he suggests, significant investment would flow into the promotion of it (Haldane, 2021).

Nevertheless, through a large range of surveys of households and individuals, we have around four decades of data on volunteering in the UK. Surveys of the use of time by individuals put the direct economic value of volunteering at circa £22 billion (ONS, 2017; see also Chapter 2 for further estimates and comparisons). Significant proportions of the population (generally around two-fifths) give some time, at least on an annual basis, to formal voluntary organisations. Some of the largest registered charities mobilise several tens of thousands of volunteers; around 750,000 trustees of charities in England and Wales carry out significant, often specialised, governance tasks (Clifford, 2020). Less immediately visible in public debates about volunteering, but again embodying substantial commitments, are the distinctive roles played by volunteers in supporting public services;

by some estimates, around 23 per cent of those engaged in volunteering do so in public sector settings (Low et al., 2007: table 4.2).

By any standards these are large numbers of people and substantial amounts of effort. The UK figures also compare reasonably favourably with those of other states (Chapter 2). Writing in 1948, William Beveridge's authoritative survey of voluntary action was confident that the 'spirit of service' was 'in our people' (Beveridge, 1948: 151). Reliable social survey data show that that spirit is still present in substantial proportions of the population. So there is a success story here. Unsurprisingly, governments have been keen to claim credit for their efforts in promoting voluntary action, and they have latched on to the potential benefits that volunteering might provide for society. They have done so because of diminishing returns in existing policy frameworks. As social policy analyst Malcolm Dean put it, 'it took the first half of the twentieth century for the country to recognise that charities could not provide the services that modern society needs; and the second half to realise the state by itself could not do so either' (Dean, 2013). For around half a century, governments have promoted voluntary action, albeit with varying degrees of energy and in different ways. This includes Labour governments, whose alleged historic hostility to the voluntary sector has been shown to be a myth (Deakin and Davis Smith, 2011). The Blair and Brown administrations were characterised by active engagement with the voluntary sector (Chapter 12), and voluntary action is arguably a decontested space as far as the main political parties are concerned (Kendall, 2009).

Governments therefore place faith in voluntary action and they also claim credit for conserving or promoting it. Since at least the millennium, when Labour first began to set aspirational targets for volunteering, the proportion of the population volunteering has been closely watched by both major parties when in government, and any signs of increases have been enthusiastically welcomed. In an early example, David Blunkett, the then Home Secretary, trumpeted a rise of 1.3 million in the number of people engaged in volunteering in 2003. By 2006, in his capacity as the Minister of Communities and Local Government, David Miliband claimed that the Blair government's promotion of a 'stronger culture of volunteering' had led to an increase in the proportion of the population volunteering through organisations from 47 to 51 per cent in four years (BBC News, 2004; Miliband, 2006). However, by the end of Labour's period of government in 2010, volunteering rates were statistically indistinguishable from where they had been when the survey that measured them was first conducted.

One might have expected the Coalition government to monitor volunteering closely, given the 'Big Society' policies promulgated by David Cameron (Prime Minister, 2010–16). Those policies clearly envisaged an expansion of the extent of voluntary action by citizens, but the government swiftly cancelled the Citizenship Survey, the key instrument for measuring volunteering in England and Wales, as part of austerity measures. This was on the grounds that it was more important to provide financial support to charities than 'hand out blank cheques to opinion polling companies'. The UK Statistics Authority disagreed (BBC News, 2011). Ministers were pressed on their own commitment to voluntary action, sometimes with embarrassing results during live interviews (BBC Radio 4, 2011; Street-Porter, 2011).

Though it was launched and relaunched on several occasions, the Big Society did not gain traction. The profile of volunteering was raised by the visibility of the distinctively attired unpaid volunteer 'Gamesmakers' in the 2012 Olympic Games. A short-term boost in volunteering rates was then evident in the first wave of results from the Community Life Survey (successor to the Citizenship Survey) in early 2013, leading David Cameron to welcome the evidence that 'millions more people' were engaging and Nick Hurd (the then Minister for Civil Society) to celebrate the reversal in the decline of volunteering (Gov.uk, 2013). Gushingly, Cameron announced in February 2013 that 'volunteering is up, charitable giving is up, and the big society is getting bigger'. In a 2015 debate, Conservative MPs claimed that the government had 'successfully reversed a long-term decline started under a Labour government' and that the 'volunteering legacy [was] one of the most extraordinary achievements' of the Olympic Games (Lindsey and Mohan, 2018: 70). In fact, this alleged increase was never more than a minor blip that was not statistically significant or sustained. Cameron may have hoped for a significant increase in volunteering but it failed to materialise. Instead, volunteering rates soon flatlined again. Although Theresa May (Prime Minister, 2016–19) expressed the hope that volunteering could be encouraged as part of her vision of a 'shared society' (May, 2017), the travails of her government, and acrimonious debates about Brexit, soon came to crowd out discussion of voluntary action, until COVID-19 brought it back to centre stage. There was an initial surge of interest in volunteering in the early stages of the pandemic but history repeated itself. The increase was celebrated, and proclamations were made about a turning point and a revived and more expansive vision of voluntary action, but the numbers of volunteers soon subsided and continued to do so (Chapter 13).

Think-tanks and prominent public commentators also contributed to the discussion. As with politicians, there were some overenthusiastic readings of evidence. The 'Red Tory', Phillip Blond, claimed (without providing clear evidence) that volunteering rates had doubled in the early post-2010 election period (Blond, 2010a), which he took to be a public endorsement of the Big Society. The historian Niall Ferguson put forward a declinist narrative in his 2012 Reith Lectures. He observed some year-on-year reductions in volunteering and noted that 'only one quarter' of the population engaged in formal volunteering through organisations on at least a monthly basis. He attributed this to a crowding out of voluntarism by the 'excessive pretensions' of the state (Ferguson, 2012). He really needed to show both that volunteering had declined and that that decline was attributable to state expansion. However, since voluntary action has continued to decline in a context of substantial post-2010 shrinkage in the size of the state, his contention stands in need of qualification.

What was to be done? The post-1997 Labour governments set targets of various kinds. Their vague aspirations (e.g. 'making substantial progress ... towards actively involving one million more people') were soon refined. The Home Office was expected, for example, to oversee an increase in 'voluntary and community sector activity, including increased community participation, by 5% by 2006' (Prime et al., 2002; HM Treasury, 2002). The post-2010 governments have avoided such directive aspirations, arguing, for example, that the form through which people contributed to their communities did not matter. Eschewing the targetry of New Labour, they have instead enlisted everyone in the cause, making indirect rhetorical statements such as the wistful use of the third-person pronoun – 'we could do so much more' – from the 2010 Giving Green Paper (Cabinet Office, 2010: 4). It's a rallying cry but also an excuse: it implicitly enlists the entire population in the cause, while saying little about the potential contribution that governments might make to creating the conditions in which citizens are able to engage actively in their communities.

Many supporters of voluntary action have focused on the importance to society of engaging rising generations in something which is so important to national identity. They are therefore supportive of investment in programmes to inculcate good civic habits. The underlying theory of change is that if under-represented groups are not presented with opportunities to engage, the country will witness an erosion of its social capital. Young people and the unemployed are key targets here, with substantial investments in youth-volunteering initiatives irrespective of which party has been in government since

1997. The risk, according to an influential commentator on the voluntary sector, is that such approaches involve strong overtones of social discipline and control. The policy repertoire imposes on young people combinations of 'supervised homework, national service, the cat [o'nine tails – a whip formerly used in the British Navy] or an avenging God, ... showing zero tolerance or at most compassion with a hard edge toward those who do not conform' (Deakin, 1999: 190). Such unreconstructed social control can be off-putting but it doesn't seem to stem the regular supply of proposals for the return of some form of national service (Valentin and Hawksbee, 2023) – the most recent instance of which being the 2024 Conservative manifesto.

What can reasonably be expected of citizens? It has been argued that rights are accompanied by responsibilities. In his influential conception of citizenship, T. H. Marshall argued that the extension of social rights through the welfare state carried with it a 'general obligation to live the life of a good citizen, giving such service as can promote the welfare of the community' (1950: 78). Should we, therefore, expect that those who receive state support should be penalised if they fail to become involved in their communities? The issue has occasionally surfaced. For example, and without a great fanfare, some local authorities began to consider rewarding the contributions people make to the community in prioritising housing allocations, by redefining working households as including those who volunteer at least 16 hours per week.[1] That is an interesting approach to enforcing responsibilities among citizens, which contrasts with the absence of rights enjoyed by volunteers in law (see O'Brien, 2011). The crossbench peer Lord Bichard controversially suggested that a pension penalty might be imposed on those elderly people who were 'not contributing in some way' to civil society. The obvious retort was that the great majority of that demographic group had paid their dues through taxation and national insurance and were already contributing extensive support to their family, neighbours and community organisations (House of Lords, 2013).[2] (Bichard later stated that he had merely been floating an idea rather than making a concrete proposal.)

---

[1] See *Municipal Journal, 15 June 2011*; for one example, see www.thurrock.gov.uk/finding-somewhere-to-live/prioritising-housing-applicants.
[2] See www.bbc.co.uk/news/uk-politics-20044862 for the reaction.

The challenge with public debate on volunteering is that it strongly focuses on headline figures, leading to unproductive exchanges of soundbites or controversial proposals involving degrees of compulsion. There is then an oversimplification of the extent of variation in engagement, and reductionist accounts of the causes of such variation. In turn this has the potential to lead to stereotypical representations of non-engagement and unrealistic expectations of individuals and communities, which carry risks if translated simplistically into practical recommendations. If we delve beneath the surface of what looks like a satisfactory aggregate picture in terms of levels of engagement – after all, significant fractions of the adult population engage in volunteering in the UK – there are substantial gradients and inequalities.

Structure of the book

In order to explore the contours of voluntary action the book begins with the question of definition. Voluntary action is not a simple concept with a universally shared definition. Social scientists distinguish between volunteering as unpaid *help* or unpaid *work*, and between *formal* and *informal* volunteering, and they also argue that the boundary between volunteering and other forms of unpaid work, such as caring, is a fluid one. I introduce key literature on the definition of volunteering and relevant conceptual frameworks for understanding it in Chapter 1. From there, Chapter 2 provides an overview to aid our understanding of trends in the amount and distribution of voluntary action. Trends over various time frames are considered, which is particularly important for a discussion of short-term impacts (such as those of the London Olympics or COVID-19).

The remainder of the book is divided into three parts. First, the *contours* of voluntary action are explored (Chapters 3–6). The presence and level of the spirit of service – to adapt Beveridge's phraseology – varies between people and places and over time. These chapters offer overviews of key structural features of voluntary action: who participates in it, the activities they carry out and the roles and responsibilities they hold (Chapter 3); how much effort people contribute, who contributes the most (what has been termed the 'civic core') and conversely who is not involved at all (Chapter 4); community-level variations in the extent to which residents participate in volunteering (Chapter 5); and the trajectories through which individuals pass, between engagement and non-engagement or between varying levels of engagement, over time (Chapter 6).

These chapters indicate substantial variations in voluntary action, but these alone do not justify intervention in an activity which by definition is about the choices of private citizens. What are the arguments for policies to support volunteering? And what do governments hope to gain through such policies?

The International Labour Organization has argued that volunteering is an 'essential renewable resource' for social development (UN Volunteers, 2022). That resource is valued because of its direct and latent benefits. The obvious direct benefits of volunteering are visible in terms of the volume of effort and the activities carried out, and we possess extensive data on numbers of volunteers and the imputed economic value of their activities. However, it's the indirect – or *latent* – benefits of volunteering that make the activity so attractive to policymakers, because of its apparent ability to contribute to wider goals of public policy. By latent benefits, I mean outcomes of an activity that were unintended and which emerge indirectly from a group or its collective activities. The indirect benefits of the activities of the bookbinders might be that those seeking work acquire new skills. Alternatively, group members see improvements in their well-being thanks to having both a sense of purpose and the social enjoyment of meeting with the group regularly. Other latent benefits claimed for volunteering could include increasing levels of political interest and civic engagement as a result of exposure to the perspectives of a broader range of people (see Chapters 8–10).

Such potential impacts have been seized upon and sometimes stretched a long way. For what is in many cases fairly routine social action, the claims for volunteering's benefits can appear implausibly grandiose, moving dramatically from the material (how much, where and when) to the ineffable (the transformative power of the voluntary spirit). In an introduction to the publication *Volunteering Works* (Ockenden, 2007) – a title which appears to answer its own question – Julia Neuberger made the following statement:

> It is this very elusiveness, the power of volunteering to act upon people in mysterious ways, that makes it *so powerful an intervention* – for those who volunteer, those who are helped by volunteers and the community generally that benefits from the contribution of volunteers.

However, before we get completely carried away, note that she added the rider, 'and that makes it so frustrating for government', recognising that whether or not those benefits actually accrue in practice is highly contingent and that there was a considerable divergence of views on how best to promote volunteering.

To introduce Part III on impacts, Chapter 7 discusses the general challenges that confront efforts to assess the latent benefits of volunteering. The substantive chapters consider the relationship between volunteering and labour market outcomes for volunteers (Chapter 8), the connections between voluntary activity, health outcomes and individual well-being (Chapter 9) and the impact of volunteering on interest and engagement in politics (Chapter 10).

These claims all rest on the latent benefits of voluntary action. It is unlikely that many individuals became involved in volunteering because they thought it would reduce their blood pressure or raise their level of political engagement, though some do report their belief that volunteering would enhance their employability. But through participating in such activities, it is claimed, individuals and their communities stand to benefit in those ways. That said, the evidence is not always conclusive: if volunteering were to be prescribed as a vitamin supplement ('vitamin V': Bekkers and Verkaik, 2015) we wouldn't really know what the appropriate duration, size and efficacy of the dosage ought to be, and no regular pharmaceutical intervention would get past the regulators if that were the case.

Part IV explores changing contexts for voluntary action in the future. Spirits – in the alcoholic sense at least – require careful conservation and distillation, under controlled conditions. That does not sound like a description of recent periods in British history. Consideration of what might happen to volunteering requires thought about interactions between demographic change, the attitudes of individuals and economic circumstances. Socioeconomic changes have effects in terms of changes in claims on the time of individuals and the resources they have available. Beveridge argued that there was a 'reserve of willingness to be drawn on if ways and means of dealing with people's more immediate needs can be devised' (Beveridge, 1948: 151): the economic security inaugurated by post-war welfare reforms would underpin the ability of individuals to contribute to society. But those circumstances no longer apply. In any case, people and communities 'do not always come when they are summoned' (Clarke, 2014) so we need to understand attitudes to engagement, especially in a context in which governments are asking their citizens to do more (Chapter 11). This is followed by reflections on the broad themes evident in government policies to support voluntary action, with an emphasis on the underpinnings of policy and the broad principles of it rather than on the detail of specific measures (Chapter 12).

Next, I reflect on voluntary action in the time of COVID-19 (Chapter 13) before drawing this volume to a close with a return to Beveridge's spirit of service and some scenarios for the ways in which volunteering might be supported in the future. The argument made is that considerable thought needs to be given to promoting an environment in which individuals have opportunities to engage in voluntary action and access to resources which enable them to take up those opportunities, rather than presenting volunteering as a necessity or obligation.

Part I

Frameworks

1

Concepts and definitions: hunting Snarks and 'mapping volunteerland'

Introduction

What is meant by the terms 'volunteer' and 'volunteering'? Let us revisit the illustration from the Introduction of a setting in which people are repairing old books and consider in more detail the social relationships within which that activity is embedded. First, the bookbinders receive no remuneration, though it is possible that some reasonable expenses are paid. Nor do they themselves benefit directly from the output of their activities, though there might be latent or indirect benefits such as the 'warm glow' impact of participating in voluntary action (Andreoni, 1990), which may have associated pay-offs in terms of improved individual well-being (see Chapter 9). The direct benefits accrue to the library and to those who are enabled to read the books. There is no compulsion in the relationship: the bookbinders are undertaking this activity freely and they can leave at any time. Finally, the activity is structured – it takes place in an organisational setting, run by a formally constituted voluntary organisation. As a result, it would conventionally be referred to as 'formal' volunteering rather than 'informal' or 'direct' volunteering (i.e. support given directly to individuals).

What the bookbinders are doing can therefore be said to satisfy the definition of volunteer work adopted by the International Labour Organization (2011: 13):

> [U]npaid non-compulsory work: that is, the time individuals give without pay to activities performed either through an organisation or directly for others outside their own family.

The term 'volunteer' originates in a Hebrew word meaning 'to willingly give' (Cnaan et al., 1996), so any activity that had entailed compulsion, in any form, would be ruled out. Extensions of such definitions might also include the requirement that some form of public benefit is generated by the activities in question, over and above the benefits to the volunteers.

This apparently simple definition belies the challenges that arise in terms of achieving an agreed understanding of volunteering which can then be deployed to estimate its scope and contribution. That is the subject of this chapter. We commence with a discussion of what people think volunteering is, by summarising the results of studies in which scenarios are presented to individuals about whether particular sorts of activities are considered to constitute volunteering. While pointing to broad common ground, these studies also indicate areas of uncertainty and debate. Then we consider how volunteering is measured in national social surveys, pointing to some of the risks and challenges posed in terms of imposing some sort of unity on this complex phenomenon. This takes us to a discussion of what are commonly referred to as key 'paradigms' in the interpretation of volunteering and a consideration of perspectives which have sought to explain patterns of volunteering, drawing on what are known as 'resource' and 'dominant status' models, and on the utility of notions of various forms of capital in the explanation of volunteering. These approaches have a tendency to treat volunteering as a unified and distinct object of study. Recent sociological work has challenged this view, seeing volunteering as an instance of work – only, in this case, work that happens to be unpaid – and argued that this is a more productive approach than analysing volunteering in terms of the motivations or psychological properties of volunteers such as character or a disposition towards altruism. As Taylor (2005: 122) puts it, 'altruism does not define the volunteer any more than self-interest defines the employee'. Finally, there is a discussion of the politicisation of the analysis of volunteering: which sorts of activity are prioritised and which are not?

What people think of as volunteering

Studies of the public's understanding of voluntary action offer participants a list of activities and ask them which they would regard as volunteering. The 1991 UK National Survey of Volunteering (NSV) offered brief descriptions of 11 activities and asked how strongly respondents considered that these constituted volunteering, with response options on a five-point scale (Lynn and Davis Smith, 1991). A subsequent US study by Cnaan et al. (1996) offered over two dozen scenarios of varying degrees of complexity. Dean and Verrier (2022) replicated elements of Cnaan et al.'s work on a student sample in the UK. The studies differ in the methods used but there is some consistency across them. Perceptions of some activities are unambiguous – in the 1991 NSV, only very small proportions did not regard blood donation as voluntary work; in Cnaan et al. (1996) the top-ranked item was being a Big Brother or Sister (this is a very prominent mentoring initiative in the USA). Others divided opinion; some three-fifths of respondents to the NSV stated that being a local councillor was 'probably' or 'definitely' not voluntary work (notwithstanding that it involves extensive unpaid commitments of time). Responses were clearly shaped by what Cnaan et al. referred as the perceived 'purity' of the actions described. That purity has several dimensions.

Thus, free choice is intrinsic to the whole concept of voluntary action, so one would therefore anticipate that unpaid work which involved compulsion would receive at best qualified approval. Perceptions that compulsion was involved led to items being regarded as less 'pure' forms of voluntary action. Indeed, community service mandated in lieu of a custodial sentence was placed at the bottom of the rankings in Cnaan et al. (1996) and Dean and Verrier (2022). However, compulsion doesn't just involve judicial sanction: what about community service that is required in some secondary education programmes in the USA? And to what extent do employees really have a choice in the case of a company that prides itself on employer-sponsored volunteering? Even where not mandated in school curricula, in recent times there has been so much emphasis on the value of volunteering in relation to post-secondary education – for instance, its importance in personal statements for university applications – that we can regard this as an area of moral compulsion.

As to rewards, there was general agreement in the NSV that 'helping people who have a special problem' counted as volunteering, but only around two-fifths agreed that that was the case when the qualification that those involved had received expenses or a small fee was added. That was three decades ago and few would now disagree that payment of expenses for volunteers is appropriate and necessary to overcome financial barriers to engagement. But what about free concert tickets, living allowances for residential volunteers, or educational scholarships or tuition rebates as a reward for service? Such incentives attached to particular forms of volunteering resulted in the items slipping down the rankings in the studies by Cnaan et al. (1996) and Dean and Verrier (2022). Incentive schemes – such as tuition remission in the USA, or even programmes in which students receive a basic living allowance – may be judged necessary to help reduce socioeconomic gaps in participation, but the element of reward means that the activity is not viewed by the public as being undertaken for its own sake. There are also cases where the reward is not financial, as in some educational qualifications which mandate service, such as the International Baccalaureate; the educational argument being made here is that there are wider societal benefits from an engaged and informed citizenry, but it remains the case that the individuals benefit from the qualifications they have obtained.

When it comes to the consideration of scenarios that included some element of benefit to the volunteer, all three studies showed that respondents were prepared to acknowledge that such benefits (whether to the volunteer, members of their family or even close personal friends) did not disbar an activity from being regarded as volunteering. The question of benefit to the volunteer was, however, of far less concern to study respondents compared to issues of compulsion and rewards.

Help, work, social action and the meaning of volunteering

If a social researcher were to approach you and ask whether you had undertaken any voluntary action in the past four weeks, without offering you any further guidance to assist your deliberations, you might struggle with the terminology. If contributing without pay to the activities of an organisation was an ingrained habit – perhaps a pleasurable activity indistinguishable from a hobby or a contribution that formed an integral component of religious observance – then a respondent might not identify it as a separate and distinct activity. Alternatively, you might be juggling, alongside your paid job, such a large number of unpaid roles that you could be forgiven for being unable to reflect in great detail about whether or not any or all could be thought of as voluntary action, and you might end up ticking the 'not applicable' box. Qualitative research does find examples of people who respond to social surveys by declaring that they do no voluntary work, yet in detailed accounts of their lives they provide ample evidence that they do (Brookfield et al., 2018a; Lindsey and Mohan, 2018).

Because there is no shared understanding of the meaning of the term, robust surveys take an indirect approach to questions about whether individuals have engaged in 'volunteering'. In the case of the Citizenship and Community Life surveys in England, respondents are first offered a list of types of organisation and asked about their involvement in them. Follow-up questions then ask not whether they have volunteered but about giving *unpaid help* to the organisations in which they claim involvement. Again, to prompt recall, they are offered a menu of possibilities, such as raising funds, engagement in committees, mentoring, providing transport and so on. Positive answers are taken as indications of *formal volunteering*: activities undertaken through formal organisational structures. To capture *informal volunteering*, which takes place in non-organisational settings, respondents are asked to recall acts of a more spontaneous kind oriented directly to support of individuals, such as providing advice, DIY, car repairs, cooking meals or assisting with shopping. The latter is sometimes characterised as 'direct' volunteering (Salamon et al., 2011).

The foregoing surveys are sometimes referred to as 'topical' surveys as they have a focus on a quite specific topic (such as dimensions of citizen engagement), so they are able to probe phenomena such as volunteering in some depth. This is in contrast to 'generalist' surveys such as the British Household Panel Study (BHPS), which gather data on a wide range of topics and consequently have less scope for detailed probing of specific issues. In that survey, respondents were asked about whether they carry out *unpaid voluntary work* as one of a series of options in a question about how they spent their *leisure* time. Note the inclusion of leisure and work in the same topic – potentially a source of uncertainty for the respondent, though no further contextual information was offered. The successor to the BHPS, the UK Household Longitudinal Study (UKHLS, from 2008) included a separate module on voluntary work and phrased its question differently. Respondents were asked whether they had 'given *any unpaid help or worked as a volunteer for any type of local, national or international organisation*'. There are clearly differences between the two ways of measuring volunteering ('unpaid voluntary work' versus 'unpaid help or work'), although in fact the estimate of the proportions involved is broadly similar across these two surveys.

These examples demonstrate variation in the different terminology used to measure voluntary action in surveys. Some surveys refer to unpaid *help*; in others volunteering is characterised as unpaid *work*. This is a field where 'methodology is destiny': the questions asked influence the results that are generated. It is known that individuals are more or less likely to recall certain elements of voluntary activity, depending on whether questions are posed in terms of unpaid work or unpaid help. Respondents do not necessarily possess a common, shared understanding of the distinction between unpaid work and unpaid help, and therefore surveys can generate quite different results depending on the methods and definitions used (Tarling, 2000; Rooney et al., 2004; McCulloch, 2011).

There are further measurement challenges. Notions of engagement are malleable (Sampson et al., 2005) and may change over time. Recent British discussions refer to a broader notion of 'social action', which appears to suggest a greater range of prosocial behaviours (Cabinet Office, 2015; DCMS, 2016). To capture this, additional questions have been incorporated into the annual Community Life Survey (in England), asking about unpaid activities such as setting up new services or resisting the closure of others, running local services on a voluntary basis and organising community events. There is particular government concern with the encouragement of social action among young people, defined very broadly as 'activities that young people do to make a positive difference to others or the environment' (#iwill, nd). A government-commissioned National Youth Social Action Survey helpfully offered respondents 26 prompts to help them recall whether they had undertaken such action. Notably, prompts in a section on 'campaigning for something in which you believe' specifically *excluded* party-political engagement (Ipsos MORI, 2014). Clearly, the inference to be drawn was that volunteering was a non-political sphere of activity.

There is also the question of the depth of engagement in voluntary action. Recent literature (Hustinx, 2001; Hustinx and Lammertyn, 2003; Macduff, 2005) has spoken of short-term and one-off voluntary acts: 'episodic' volunteering associated with reflexive and individualised approaches to voluntarism. It has also been argued (see Sampson et al., 2005, based on their longitudinal study of Chicago) that social action (particularly protest and campaigning activity) increasingly takes the form of one-off acts of mobilisation rather than regular participation through formal organisational structures. Survey questions based on the number of hours committed to volunteering, or the frequency with which it occurs, may not necessarily pick up such participation. There is something of a fascination with 'microvolunteering', or people doing small-scale voluntary acts while engaged in something else, but little systematic evidence on its scale (Heley et al., 2022), nor about online volunteering, through reliable national surveys.

Paradigms of voluntary action

How do we theorise and analyse voluntary action? One view is that three key paradigms – or analytical frameworks – for the analysis of voluntary action can be identified in academic debate: the dominant, civil society and serious leisure paradigms (Lyons et al., 1998;

Rochester et al., 2010; Lindsey and Mohan, 2018: 7–8). These three perspectives differentiate between voluntary acts in terms of motivation, organisational setting, field and scope for agency on the part of the volunteer.

The *dominant paradigm* is held to have been highly influential on public policy, although it is also criticised for its unduly narrow perspective on voluntary action. First, in terms of motivation, volunteering is merely presented as an altruistic act. Second, the areas in which voluntary action occurs are relatively narrow, namely the field of social welfare, to the exclusion of many other settings (recreational clubs and associations or campaigning and advocacy groups) for voluntary action. Third, the organisational context is one in which the activities of volunteers largely take place in the highly structured settings of large, professionally structured organisations. This belies the reality – in the UK – that the median income of charities (the principal organisational form for entities large enough to make financial returns to regulators) is around £20,000 and that most operate entirely through volunteers (not paid staff). Finally, these organisations confine the scope for agency on the part of volunteers, whose tasks are pre-specified in advance; they are treated as an unpaid element of the workforce. The implication is clearly that volunteering is an activity which exists primarily to support the delivery of public services in the government's task of enabling people to overcome social and economic obstacles, principally by driving up productivity in public services. While public funding was a key area of growth for the voluntary sector at the time Rochester et al. (2010) were writing about the dominant paradigm, barely one-third of voluntary organisations received it, and the great bulk of it was concentrated in a small number of large organisations (Clifford et al., 2013; Clifford and Mohan, 2016). Many millions of volunteers were engaged in organisations that had no public funding, nor were they at all engaged in relationships with the state. Yet such groups and activities received little attention, although some recent work has sought to correct this imbalance. The dominant paradigm may have been a valid characterisation of the thinking underpinning Labour government policy but in terms of research priorities there is a substantial body of work on small-scale voluntary organisations, which do not conform to the dominant paradigm stereotype (Dayson et al., 2018; McCabe and Phillimore, 2017).

Second, there is the *civil society paradigm*. Here, the motivation is not altruism but instead self-help or mutual aid, based on the ability of people to work together to meet shared needs, offer each other mutual support and campaign for social and political change. The organisational context is likely to be volunteer-run organisations or self-help groups, not agencies with paid managerial personnel; and members are not brought in to play particular, pre-specified roles. This leaves much greater scope for agency: those involved are as likely to be activists as volunteers: 'volunteers target people while activists target structures. The activist changes, while the volunteer maintains' (Musick and Wilson, 2008: 18). There is an argument that such forms of action have not always received the attention they deserve and that the space for critical debate in the UK's voluntary sector has in recent years been squeezed by an unsympathetic government (Aiken and Taylor, 2019), although the COVID-19 pandemic did result in the emergence of many mutual aid groups which have been the subject of some work (see Chapter 13).

The third paradigm is referred to as *serious leisure*: the systematic pursuit of a hobby or interest, which may be casual or more project-based (Stebbins, 2007). The motivation is intrinsic, not extrinsic: an enthusiasm for a specific form of involvement and commitment. It is particularly common in fields such as the arts, culture, sports and recreation. Volunteer roles can be as performer, practitioner, participant and/or administrator. The context may be large or small: an informal hobby group or a formal cultural organisation. There is little doubt that this field of activity is very large, but whether it is neglected is another matter. Lindsey and Mohan (2018: table 5.1) point out that sports groups and a broad range of groups characterised as 'hobbies, recreation and arts', as well as children's education (most likely parent–teacher associations (PTAs) and other voluntary actions in support of schools), are consistently at or near the top of rankings of the types of entity supported by volunteers in British surveys over four decades. There is extensive work on volunteers in fields such as arts, sport and recreation, which again somewhat contradicts the view that 'serious leisure' has been neglected as an object of research.

These broad classificatory paradigms are used to characterise the settings in which volunteering takes place and the kinds of actions carried out by volunteers. At times the dominant paradigm thesis can be overplayed: it is an attractive argument for pro-voluntarists as it rightly emphasises the agency and independence of voluntary organisations, but even at the height of the New Labour period only a minority of organisations received public money and were delivering public services under contract. And there is certainly an argument to be had about the shrinking space for voluntary action, with constant attacks on the allegedly politicised activities of charities, but again that is some distance from the concerns of the great majority of small, locally focused and volunteer-led organisations that make up the voluntary sector.

These paradigms provide a broad overview of the structure of the voluntary sector, but how exactly do individuals come to occupy volunteering positions? At times it feels as if the study of this process is reduced to analyses of psychological propensities and individual motivations. Long before the development of large-scale surveys of volunteering, Richard Titmuss expressed the concern that revealing the complex background to blood donation by individuals would require 'the insights of a Freud, a Jung and a Levi-Strauss' (Titmuss, 1970: 235). Since Titmuss was writing, a body of research by psychologists has emphasised the range of functions which can be fulfilled by volunteering, mapping these in the Volunteer Functions Inventory (Clary et al., 1996). The focus is on volunteers' perceptions of the benefits (personal growth, enhancement of skills, social integration, career benefits, protective (e.g. therapeutic) functions and having the opportunity to enact their personal values) that they themselves will gain from volunteering. The assumption seems to be that volunteering will take place if, having weighed up the costs and benefits, an individual concludes that net benefits will occur. As well as uncertainty as to whether these benefits accrue (Ellis Paine et al., 2013; Bekkers et al., 2015), one might question whether volunteering can be reduced to this type of calculus. Moreover, research on public perceptions shows that people are more likely to be perceived as a volunteer to a greater extent if their actions are seen to have a net cost to them, rather than a benefit (Cnaan et al., 1996).

These are also very broad typologies which may conceal as much as they reveal. They combine motive, setting and activity in a very generalised way. They differentiate between volunteering as altruism (whether pure or impure, in economic terminology) (Andreoni, 1990), a social phenomenon (involving relationships with others, including recipients of assistance, in which the question of social bonds and social solidarity is uppermost), a psychological phenomenon (a sustained or planned form of behaviour, which is influenced by personality traits) and actions informed by a sense of participation in an active democracy. As Hustinx et al. (2010) suggest, we should be wary of overarching theories of voluntary action because of the complexity of the topic, involving a range of acts in different contexts which have very different meanings to individuals, and because of the disciplinary range of perspectives on voluntary action.

These characterisations of voluntary action overlap, and the richness and multidimensional character of voluntary action is not reducible to these broad categories. Qualitative studies of volunteering characteristically find that respondents (such as those in studies by Brookfield et al., 2014 or Lindsey and Mohan, 2018) describe and characterise the voluntary action they undertake in ways which are not easy to pigeonhole. Altruism may or may not be recognised by participants in studies of volunteering; volunteers certainly characterise what they do as a social phenomenon, involving convivial interaction with individuals in much the same way as does any other leisure activity; and, as to active, participatory democracy (Eliasoph, 2013), respondents in what look like large-scale service delivery activities are vocal about the political dimensions of voluntary action (Lindsey and Mohan, 2018: chapters 5, 6; Roberts and Devine, 2004). Many voluntary activities that resemble work are not regarded as such by those who engage in them – though they could be a replacement for paid work, a route into or out of it, or a source of skills through which a volunteer might hope to gain paid work. Volunteers may characterise what they do as leisure even though its outward appearance is that of work – but maybe the activity that they regard as leisure is taking place in a different setting where the participant enjoys spending time, thereby contributing to well-being, or is offering an opportunity to extend the use of skills developed in a hobby. As an example, a continuum between leisure and work was an important theme of Naomi Harflett's (2014) study of National Trust volunteers – indeed, the activities of some of her interviewees could easily have been classed as either or both. The idea that people arrive at a particular volunteering position in an organisation purely as a rational choice expression of altruism is also undermined when one looks at case studies of individual organisations (see also Chapter 3). People occupy similar roles but have come to do so for multiple biographical reasons. Altruism, yes – but personal interests, self-interest and attachments to a cause, place or organisational setting will all help account for why an individual 'chooses' an activity. But this still poses the question of what resources are required for various forms of participation and who has the resources to engage. To understand that, recent work has begun to take a broader perspective on individuals' longitudinal journeys into volunteering.

Volunteering, work and the total social organisation of labour

A growing body of sociological research (Taylor, 2005; Hustinx et al., 2010) argues that research which focuses on functions that volunteering serves for individuals, and the motivations of those individuals, overlooks the contexts in which volunteering originates and takes place. Volunteering is inherently multidimensional and its study needs to be situated in the broader social, structural and cultural environment of the lives of those who engage in it.

Therefore, it has been argued that we should consider volunteering as part of the 'total social organisation of labour' (Glucksmann, 2005): all forms of work and non-work, paid and unpaid, are interconnected and have shifting boundaries. Volunteering cannot be studied as separate and distinct from other forms of work (such as unpaid care) and leisure. By and large, according to Rebecca Taylor, volunteering has been treated in an impoverished and narrow way. She argues that the concept of 'work' has been equated solely with paid employment and assumed to be solely about a self-interested search for economic reward, in contrast to unpaid work conducted almost entirely by women in the private sphere of the home. If volunteering is considered at all in such a framework, it is viewed as a 'selfless activity motivated by rewards that must be disinterested and, by definition, not work'. Taylor argues that this then leads to a reductionist view in which volunteering is treated as a matter of psychological disposition, character or altruism, and potentially presented as a natural urge that people have. It is thus placed beyond the reach of critique (Taylor, 2005: 122).

Such views sit uneasily with the complexity of the ways in which individuals become involved in voluntary action; with the complexity of motivations, both altruistic and self-interested, leisure and work, which underpin individual actions; and with the complexity of individual biographies (O'Toole and Grey, 2016). First of all, 'voluntary work, like domestic labour, has to be supported economically' (Taylor, 2005: 135). This requires understanding a person's unpaid work in relation to their paid work and their economic and social position. For this reason, Taylor calls attention to the limitations of approaches which treat volunteering as a unified phenomenon in a way that does a disservice to the distinctions between social classes in terms of unpaid work, between formal and informal voluntary activity and indeed between those who refer to themselves as volunteers and those who do not.

Why, after all, should the sheer range of activities that are carried out be subsumed under a collective soubriquet: volunteering? We might include 'any activity in which time is freely given to benefit another person, group or organisation' (Musick and Wilson, 2008), but the range of tasks encompasses governance roles for which high-level professional experience might be essential, actions to support vulnerable people through health or personal crises that require great sensitivity and empathy, occasional litter-picking in parks, and roles in rescue activities that are impossible without a high level of fitness and may entail severe personal risks. Accountants, lawyers, counsellors, local authority maintenance operatives and mountain or sea rescue personnel wouldn't be placed in the same categories of government socioeconomic classifications, so why does the study of volunteering persist in operating as if they did? Yet these differences are elided or ignored in the way that volunteering is analysed. Moreover – at least in those parts of the voluntary sector that have employees – volunteers and paid workers will be found operating in the same spaces. Overgaard (2019) gives the example of a social care volunteer helping a paid worker change bedding in a care setting. Both are doing the same work but one has done it for 30 years without financial reward. This raises important points about the definition and status of voluntary work. The fact that volunteering is unpaid, argues Overgaard, is simply accepted; what is not accepted is that volunteering 'is the unpaid opposite of paid labor', and therefore ought to be analysed in the same way. That is, in terms of the social relationships within which it is embedded. Overgaard suggests, therefore, that a more logical way to look at this is to consider the type of work that someone does, and then go on to ask whether that work is paid or unpaid. Rather than comparing unpaid volunteering in a religious organisation with volunteering in sport or outdoor recreation, instead ask how unpaid work within a specific domain compares with paid work within that domain (e.g., in Overgaard's example, are there substantive differences in the work done by volunteers from work done by paid employees?). A counterargument to Overgaard's view is that expressed by Musick and Wilson: if volunteering is thought of solely as unpaid productive labour then we lose its essential quality, as a gift of time, and we neglect its diverse meanings (Musick and Wilson, 2008: 6).

If we accept Overgaard's argument that 'volunteering is, in fact and above all else, unpaid labor', then ought volunteers to have the same rights and protections as employees? Conversely, how are employees to be protected from being undercut by unpaid volunteers? There are some guidelines to prevent job substitution so that, for example, if public services are transferred to voluntary control, any employees transferred have their current conditions protected. But what about the position of volunteers? Several British legal cases have determined that since employment requires remuneration, volunteering cannot be considered employment – even when obvious parallels with the nature of paid work have been drawn, such as the activities carried out or the presence of a contract (Morris, 1999; Royston, 2012). Overgaard and Kerlin (2022) show that US Fair Labor Standards legislation is in principle supportive of employment rights and remuneration for unpaid workers if they are engaged in activities that generate a surplus for their organisation (unpaid positions in retail activities would, strictly speaking, be regarded as engaging in a commercial activity and the authors point to the ambivalent position of certain categories of social enterprises). O'Brien widens the argument to a broader spectrum of rights for volunteers. She finds that European Union policy promotes volunteering on many fronts as long as they are not 'economically demanding, [thereby] placing the cost implications on citizens' (O'Brien, 2011: 74). In short, volunteering may be described as work, and it may have many characteristics of work, but those who engage in it do not have the protections of paid employees. Those who engage in it as a constructive activity while they are seeking work have also occasionally found that volunteering ranks behind working for a major retail chain for next to no remuneration, at least in the eyes of the employment services (Grice, 2013).

Explaining patterns of volunteering

As Taylor points out, volunteering requires resources, and an established finding is that volunteers are highly educated and have a high occupational status and high income. These patterns have been explained through what is termed a 'resource model' (Musick and Wilson, 2008; Wilson, 2000; Wilson and Musick, 1997). Voluntary work is simultaneously said to encompass productive work that requires human capital, collective behaviour that requires social capital and ethically guided action that requires cultural capital (Wilson and Musick, 1997: 694). As is the case with other forms of work, these practices require resources that are not evenly distributed across the population – hence Musick and Wilson's emphasis on the 'enabling resources' which are useful or essential for the performance of voluntary work (Musick and Wilson, 2008: 113) – and hence the uneven distribution of voluntary action across the population. In a related argument, David Horton Smith has argued that a 'dominant status model' can help explain why certain people are more likely to volunteer when they are characterised by socially approved or dominant statuses. The suggestion is that volunteering itself is a characteristic which adds to a person's prestige and respect (Wilson, 2000), or that those of dominant status are more desirable to organisations (Hustinx et al., 2010).

Resource theory seeks to account for the division of tasks and positions in voluntary organisations in terms of the differences in levels of competence and resources required for those positions. In contrast, dominant status theory focuses on symbolic power struggles inside volunteer organisations, with high-status and more powerful individuals occupying the most prestigious positions. While the case can be made that – at least in relation to socioeconomic gradients in engagement (Chapter 3) – the links between economic capital and volunteering are clear, there are challenges in terms of the operationalisation of concepts of social and cultural capital. Researchers therefore turn to the work of Bourdieu on these, and other, forms of capital to provide further insight.

Bourdieu argues that individuals' unequal access to resources will determine their position in a social hierarchy and the control they have over their own situation. Bourdieu distinguished several forms of capital – *economic, cultural, social* and *symbolic capital* – and his arguments have been applied in the discussion of volunteering (Eimhjellen, 2023; Meyer and Rameder, 2022; Harflett, 2015; Dean, 2016). *Economic capital* concerns not just income but other monetary resources and assets over which an individual may have control. *Cultural capital* can take various forms; it encompasses resources in the forms of knowledge, competence, tastes and practice. *Social capital* is related to an individual's social network, friendships and broader networks of connections, which may provide routes for individuals to access opportunities or resources. Bourdieu also developed the concept of *symbolic capital* to denote traits or characteristics which burnished the reputation or prestige of the capital holder. In the context of volunteering, such resources enhance the likelihood of accessing positions in voluntary organisations (Meyer and Rameder, 2022; Wilson and Musick, 1997: 709) in a manner which enables those who possess such capital to reinforce and enhance their status. Somewhat as anticipated in the dominant status model, recruitment of volunteers then reproduces social inequalities, by selection of people who share the characteristics and world view of those who are already over-represented among existing volunteers. Perhaps counter-intuitively, as Dean (2016) shows, even those charged with running projects designed to enhance access to volunteering end up recruiting precisely those individuals who seem most likely to fit in and accomplish tasks, rather than being those in most need of the opportunity to engage. Bourdieu's 'capitals' now form the basis for a growing body of work on patterns of inequality and stratification in volunteering, which points to the limitations of resource-based accounts of volunteering.

An emphasis on the role of social capital in enabling volunteering places substantial explanatory emphasis on the extensiveness of people's social networks and arguably reproduces a resource model (people of higher socioeconomic status join more organisations, and people with higher levels of human capital have more social ties; as

Concepts and definitions 29

these people have more extensive social networks and ties they then expose themselves to being asked to volunteer; Wilson, 2000; Wilson and Musick, 1997). Hence a key reason why 'some factors are associated with volunteering is that they increase the chances of being asked' (Musick and Wilson, 2008: 293). Arguably this privileges social capital and does not fully recognise the role of other forms of capital in enabling volunteering. Second, the suggestion is that higher levels of human capital are related to higher levels of volunteering because people with high levels of human capital have more social ties (Wilson, 2000: 224). The emphasis here is on the social capital that is created by human capital, which underplays the enabling elements of human capital in terms of skills and knowledge. The operationalisation of human capital may also be problematic. Some researchers have deployed income as a measure of human capital (Bennett and Parameshwaran, 2013; Wilson and Musick, 1997) rather than as a measure of economic capital. The issue here is that it may be the financial resources themselves which enable volunteering rather than the human capital with which they are associated.

A third limitation of the resource model is the restricted operationalisation of the concept of cultural capital, which is often framed in terms of religious belief and observance, on the grounds that a 'culture of benevolence is institutionalised in churches' (Wilson and Musick, 1997: 697). Even if (in a UK context) religiosity was not steadily declining, this would seem to neglect other aspects of cultural capital such as cultural tastes and practices. Nevertheless, these concepts are gaining currency in emerging qualitative and case study work in the field.

Visions of voluntarism: politics, inequality and voluntary action

There are disagreements not just about which elements of volunteering should be studied and how they ought to be studied. There is also contention about the interpretation of changing patterns of voluntary action, the role of state and corporate actors in promoting particular visions of change and the importance of measurement.

Informal and formal volunteering

First, much of the emphasis in studies of voluntary action is on *formal volunteering* – that which takes place only through structured organisational settings. An emphasis on formal engagement at the expense of informal volunteering – involving reciprocal help and direct support to neighbours – arguably underplays the significant contributions made by the latter to community functioning, reinforces an emphasis on middle-class conceptions (and perhaps stereotypes) of voluntary action and neglects other emerging forms of engagement (Taylor, 2005: 125–6). Informal volunteering largely involves direct interactions with people one knows – hence Salamon et al. (2011) speak of 'direct' volunteering. Such activity is particularly important to the extent that it enables disadvantaged neighbourhoods to deal with poverty, unemployment and social exclusion (Forrest and Kearns, 2001: 2141; Williams, 2003; see also Chapter 5). Socioeconomic dimensions of the difference between those who engaged in formal and informal volunteering are discussed by Egerton and Mullan (2008) and also in Chapter 3.

There are policy and political implications of the neglect of informal activities. In policy terms, there is little attention given to how (if at all) informal volunteering might be encouraged. Partly this is because the ad hoc and sometimes unplanned nature of informal volunteering, which may involve actions of short-term duration not taking place (by definition) in an organisational setting, does not lend itself to easy quantification. Nor, perhaps, as Dean (2022) suggests, does informal volunteering lend itself to developmental narratives regarding its instrumental value – for example, in relation to employability. Informal volunteering may well demonstrate a young person's possession of human qualities such as empathy and patience; it may be judged less likely to support the acquisition of skills that are directly transferable into paid work. This may be the reason why policies tend to focus on formal volunteering but, Dean argues, the result is that communities are criticised for what they lack – formal volunteers operating through organisational settings – rather than acknowledgement being made of the support networks that exist within them.

The political implications of the secondary importance attached to informal volunteering are thus that it devalues the contributions of large numbers of people. Ironically, of course, this argument was turned on its head during COVID-19, when there was an outpouring of mutual aid and of informal volunteering, as people turned out in large numbers to support residents in their immediate communities (Chapter 13). If, in a post-Covid future, society returns to business as usual, prioritising formal volunteering for its ability to enhance human capital and shore up impoverished public services, much will have been lost (for a similar – though earlier – argument, see Dowling, 2016).

The hybridisation of volunteering?

The nature of volunteering is changing as a consequence of social, economic and political forces, and Shachar et al. (2019) suggest that volunteering is taking on a hybrid character (Hustinx et al., 2010), as initiatives are introduced which, to a greater or lesser degree, test the limitations of the notion of volunteering as the exercise of free choice by individuals, pursuing causes motivated by altruism. Illustrations might include compulsory community service orders for convicts, conditionality attached to benefit payments, the moral suasion of university application forms and the 'fantasy of employability' promoted by educationalists (Chapter 8). Schemes that promote volunteering deploying various forms of incentives might also be included here. The promotion of corporate social responsibility initiatives might also be thought relevant, because of questions about how genuinely 'voluntary' they are. Some argue that the implied compulsion in such initiatives means we should recognise a new category of action: 'voluntolding' (Kelemen et al., 2017: 1253). Hybridisation also means that volunteering takes place in a range of organisational settings (Shachar et al., 2019: 252) and that new incentive structures are in place to reward volunteers (stipends, tickets for concerts, etc.). Because of the associations between volunteering and employability, or between a volunteer and his/her employer in the case of corporate volunteering initiatives, there are also questions about hybridised motivations. A novel feature has been the growth of 'third-party' initiatives to boost volunteering, led by governments, corporations, think-tanks and educational institutions (Haski-Leventhal et al., 2010). These initiatives may be pursued for their intrinsic value – such as strengthening the social fabric – or they may be associated with more instrumental goals, such as the burnishing of corporate reputations or the imposition of stricter conditional requirements on those in receipt of benefits.

Renewable resources

There are also competing interpretations of, and therefore policy responses to, the implications of these trends. Some researchers define their focus in largely managerial terms. They see volunteering as a renewable societal resource and, as with the resources that sustain life on the planet, are concerned about detecting unexploited reserves. Hence there is a stress on 'volunteerability' – mirroring neoliberal discourses about employability, this concept embraces whatever might need to be done to increase volunteering opportunities, to support and train those who might occupy them and to break down barriers that prevent people from engaging. In a recent extension of these arguments, Koolen-Maas et al. (2023) argue that volunteers can be thought of as a natural resource which is 'harvested, [and] requires different forms of management based ... on resource levels, propagation methods and sustainability needs'. As with the natural environment, they worry about the potential for pollution of the resource base. Possibly overextending the natural resource analogy, they distinguish three types of volunteer resource: wild salmon, farmed fish and marine zooplankton. Only one of these is flattering – the 'wild salmon', which refers to those highly prized but increasingly scarce traditional volunteers. The 'farmed fish' are the identikit products of standardised initiatives (corporate volunteering, university service-learning), while the 'zooplankton' float in the water, occasionally being sucked in large numbers into one-off initiatives (the 'Big Help Out' for the Coronation, perhaps). These all differ in terms of commitment, expertise and quality of service. The issue for volunteer-involving agencies is how best to identify, recruit and retain these types of 'fish' and provide an environment for them that supports their development.

This characterisation of volunteering as a matter of resource availability and the management of supply and demand is resisted by others, who point to the political and corporate interests behind the framing of volunteering policy as an issue for intervention. In such framings, volunteering is presented as a panacea for a large range of social problems. The solution, first of all, is to make more people aware of it. Thus, Salamon et al. (2004, 3) described the non-profit sector, including voluntary action by individuals, as a 'lost continent' on the socioeconomic map of the world, and prominent British public figures have taken up the cudgel. The former deputy governor of the Bank of England has argued that if only the true value of volunteering were represented in the national accounts, and its contribution genuinely recognised, investment in voluntary action would flow (Haldane, 2021). Then there are the multiple social problems to which volunteering can provide the solution – hence ad hoc campaigns promoting volunteering in key public services or pronouncements by think-tanks and individual members of elite groups about the ability of volunteering to resolve pressing social challenges. Such claims can be highly instrumental in character – as we see in Chapters 8–10, with the discussion of the impacts of volunteering. What these operate with is an unproblematic assumption that volunteering is a solution to the world's ills, and that what is required is more of it, without recognising the limits to such policies. As Shachar et al. (2019: 247) put it, there has come into being an assemblage of networks, mechanisms and discourses that makes volunteering a phenomenon that is 'delineable, stabilised and utilised' and is therefore amenable to political promotion. But these are also claims and proposals that operate within a narrow frame of reference, calling for greater engagement without simultaneously considering what sort of broader changes to patterns of work and social security support might be needed to support it.

By now it should be clear that volunteering is a multifaceted activity which resists easy classification, measurement and interpretation. Given the terminological profusion and confusion – help, work, action, altruism, activism – it is tempting to reach for the social science equivalent of Lewis Carroll's *Hunting of the Snark*. This allegorical poem describes an expedition which sets off in search of a mythical creature, the nature of which is poorly understood, although the leader of the expedition insists that there are 'unmistakeable marks' by which it might be identified; the search sets off guided by the most vague of maps; venturing deeper and deeper into the mist, the crew think they can see some sort of creature, but they are not quite sure what, and it vanishes as soon as they have seen it. Despite these challenges there remains confidence that the landscape of voluntary action can be mapped. Salamon et al. (2011) argued that, were all the world's volunteers resident in a single country – 'volunteerland' – it would have the largest adult population in the world. What do the contours of the volunteer landscape look like? That is the subject of the following chapters.

2

Trends in voluntary action

Introduction

According to the International Labour Organization, voluntary action represents an 'essential renewable resource' for social development (ILO, 2011). If it is indeed renewable, that might lead us to anticipate at least stability in rates of engagement. There are competing views about the ways in which such stability might be achieved. For conservative writers, the post-war advance of state intervention in welfare provision prompted claims that voluntary initiative would be crowded out. On the other hand, there was the view that supportive welfare state programmes would facilitate engagement. As the influential social policy academic Richard Titmuss put it, 'the ways in which society organises and structures its social institutions ... can allow the "theme of the gift" to spread among and between social groups' (Titmuss, 1970: 225). The argument was also made that rising living standards and the widening of access to educational opportunities would generate a ready supply of people with the time and resources to engage in volunteering. Such views were certainly evident in the public utterances of Margaret Thatcher and Conservative ministers from 1979 onwards (Brenton, 1985).

Testing whether long-term changes have taken place is not straightforward. There is no way of establishing a baseline, comparable with a modern social survey, about levels of volunteering in the early post-war decades. Hilton et al. (2012: 50–1) discern an apparent upturn in engagement by plotting 31 estimates of levels of volunteering between 1948 and 2010 and drawing a trend line through them. However, their figures were drawn from a disparate set of studies, often small scale and local, carried out for different reasons in different places and not employing a consistent methodology across survey sites or over time (Hilton et al., 2012: 50–1). It is difficult to draw firm conclusions from this set of surveys. This problem continues to be challenging. In a more systematic international review, researchers found variations in reported levels of volunteering in the UK ranging, from 1997 to 2010, between 2 and 48 per cent of the adult population. While they drily acknowledged the possibility that this signalled a 'dizzying array of gyrations' in volunteering rates (Salamon et al., 2011: 217), the sober explanation is that the variations were a function of survey methodology. The upper estimates came from a specialist survey of volunteering which provided respondents with as many as 39 prompts to aid their recall; the lower ones were drawn from time use diaries where individuals were simply asked to record what they had done in the preceding week, and those descriptions were subsequently classified by researchers.

Arriving at valid and reliable estimates of volunteer effort is important; prominent academics and stakeholders argue that, otherwise, its visibility is reduced, its economic weight is obscured, the scale of the contribution that volunteers make is not recorded and the country's ability to manage voluntary work is inhibited (Salamon et al., 2011). Aside from the direct benefits and economic value of volunteering, there are arguments that a strong tradition of engagement in voluntary action has latent benefits for societies through the production of social capital – the networks, norms and trust that facilitate collective action and social cohesion (Hall, 1999; Putnam et al., 1993; Putnam, 2000). The core of the argument is that social networks increase levels of public trust and enhance societal capacities for collective action. Citizen commitment to voluntary work featured as a component of Hall's influential work on social capital in the UK (Hall, 1999: 425). Measuring trends in voluntary action therefore forms an important part of an effort to capture its wider benefits. What do the data tell us?

This chapter reviews evidence from four key sources which shed light on different aspects of the anatomy of voluntary action in the UK. I begin with a consideration of survey data on volunteering (next section). The primary focus is on cross-sectional surveys of formal and informal volunteering by individuals, although some findings from longitudinal surveys are also discussed (in Chapter 6). Then I place these findings in international context by examining country-level variations and some of the underlying reasons for them (third section). This is followed by economic estimates of the scale of volunteer work, drawing principally on surveys of time use by individuals (fourth section). Finally, there are data on the settings in which voluntary action takes place: to what extent is volunteering occurring only or principally in voluntary organisations, and to what extent are these organisations (and the wider voluntary sector, of which they are a part) to be considered as 'voluntary' (fifth section)?

Aggregate trends in voluntary action, 1981–2022

While there has been a high degree of stability in volunteering rates for a large proportion of the past four decades, there is now evidence of a slow but steady decline. No individual survey has been conducted throughout that period, but from 1981 onwards numerous large-scale surveys, repeated at intervals, allow reasonably reliable statements about trends in volunteering over time. Most key surveys focus on England but others cover the whole UK, such as the BHPS/UKHLS, albeit not for the entire time period. Here I summarise the main trends; for more details and further discussion of trends see Lindsey and Mohan (2018: 61–71).

For cross-sectional surveys, data are available from various waves of the NSV (1981, 1991 and 1997); their successor, the Helping Out Survey (Low et al., 2007); the General Household Survey (GHS) (1981, 1987 and 1992); and the Citizenship Survey (2001–11) and its successor, the Community Life Survey (Gov.uk, 2012–). As for longitudinal sources, the BHPS asked individuals about volunteering activities at two-year intervals from 1996, as does its successor, the UKHLS. Beginning in 1981, with the NSV and GHS, we typically have at least one survey-based measure of voluntary action at the beginning and midpoint of each decade, and sometimes more than one. The main estimates of volunteering for the 1980s and 1990s are presented in Lindsey and Mohan (2018: table 4.1).

There are considerable variations in the estimates. Consider the proportions engaged in formal volunteering. The NSVs (1981, 1991 and 2006) reported the proportions involved in formal volunteering of between 44 and 59 per cent for annual engagement and up to 39 per cent for monthly volunteering. The GHS (1981, 1987, 1992) asked about voluntary work and generated estimates of around one-quarter of the population for annual involvement through the 1980s and early 1990s. The BHPS and Understanding Society give figures, since 1996, for the proportions engaged in unpaid voluntary work at least annually of around 20 per cent and circa 10 per cent for monthly engagement. In the Citizenship Survey (2001–11), reported rates of giving unpaid help to organisations are between 40 and 45 per cent (at least annually) and between 25 and 29 per cent (at least monthly). The Community Life Survey (2013–) for England shows, in recent years, a lower and now declining rate.

Much of this variation is a function of differences in the survey instruments used and questions posed to respondents (Lynn, 1994; Tarling, 2000; Rooney et al., 2004; Staetsky and Mohan, 2011). Lower estimates are from surveys in which volunteering has been measured with a single question, perhaps as one option offered in a question about leisure time, with little auxiliary information to aid respondents (BHPS, GHS, UKHLS). In others, a set or a sequence of questions was presented, including extensive prompting for recall of organisations in which the respondent was a participant and the nature and frequency of the activities they carried out (NSV, Citizenship Survey, Community Life Survey). We would therefore expect a higher level of recall and reporting of volunteering in those surveys than in the BHPS or UKHLS.

Thus, there is no single 'true' estimate of volunteering. However, we can confidently say that there has been much stability over time, because various surveys applied a consistent methodology for at least a decade and *within each of these surveys* estimates of voluntary activity varied very little. The GHS and the NSV both illustrate consistency for the Conservative administrations of 1979–1997; the BHPS shows little fluctuation in volunteering from 1996 onwards. The detailed investigations of the Citizenship Survey from 2001 to 2011, and the Community Life Survey, have shown relatively little variation over time until recently.

For the present analysis I use data for England from the Citizenship and Community Life surveys. There are more or less annual data, gathered in a broadly consistent way for over 20 years (with some variations, such as the move from interviews to a mixture of postal and web-based modes of delivery). Sample sizes are large – typically 9,000–10,000. I consider both formal and informal volunteering by frequency. The Citizenship Survey (2001–11) asked questions about formal volunteering (unpaid help given in an organisational setting) and informal volunteering (help given directly to individuals in the respondent's community) (see Chapter 1, and also Staetsky and Mohan, 2011). The subsequent Community Life Survey retained the same questions on volunteering.

Between 2001 and 2005 there were small increases in the proportion of the population engaged in formal volunteering, whether undertaken on a monthly or annual basis. There followed a slight decline to 2008–9, a sharper dip from 2008–9 to 2009–10 and a levelling out between 2009–10 and 2010–11. These changes were less obviously evident for informal volunteering, regardless of frequency. The more notable feature for informal volunteering is the drop from 2008–9 to subsequent years (see Figure 2.1).

The graph of change over time points to two periods in which more visible changes took place. The first is the period of recessionary conditions from 2008 onwards, which were associated with a significant reduction in the rates of informal volunteering, whether on a monthly

38 Frameworks

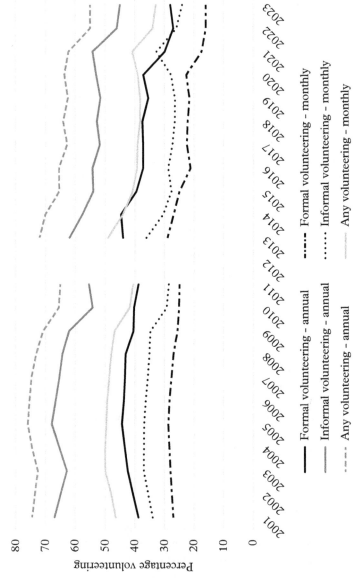

Figure 2.1 Trends in volunteering, 2001–23. Source: Citizenship Survey (2001–11); Community Life Survey (2013–23). Figures are percentages of adults aged over 16.

or less frequent basis. The proportion engaged *regularly* in informal volunteering dropped from 37 to 29 per cent between 2005 and 2010–11, while the equivalent figures for those engaged *less frequently* fell from 68 to 54 per cent. More fine-grained analyses point to the impact of recession on engagement (discussed further in Chapter 11).

To what degree was there evidence of a decisive subsequent upwards shift in engagement in the post-recession period and (simultaneously) after the 2010 election? If the public had been fired with enthusiasm for the Big Society we would have expected an increase. The first results from the Community Life Survey (2012–13) – covering the period August–October 2012 – appeared to indicate that volunteering had gone up, but note that those figures were for a period when the Olympics and the Paralympics gave volunteering a high public profile through the volunteer 'Gamesmakers'. It is possible that this was in the minds of respondents, prompting a certain amount of social desirability bias in their question responses. The full-year results showed that the 2012–13 figures were significantly higher than those reported for 2001 but otherwise indistinguishable statistically from most of the Citizenship Survey results for the post-2001 period.

The initial Community Life Survey results were greeted enthusiastically by Conservatives (see the Introduction). One claim made was of a decline under the Labour government, which had some statistical foundation, because volunteering rates for 2009–10 were, statistically speaking, significantly lower than those of five years previously. On the other hand, as convincingly shown by an analysis of quarterly survey data covering the period of the recession following the financial crash, much of the reduction after 2008 was due to exogenous economic events (Clark and Heath, 2014; Lim and Laurence, 2015; see also Chapter 11).

Despite what might be regarded as trendless fluctuation – year-on-year comparisons rarely indicated that changes from one year to the next were statistically significant – public pronouncements by government ministers and Conservative MPs hailed volunteering rates as a vindication of their policies (as we saw in the Introduction). In this regard they were no different from their Labour predecessors, who had also welcomed short-term increases in the mid-2000s. The best that can be said about these claims is that they are going somewhat beyond the limits of the evidence – it was indisputable that volunteering rates had changed, though the changes were not substantial or statistically significant; the question was how much of the change could be attributed to government action.

Subsequent Community Life Surveys have shown that volunteering levels initially flatlined for the period up to 2019. The COVID-19 pandemic provided another boost to voluntary action but its impacts differed in important qualitative senses, which are considered in more detail in Chapter 13. COVID-19 was associated with a rise in informal voluntary activities, notably through people providing direct support to their neighbours. Conversely, lockdown restrictions meant that much formal volunteering, of the kind that took place in organisational settings, was restricted. As a result, Figure 2.1 shows the second most notable feature of changes in volunteering rates in recent times: an upturn in *informal* volunteering in 2020 mirrored by a decline in the level of formal engagement, though for both types of volunteering there was a return to previous levels of engagement in 2021. Data for 2021–2, however, then suggest further, and quite dramatic, reductions, particularly in monthly formal volunteering, which fell to one-sixth of the adult population. To give an idea of the scale of these reductions, this figure equates to 55 per cent of the largest ever reports of monthly formal volunteering (29 per cent in 2005 and 2012–13). For annual formal volunteering, the 2021–2 figure (27 per cent) is now three-fifths of the proportions recorded in 2005, 2012–13 and 2014–15 (44, 44 and 45 per cent respectively).

It is possible that this could reflect changes in the way people classify their activities. The monthly figures for formal and informal volunteering move in opposite directions between 2019–20 and 2020–1, which would presumably reflect the impact of lockdown and social distancing restrictions on formal (i.e. organisation-based) volunteering. We know that voluntary organisations adapted swiftly to the pandemic (Chapter 13), delivering many services in different ways (not all online), so we cannot rule out the possibility that survey respondents placed, in the 'informal' volunteering category, activities that had previously taken place in organisational settings ('formal' volunteering). We might therefore prefer to examine the proportion of people engaged in helping others – regardless of whether they were doing so 'formally' or 'informally'. This is now some 55 per cent of the population – or approximately three-quarters of what it was in 2012–13.

In short, bringing together a comprehensive range of survey datasets, there is evidence, broadly, of stability in volunteering rates over most of the post-1979 period, as measured in terms of the proportion of the population engaged in volunteering. Within the overall trends some short-term changes can be detected – such as clear recessionary impacts around and after 2008, a small upward shift in 2012 and an initial response to COVID-19 which does not appear to have been subsequently sustained. There is nothing to support claims from post-2010 governments that their policies have reversed decline, let alone produced a significant increase in engagement. If anything, the opposite is true: the recent waves of Community Life Survey data suggest a net decline on a scale not seen at any point since that survey's predecessor, the Citizenship Survey, was established in 2001. The Community Life Survey was not run in 2022–3 but figures for the latter part of 2023 are now available, and these show no distinguishable change from the levels recorded in the 2021–2 survey (Figure 2.1).

Countries don't volunteer: people do

Few politicians or governments engage in comparisons of variations in rates of prosocial behaviours, but the Coalition government's first version of a White Paper on giving of time and money recorded that the UK was only 29th in the international ranking of countries as measured by reported levels of volunteering (Cabinet Office, 2010: 4). Before lamenting yet another example of civic decline, the authors might have been advised to look more closely at the countries placed above the UK. They included bastions of freedom such as Myanmar and several other authoritarian countries, where any statistics on the voluntary activities of citizens really ought to have been taken with a pinch of salt (Stevens, 2011).

Comparisons of volunteering rates between countries are inherently hazardous. Nation states may vary in the freedoms granted to their citizens and in levels of economic development; there may also be variations in cultural understandings of what counted as volunteering. But even when a more restricted range of countries is considered, such as those in Europe, there remains considerable variation: rates of formal volunteering sometimes approach or exceed 50 per cent of the adult population in Nordic countries in Europe but fall to below 10 per cent in certain southern European societies and former Soviet bloc states (Bennett, 2015; Plagnol and Huppert, 2010). Given the range of ways in which questions about volunteering are posed, it is sensible to focus on relative positions rather than absolute levels of engagement. When formal volunteering through an organisation is considered, the UK typically features somewhere in the middle of the rankings – below Switzerland, Germany, Austria, the Netherlands and Scandinavian countries but clearly ahead of countries in eastern and southern Europe. Low rates in eastern Europe are sometimes treated as exceptional, being attributed to a combination of the collapse of the infrastructure that mobilised participation during the Communist era and the effects of economic 'shock therapy' on individuals (Purdam and Tranmer, 2012: 393–41; Plagnol and Huppert, 2010: figure 1; Enjolras, 2021).

How are these variations to be explained? Countries don't volunteer, their citizens do, so analyses need to adjust for individual, compositional factors – the mix of individuals within countries. But even after allowing for these influences, country-level variations remain significant. So what else might account for them? The research focus is on how the larger sociocultural context impacts volunteering rates. For example, Bernard Enjolras (2021) argues that the extent to which individuals are able to exercise a choice to volunteer – what he describes as a capability approach to volunteering – is a function of structural features of the societies they inhabit. He therefore explores the influence of country-level variations in gross domestic product (GDP), income inequality, religiosity, social trust, civil liberties and welfare provision. These characterise the context in which people make decisions about whether or not to engage. After allowing for individual characteristics, Enjolras's analysis shows that GDP per capita has a positive effect on volunteering levels while the Gini coefficient, a measure of inequality, has a negative effect. Measures of social trust, belief in the rule of law and the quality of democracy all have positive effects. The degree of religiosity of a country, however, has a negative effect on volunteering, echoing other findings (Damian, 2019; Bennett, 2015).

Enjolras points to plausible mechanisms that may be at play here. Contextual economic capabilities (GDP) reinforce the effect of individual economic resources on engagement: the wealthier the country, the higher the level of volunteering. Lower levels of economic inequality and higher levels of social trust might enhance shared goals and cooperation, motivating people to engage in unpaid activities (Enjolras, 2021; Kamerāde et al., 2016). His emphasis on the relationship between volunteering, inequality and social trust points to important differences in how welfare arrangements assign tasks and responsibilities between the state, the market and the family. Enjolras differentiates between Nordic, Continental, Anglo-Saxon, Mediterranean and post-Communist regimes. In the Nordic and Anglo-Saxon countries of Europe, high levels of social welfare spending coexist with high levels of volunteering; Continental states combine higher levels of social expenditure with medium levels of volunteering; Mediterranean societies exhibit lower welfare expenditures and voluntary action; post-Communist countries are characterised by the lowest levels of welfare support and volunteering. It is the regimes that 'redistribute the most and therefore, are able to reduce inequality, that have higher levels of social trust and formal volunteering' (Enjolras, 2021: 1203).

This is of relevance to recent debates in the UK. The core of the 'Big Society' discussions was the assumption that an expanded state had squeezed out voluntary initiative and that state shrinkage would result in the efflorescence of volunteering. European comparisons suggest that such an assessment is overly simplistic. The relationship between welfare state expenditures and volunteering is not a simple one of crowding out: in some circumstances welfare spending can support engagement, particularly among low-income groups, thereby closing gaps in volunteering rates and helping to sustain volunteering in disadvantaged areas. This has been demonstrated by researchers who have studied those areas of voluntary initiative that are most closely linked to state welfare policies and the effects of welfare policies on particular groups in the population (Stadelmann-Steffen, 2011). Redistributive programmes can boost engagement for those who 'are most constrained in their choices: the less well-educated, the poor and children' (Van Ingen and van der Meer, 2011); and the specific design of welfare policies matters for the production of social capital: personal experience with selective, means-tested institutions reduces interpersonal trust which, other things being equal, will reduce the likelihood of active citizen engagement (Kumlin and Rothstein, 2005).

The economic value of voluntary action

An emphasis on rates of engagement neglects the question of how much time individuals put into volunteering. Depending on how these two factors interact with the size of the population, one or both of them could be in decline while the absolute amount of time spent volunteering rose. The size of the post-war baby boom generation in the UK has meant that the country has benefited in recent years from a bulge in precisely the age groups that are most heavily engaged in volunteering, but demographic changes could mean that eventually this group accounts for a smaller proportion of the whole population.

There are long-running efforts to develop systems through which unpaid work is appropriately recognised in national accounting systems (ILO, 2011). It would be desirable to measure outputs, but volunteering is such a heterogeneous phenomenon that a very wide range of outputs might result directly from it, to say nothing of the indirect or latent benefits that are claimed. Consequently measurement efforts have generally focused on inputs – that is, the amount of time devoted to the activity, combining an estimate of the population involved with an estimate of the amount of time they contribute.

Estimates have been produced by the UK's Office for National Statistics, which concentrated on regular formal (at least monthly) volunteering. While the proportion of men and women volunteering rose slightly between 2000 and 2015, the mean amount of time they volunteered per day dropped. For men the net result of this was a reduction in the total amount of time contributed of the order of 8–9 per cent. The population had grown over the period in question but not by enough to outweigh the reduction in time committed. As a result, the value of formal volunteering was estimated to have dropped slightly, from £23.6 billion to £22.6 billion (ONS, 2017). An extension of this work to 2019 indicated an ongoing reduction in the hours devoted to volunteering; nevertheless, this study still estimated a total of some two billion hours of voluntary effort each year (Martin and Franklin, 2022). Despite this impressive contribution, commentators regard it as unacknowledged and undermeasured, and they resort to characterisations of the lost country of 'volunteerland' to emphasise its scale (Salamon et al., 2011: 219).

In attempting to quantify the value of volunteering there are various methods of attaching a monetary estimate to the direct and indirect benefits of all this effort. One approach has been to estimate the 'replacement cost' of the activity – the wage that would be paid to those occupying roles deemed equivalent to the roles undertaken by volunteers. There are challenges with this approach. First, volunteering is not free, so a full account would require measurement of the costs incurred in recruiting, investing in and supporting volunteer roles, and then deducting these from the assumed monetary benefits. Second, not all volunteer roles, almost by definition, have a precise equivalent in the world of paid work. Some volunteers do carry out tasks done elsewhere by paid personnel but their enthusiasm and commitment may not compensate for their lack of skill. A replacement cost approach may overestimate the value of the volunteer. Third, the replacement cost method was based on analysis of regular (at least monthly) formal volunteering; this most closely approximates to workplaces, with which volunteering is usually being compared in such estimations. However, this does mean that infrequent or informal kinds of voluntary action are excluded, leading to substantial underestimation (Haldane, 2014). It has been argued that the value of informal volunteering and other currently unmeasured components of prosocial behaviour means we should double the estimate of the direct value of volunteering, to around £44 billion (Nicol Economics, 2019). The focus on economic output could be seen as perpetuating a view of volunteers as constituting nothing more than a free human resource, but such economic metrics constitute only one conception of value.

Other work goes beyond the estimation of the direct value of volunteer time, producing a financial estimate of the well-being benefits of volunteering to volunteers. There are some demonstrable benefits to subjective well-being from volunteering (measured through self-reports) (Bekkers et al., 2015; see also Chapters 7 and 8). One such is that volunteers' life satisfaction is approximately 1.9 per cent higher than that of non-volunteers. The method used to quantify the value of this assesses how much monetary compensation individuals would need to *maintain* that level of well-being in the event that they were to cease volunteering. Various estimates have been produced. Haldane (2014) quotes one estimate of £2,400 per person, or well over 10 per cent of the typical household income at the time. A more conservative and more recent estimate suggests a figure of £911 (Lawton et al., 2021).

The extrapolations do not stop there, though. Haldane went on to identify the wider social impacts of the activities of voluntary organisations – note, not of volunteers per se – by quoting figures on the social return on investment of specific interventions. Likely such returns would include savings to the taxpayer consequent on not having to incarcerate individuals who'd been supported by volunteers, savings on emergency accommodation if people were prevented from experiencing crises in the first place and so on. On the basis of this approach, Haldane postulated that the wider social benefits of volunteering might be several times more valuable than the direct benefits resulting from the services of volunteers and the private benefits to individuals in terms of well-being. The size of such estimates, and whether they could be achieved in practice, depends on what assumptions are made about whether support would have been available from other sources, such as the public sector.

Voluntary action and the voluntary sector

Volunteering takes place across all sectors of society and not just in voluntary organisations. The last national survey to explore this (Low et al., 2007) reported that two-thirds of volunteers reported that they were supporting a voluntary organisation; just under one-quarter volunteered in the public sector. This is an important reminder that public services engage large numbers of volunteers and that a strong public sector can contribute greatly to the promotion of volunteering.

Finally, 10 per cent of respondents said that they were volunteering in the private sector. That is incompatible with the usual definitions of volunteering, which emphasise that it has societal, not private, benefits; how can such efforts be distinguished from unpaid overtime, contributing to company profits?

Exactly how many people volunteer in formal organisational settings is a matter for debate. With some two-fifths of adults volunteering on at least an annual basis, this equates to around 21 million people. If we apply the sectoral breakdown given above it suggests that two-thirds of these, or 13.6 million people, volunteer in the voluntary sector. How does that compare with estimates from other sources?

First, consider registered charities. The Charity Commission asks charities to report the numbers of volunteers they engage, minus their trustees. Some 90,000 such returns for charities in England are available in recent years, with a mean of around 56 volunteers, so grossing up these figures would give some nine million volunteers (based on around 160,000 charities being registered). That leaves us four million short of the survey estimate of volunteer numbers. People also volunteer through other non-profit organisations, including community interest companies (CICs), companies limited by guarantee (CLGs) and industrial and provident societies. Estimates derived from two substantial surveys of these organisations in England (2008 and 2010) suggest that charities account for some four-fifths of the total number of volunteers engaged with formal organisations.[1] Therefore, multiplying the numbers for charities by 1.25, there are around 11 million volunteers engaged with entities that are registered with one or another of the relevant regulators for the field.

Many voluntary organisations, however, do not appear on regulatory radars; some extrapolations (now dated, though repeatedly cited) suggest that there may be between 600,000 and 900,000 such entities (Macgillivray et al., 2001). Based on the national Charity Commission data, the median number of volunteers per charity is 12, suggesting a total of over seven million in these 'below-radar groups'. This would take the number of volunteers to between 18 and 21 million.

---

[1] These were the National Surveys of Third Sector Organisations (NSTSO, 2008) and of Charities and Social Enterprises (NSCSE, 2010) https://beta.ukdataservice.ac.uk/datacatalogue/studies/study?id=7347. Data and survey documentation are available at https://beta.ukdataservice.ac.uk/datacatalogue/studies/study?id=6381.

These are volunteering *positions*, and – returning to Low et al.'s (2007) study – around 40 per cent of volunteers support only one organisation; the majority of volunteers are involved in two or more. The organisational estimates are therefore broadly compatible with the idea that a substantial amount of voluntary action takes place through small, community-based groups, especially if we recall that there are many organisations (e.g. sports clubs) which are unlikely to appear on the Register of Charities.

Why does this matter? This evidence emphasises that the great majority of voluntary organisations are very small, entirely volunteer led and local. Estimates derived from the 2008 National Survey of Third Sector Organisations showed that nearly 100,000 of the circa 160,000 organisations considered for the survey had no paid staff and that a high proportion of these received no money from government (while public funding is a substantial component of sector income, its distribution is highly concentrated and fewer than 35 per cent of organisations receive it) (Clifford et al., 2013; Clifford and Mohan, 2016).

So where do trends in volunteering sit in relation to trends in the organised voluntary sector? First, we know that volunteering levels have been static and the number of charitable organisations has grown, though only slowly. However, the aggregate *income* of charities has grown more rapidly than suggested by the growth in the number of charities: it has risen approximately fourfold since 1980. How can this be reconciled with the picture of stability in volunteering rates and charitable giving? The economic weight of the voluntary sector is heavily influenced by transfers of large organisations from public to charitable control (e.g. the Canal and River Trust, formerly the British Waterways Board) and the registration of new providers of public services as charities or as other non-profit CLGs or CICs (e.g. individual academy schools or chains of academies, or spinoffs of former elements of the National Health Service (NHS)). Some of these organisations are huge, with charities running what were once public services, including chains of academy schools, featuring among the largest organisations (measured by income) in the broad non-profit sector (including charities and other non-profit organisations). Therefore, a significant component of apparent growth is the product of deliberate attempts to restructure the state and not the outcome of voluntary initiative. But these organisations do not always involve volunteers in substantial numbers.

Given the static levels of charitable giving, key drivers of financial growth within existing organisations have been the growth of statutory funding and of fees paid by individuals (including direct payments for services, school or hospital fees and tickets for artistic events as well as trading activities – the ubiquitous charity shops). Estimates suggest that public funding for charities became the largest single component of the income of registered charities by the end of the Labour government in 2010 (National Council for Voluntary Organisations (NCVO), annual). The reliance on fees and contracts for the delivery of services has been paralleled by a significant growth of paid employment. The addition of hundreds of thousands of paid personnel at a time of relative stability in volunteering rates clearly represents a substantial change, by any standards, in the nature of the voluntary sector.

Implicit in these aggregate statistics is therefore the effects of a shift in the boundary between the statutory and voluntary sector, in the funding base of voluntary organisations and in the balance between paid and unpaid personnel. These developments have not been without their critics, from various points on the political spectrum. There are criticisms that the reliance of voluntary organisations on public funding compromises their independence, neuters their campaigning voice and licences the existence of organisations with vested interests in criticising the government hand that feeds them. For volunteering, this means that what volunteers do is to act as cogs in machines that exist to deliver public services, with little autonomy to make their own distinctive contributions to organisations and communities (Rochester, 2013; Seddon, 2007; Snowden, 2012).

There are two potential narratives of voluntary sector futures here. In one, the voluntary sector becomes dominated by large charities delivering services on behalf of the state through paid employees. The result is a myopic view of volunteering, in which the myriad small, volunteer-led groups that in fact make up the bulk of the sector fall from view while attention is solely directed to the narrow contributions that volunteering can make (essentially, cost-saving) to public service provision. Worse, flows of public funds are accompanied by political restrictions on what voluntary organisations can do or say, limiting the ability of organisations in the spheres of advocacy and campaigning (Aiken and Taylor, 2019). According to the other narrative, a somewhat nostalgic vision of the virtues of small, local, volunteer-led organisations persists, albeit with an underlying concern that these entities are being squeezed out of being able to compete for public service contracts which would sustain their expansion (CSJ, 2014). However, this vision also coexists with ongoing adversarial actions by government to create a hostile climate for voluntary organisations (Tibballs and Slocock, 2023).

Discussion

Drawing together a substantial body of quantitative evidence, volunteering rates have clearly been stable over time, though with clear suggestions of reductions at times of stress. It remains to be seen whether there will be a return to pre-Covid levels of volunteering, let alone a post-Covid resurgence. Where there have been increases, they do not justify the enthusiasm shown by government spokespersons – and not just Conservatives. For most of the period studied in detail, volunteering rates have remained within a fairly narrow range, but the most recent surveys are painting a much more negative picture. The expectations that there would be a boost arising from the Big Society, or from COVID-19, have not been fulfilled either; again, the details of the evidence for the period since the arrival of COVID-19 in the UK are explored separately (Chapter 13).

The UK's rates of volunteering are middle-ranking in European terms, though well up the world rankings, but league tables based on a single measure can oversimplify a complex situation. A lesson from comparative research, mainly on European states, is that welfare state policies can make a difference, at least at the margins. More inclusive and redistributive welfare regimes seem to be associated with higher citizen propensities to engage in volunteering. A policy conversation about welfare policy frameworks that place a greater emphasis on economic security would be desirable and would appear to be aligned with the recognition by both Beveridge and Titmuss of the role that well-funded social security can play in sustaining meaningful participation.

This chapter has shown that the economic contribution of voluntary action is substantial – though the extent of it (in financial terms) depends on how far it is possible for credible claims to be made about the latent impacts of volunteering, as well as about its direct benefits. However, a balanced assessment of the value of these unpaid commitments does require that we factor in unpaid care – the direct benefits of which are now estimated at £162 billion (Petrillo and Bennett, 2023), compared to £44 billion for the direct value of formal and informal volunteering (Nicol Economics, 2019).

This broad consistency in the level of engagement has been taking place against a background of steady expansion in the voluntary sector, albeit one driven largely by the formation and expansion of large organisations and by the growth of government contracts and of direct payments by individuals as sources of revenue. There are divergent views on the merits of these developments, but it is notable that the wider public continue to volunteer in large numbers *irrespective of what seems to be going on in voluntary organisations themselves.* While critics are therefore correct to point to the politicisation of debates around volunteering and the voluntary sector, does this imply that, for most people and most voluntary organisations, these macro-level changes in the sector's economy and relationships with government are side issues which do not affect their everyday practice? Certainly, this is consistent with the argument that volunteering is often a sphere in which people avoid politics (Eliasoph, 1998).

These discussions of aggregate data and sector trends set the scene for what follows. The voluntary sector, and volunteering itself, are very diverse and this inevitably requires us to move from a consideration of levels of engagement to a discussion of the nature of engagement and its distribution. Chapters 3–6 therefore explore the contours of volunteering.

Part II

Contours

Introduction to Part II

'The spirit of service is in our people', wrote Beveridge in 1948. Empirically this raises some important questions about what proportion of the population are imbued with this 'spirit', who and where they are and what they do. Answers to these questions will inform consideration of the realism – or otherwise – of expectations about the contribution that voluntary action might make: is it possible fundamentally to alter the pattern of voluntary effort?

First, diversity and stratification in the volunteering population has attracted significant attention in recent years, so Chapter 3 considers socioeconomic gradients in terms of who participates, or does not participate, in voluntary action. There is a tendency at times for volunteering to be discussed purely as a matter of numbers or economic aggregates. However, the range of organisational and community settings in which volunteering takes place, and the diversity of activities carried out, call into question such an undifferentiated view. Research evidence also poses questions about whether it is at all realistic to expect volunteers to be 'representative' of the population as a whole.

I then explore the question of the concentration of effort in volunteering (Chapter 4): what I have previously referred to as the 'civic core', following an earlier Canadian study (Reed and Selbee, 2001). Reliance on relatively small subsets of the population – either for volunteering in general or for leadership roles in particular – is a long-running theme of discussions about volunteering. The UK relies on a relatively small subset of the population to carry out the great bulk of voluntary activity; this group has specific socioeconomic characteristics and is spatially concentrated. The converse of a core is a periphery, so I also discuss those who are apparently not engaged in any way with voluntary activity (Chapter 4). This discussion is followed by consideration of community-level variations. Against the background of ongoing concerns about spatial inequalities in prosperity in Britain, we need a better understanding of how significant and persistent these variations are. The evidence suggests that what appear at first sight to be substantial variations between places in volunteering largely disappear once allowance is made for the mix of people living in those places (Chapter 5). Finally, I consider volunteering *trajectories*: how do people become involved, and in what circumstances do they remain involved, in voluntary organisations – whether this be consistently, intermittently or episodically? If raising the level of voluntary effort is desirable, one way forward might be to pay more attention to these trajectories, the better to understand ways in which volunteering might be dovetailed with the circumstances of people's lives (Chapter 6).

These chapters draw extensively on large-scale quantitative analyses and this is a deliberate choice. Such approaches can be criticised for reductionism, in that (by virtue of the constraints of using large-scale survey data) they invariably relate voluntary action by individuals to a small number of characteristics and resources of individuals (Chapter 1). Criticisms have also been levelled at a tendency for a 'rather mechanical' methodological individualism, which by implication frames explanations of the decision to volunteer almost entirely as a function of individual characteristics (O'Toole and Grey, 2016), producing a statistical 'black box' in which one cannot deduce anything about process (Shachar et al., 2019). These are pertinent points, but there is much work in other fields about the processes through which people come to engage in voluntary action, some of which is reviewed below. Moreover, at times when so much is expected of voluntary action, these analyses demonstrate that variations between individuals and communities in their involvement are substantial, systematic and persistent over time. It follows that short-term changes are unlikely and that undifferentiated appeals for greater participation are unlikely to have much effect on their own. Understanding these inequalities is therefore essential – unless one believes that volunteering is solely a matter of choice and character, rather than context and circumstance.

These analyses are complemented by a growing body of qualitative research which illuminates the place of volunteering in people's lives and their routes into and out of it. In particular, that research serves to remind us of the genuinely limited extent of 'non-engagement', raising questions about the extent to which there are undiscovered reserves of volunteers remaining to be tapped. Such work further highlights the diversity of settings in which voluntary action takes place, of the range of activities that are encompassed under the banner of voluntary action and of the trajectories of individual engagement in volunteering throughout their lives.

3

Diversity and inequality in voluntary action

Introduction

When hosting two visiting European academics, who had in common a strong research interest in voluntary action, we visited a National Trust property which was historically significant as the ancestral home of a prominent Catholic family persecuted for their faith in the sixteenth century. What made a deep impression on our guests was the erudition of the volunteers at the property, who spent considerable time with our guests explaining the background to the harassment and suppression of Catholics. It was a clear demonstration of the National Trust's ability to mobilise people with considerable social and cultural capital to enhance the services they offer. Of course, in comparison with the UK population, National Trust volunteers are atypical, characteristically being older, well off, well educated and drawn from the upper tiers of the socioeconomic spectrum.

Stereotypical generalisations about a volunteer population largely composed of well-educated women from prosperous backgrounds have not been entirely banished from UK public discourse. However, there is growing awareness of the need to broaden the base of the volunteering population, as well as to recognise the range of contributions made by all forms of volunteering. At times there have been acrimonious exchanges about diversity in the voluntary sector. A press report on an investigation of the demographics of charity trustees included a facile characterisation of trustees as 'pale, male and stale'. Unsurprisingly there was a backlash, with one correspondent requesting that the authors 'stop insulting those of us who have given our time freely for decades' (Kenyon, 2018).

There are good reasons to be concerned about diversity in the voluntary sector. There is much evidence from management research of the benefits of diversity in board membership while organisations rightly believe that they are more likely to be effective in their activities if they can recruit volunteers who are similar to the people they are supporting, especially if they share lived experience. Furthermore, if volunteering is a positive experience with a potential range of benefits to individuals (though see Chapters 8–10), Charlotte Overgaard (2019: 128) suggests that 'nonparticipating groups ... are assumed to be missing out – and are therefore subject to "participatory inequality"' (Hustinx et al., 2010: 427). If there are demonstrable benefits from volunteering, it is surely desirable that such inequalities should be reduced as far as possible. Yet stratification of British society was and remains highly salient. If voluntary action depends on the capacities of and resources available to individuals, then we would expect socioeconomic stratification in the volunteer population.

To what extent can the population of volunteers reasonably be expected to reflect the country's demographic and social characteristics? For instance, can individual voluntary organisations be held responsible for ensuring their volunteers are 'representative'? If an organisation such as the National Trust aspires to be 'forever, for everyone', should its 70,000 volunteers accurately reflect the UK's demographics? That is surely setting a very high bar.

In this chapter I first explore the main strands in the existing literature on socioeconomic inequalities in voluntary action. Then I summarise analyses of UK survey datasets covering the past three decades, including an extension and updating of a previous large-scale analysis of variation in volunteering (Li, 2015). I distinguish between formal and informal volunteering – namely, voluntary effort contributed in structured ('formal') organisational settings, and that which takes place outwith such contexts, entailing direct person-to-person support in the community ('informal' volunteering; see Chapters 1 and 2). Then, considering only formal volunteering, I illustrate the diversity of organisational contexts – people select into types of organisation, and as a result we would expect to see different types of people involved in different types of organisation. Finally, there is also diversity in terms of the nature of the voluntary activities undertaken.

Stratification in volunteering: what does the literature tell us?

The most prominent focus in the analysis of patterns of volunteering draws on a combination of resource and dominant status theories. Formal volunteering through organisations is characterised as a productive activity that requires particular types of human resources, which are generally more likely to be possessed by individuals of

Diversity and inequality in voluntary action 57

higher socioeconomic status. Economic, social and cultural resources therefore strongly determine the socioeconomic composition of the volunteer population (Musick and Wilson, 2008; Wilson, 2012). Dominant status theory goes on to argue that high-status individuals are attractive to voluntary organisations in terms of symbolic capital, given their potential to enhance organisational prestige and their ability to offer high-level skills in fields such as governance, finance and management.

A substantial literature therefore deploys large-scale survey data to identify covariates associated with patterns of inclusion or exclusion in volunteering, based on the demographic and socioeconomic characteristics of individuals and households. That literature suggests a consistent picture of the relationship between socioeconomic advantage or status, and engagement in volunteering. Whether we consider educational qualifications, occupational status or income, the broad pattern is that substantially higher levels of volunteering are found for groups who possess most resources and who occupy the more elevated positions in the social hierarchy. Formal volunteering is also more likely to be undertaken by women rather than men; by younger people and more elderly groups rather than the middle-aged; by those whose health status tends to be better and those who are not living with disabilities; and by those who are actively practising their religion.

Possession of educational qualifications is generally regarded as the most consistent and substantively most significant predictor of volunteering, especially in relation to formal volunteering through organisations (Musick and Wilson, 2008: 119). Educational differences are less apparent for informal volunteering (Egerton and Mullan, 2008 – but see discussion of this work below). Since Goddard (1994), UK surveys generally show that formal volunteering rates are approximately three times as high for those with degrees as they are for those with no qualifications at all.

Differences in socioeconomic status, class and occupation are also important – not least because the kind of occupation one has is related to routes into volunteering (e.g. networks through which information about opportunities is disseminated or through which recruitment takes place) and scope to undertake it (e.g. degree of control over working hours and conditions). In UK survey datasets, the most useful index of class and status is the National Statistics Socioeconomic Classification, which measures employment relations (i.e. aspects of work and market conditions) and the nature of the labour contract. Thus it combines economic measures with assessments of the degree of autonomy and control in the workplace. The likelihood of volunteering for people in the higher occupational strata is typically at least twice those in the lowest levels. Musick and Wilson extend their discussion of occupational differences to the sector in which people work (suggesting that public sector workers, possibly because of underlying value systems, are more likely to engage in prosocial behaviours) and to particular types of occupation on the grounds that certain occupations teach civic skills, instil prosocial values and may bring strong normative pressures on employees to volunteer (Musick and Wilson, 2008: 137–46). For England, Li (2015) also found that self-employed people and small business owners are more likely to volunteer than some other groups, because they are in occupational niches which bring them into contact with others in their local community.

Unsurprisingly, the occupational composition of volunteers is partly related to the type of volunteering roles which they carry out and the field of voluntary action in which they work (Meyer and Rameder, 2022). Lambert and Rutherford (2020) argue that occupational data provide further insight into the respective roles of 'circumstances' and 'habits' in volunteering behaviour. By circumstances, they mean direct, tangible factors that may influence participation and which could in principle be changed (e.g. awareness of volunteering opportunities or changes in the accessibility of such opportunities). Habits, they argue, relate to individuals' capacities, orientations or propensities towards volunteering. These are relatively stable for individuals; they persist regardless of immediate life-cycle circumstances. Thus they are largely shaped by social background. Occupations link to and encapsulate inequalities in socioeconomic advantage (education, training, workplace autonomy, precarity, social networks) and therefore detailed occupational data provide insights into the influence on volunteering of these elements of stratification. Shared cultural orientations within specific occupational niches may also influence patterns of engagement (one example given by Lambert and Rutherford (2020) is the likelihood of participation in volunteering by highly specific occupational groups, such as finance professionals). Related to occupation, non-UK studies of the relationship between income and volunteering show, with a few exceptions, that it is positively related to volunteering.

Race and ethnicity feature strongly in the international (often US-based) literature, where the country's troubled historical legacy has left its mark on patterns of engagement by minority groups. There is a mixed picture – some work points to a lower propensity to volunteer by minority ethnic groups on the basis that they lack resources, while other accounts argue that there are higher levels of volunteering, especially among African-Americans, and that this is noticeable especially in certain forms of engagement (campaigning and activism). Apparently low levels of engagement among minority ethnic groups are sometimes interpreted as reflecting their propensity to provide aid directly to individuals on a personal basis, though there is not always consistent evidence that African-Americans are more likely to engage in informal volunteering to a greater extent than for the population as a whole (Musick and Wilson, 2008: 197–216).

If we conceptualise volunteering as part of the total social organisation of labour (see Chapter 1), then it is also important to consider *household* divisions of labour and in particular the impact of caring responsibilities on volunteering. For example, one reason why women generally are *more* likely to volunteer than men is because of the occupations they have and the connections they make through childcare. These can act in varying directions – presence of children being one way in which parents become engaged in volunteering, while unpaid care for relatives can, in some circumstances, open up opportunities to volunteer, so may be complementary to it (Musick and Wilson, 2008: 161–2, 171–96).

Religion is often thought to be strongly associated with likelihood of engagement, but in the UK at least, its effects appear marginal, though analysis is limited because few British surveys have much detail on religious affiliations and observance. The fact of adherence to a religious denomination has no discernible effect; what seems to matter more is whether someone is actively practising their religion via attendance at services. The mechanism is that they are then exposed to expectations that they ought to support the activities of the congregation and opportunities to engage in volunteering.

How these disparate characteristics of individuals combine to produce variations in volunteering is extensively debated; Musick and Wilson (2008), in the authoritative text in the field, cover the mechanisms connecting these aspects of social structure to volunteering in some detail (referring to combinations of awareness of need – related to education – socialisation, solicitation and availability of time). Finally, there is an argument that the terminology used to define and measure volunteering does not fully capture the activities of some groups, and in particular that formal volunteering is prioritised over 'informal' activities (Dean, 2022). Informal volunteering is certainly carried out by larger proportions of the population than formal volunteering through organisations (Rochester et al., 2010: 38–52), and it has been suggested that this is a form of action that is typical of working-class communities; it is 'much less a site of differential participation' than formal volunteering (Dean, 2022: 532). Whether that is the case is explored in more detail below.

Stratification in volunteering: existing evidence

There are substantial survey datasets, including questions on volunteering for the UK, which have been gathered almost annually since 2001 and at intervals before that since the 1980s. While not covering the range of 'capitals' considered in the literature (see Chapter 1), these nevertheless facilitate analysis of the broad structural features of voluntary action.

The multivariate analyses which are summarised here encompass analysis of the GHSs (1987 and 1992: Mohan et al., 2006); the Citizenship Survey for 2008–9 (for formal volunteering, see Bennett, 2013); Li's (2015) use of 10 years (2001–11) of the Citizenship Survey to analyse patterns of 'joining' (associational membership), 'helping' (volunteering) and 'giving' (donations to charity); Wheatley's (2017) work on various longitudinal and cross-sectional surveys; and my own work on formal and informal volunteering using the Community Life Surveys (2017–22). To recap (see Chapter 1), these terms refer to voluntary effort contributed in structured ('formal') organisational settings, and that which takes place outwith such contexts, entailing direct person-to-person support in the community ('informal' volunteering, see Chapters 1 and 2). In the discussion which follows I summarise my own findings from an analysis of the most recent five years of the Community Life Survey (key findings are presented in Table 3.1) which I cross-reference to previous findings to demonstrate continuities and differences. The analysis is a binary logistic regression with three separate outcome variables (respectively whether or not individuals engaged in either formal or informal volunteering or engaged in no volunteering at all). The emphasis in this analysis is on socioeconomic variations in volunteering, which influences the choice of variables in Table 3.1. Results are not always shown in the table where they are of marginal significance or effects of independent variables appear inconsistent

In terms of independent variables, in all these studies women are far more likely than men to engage in voluntary activity, whether this is formal or informal volunteering. Being married or in a partnership was not consistently related with either formal or informal volunteering (though the studies varied in terms of the classifications used). Having children is an important pathway into voluntary action since parents are presented with opportunities through schools and out-of-school clubs attended by their offspring. The presence of children in a household was found to be positively associated with formal volunteering by some studies (Table 3.1; Li, 2015; Mohan et al., 2006) but not others (Bennett, 2013) and to be either positively or negatively

Table 3.1 Analysis of characteristics of formal and informal volunteers, and non-volunteers, England, 2017–22

	Formal volunteering	Informal volunteering	No volunteering
Sex (ref: men)			
Women	0.15***	0.27***	−0.23***
Socioeconomic status (ref: never worked/long-term unemployed)			
Semi-routine/routine occupations	0.13	0.23**	−0.16*
Lower supervisory/technical roles	0.04	0.04	−0.01
Small employers/own account workers	0.28*	0.37***	−0.25*
Intermediate	0.26**	0.22**	−0.24**
Higher administrative/professional workers	0.47***	0.34***	−0.39***
Age group (ref: 16–19)			
20–24	−0.34*	0.03	0.17
25–34	−0.46***	0.14	0.06
35–49	−0.12	0.28*	−0.16
50–64	0.06	0.37**	−0.25*
65–74	0.44**	0.64***	−0.56***
Qualifications (ref: none)			
GCSE	0.54***	0.37***	−0.45***
A-level or equivalent	0.85***	0.48***	−0.65***
Higher education or equivalent	1.21***	0.65***	−0.92***
Religion (ref: none)			
Christian	0.33***	0.19***	−0.23***
Other	0.33***	0.28***	−0.27***
Caring responsibilities (ref: none)			
Yes	0.29***	0.35***	−0.39***
Children in household (ref: none)			
Yes	0.43***	0.10**	−0.21***
Ethnicity (ref: White)			
Asian	−0.28***	−0.04	0.17*
Black	0.26**	0.34***	−0.19*
Mixed/other	0.13	0.05	−0.03

* $p < 0.05$, ** $p < 0.01$, *** $p < 0.001$

Note: With the focus of the chapter on socioeconomic diversity, other variables included in the models were omitted from this table (marital status, limiting illness, housing tenure, household income (banded), length of residence in neighbourhood, wave of the survey), as these were largely of marginal statistical significance. Regression coefficients included, along with p values (asterisked) but not t-statistics.

associated depending on the age of the children. Whether the respondent was a carer was positively associated with volunteering, whether formal or informal, and not at all with non-engagement, although those reporting long caring hours were *less* likely to volunteer (Wheatley, 2017: 141).

For formal volunteering, the relationship with age varies across the studies. Mohan et al. (2006) found that volunteering rates were lowest in the 17–24 age group compared to all other age categories, peaking at ages 55–64, then dropping again for people aged over 65. This was for 1987 and 1992, and a different pattern is evident in the most recent survey data for 2017–22 (Table 3.1). Here, the youngest age group (16–19) are *more* likely to volunteer, holding other factors constant, than some of their elders. Those aged 20–24 and 25–34 are less likely than their teenage counterparts to engage in formal volunteering, though there is an upturn in the 65–74 age group. This seems to imply a change from three decades ago, potentially because young people have been more exposed to volunteering opportunities and to citizenship education, and because the expansion of higher education means that more students are deploying volunteering as a credential in the job application process (see also Chapter 8). It is possible that the high rates for those aged 16–19 reflect the presence of many full-time students in settings where volunteering is heavily promoted. Most likely the dip in formal volunteering in early adulthood is because for many people the demands of raising children and progressing up a career ladder squeeze the time available for volunteering. Informal volunteering increases with age from the mid-30s onwards – particularly for the older age groups. It might be expected that such community-based volunteering would also be associated with length of residence and hence development of familiarity with co-residents, but in fact there is no statistically significant evidence of such an association.

As regards ethnicity, early surveys (Mohan et al., 2006) were only able to contrast 'white British' people with all others; those identifying as 'white British' were more likely to volunteer. Li (2015) and Bennett (2013) found limited evidence of variations in volunteering by ethnicity. More recently, my own work shows that compared to the white population, those from Asian ethnic groups are less likely to engage in formal volunteering, but there is no difference between those groups and white people for informal volunteering; people of Asian background are more likely than others not to be engaged at all (Table 3.1). In comparison, those from Black ethnic groups are more likely to report both formal and informal volunteering relative to the rest of the population. In addition to the work reviewed here, Jump Projects

(2019: 12) use more detailed data on ethnic groups from the much larger Understanding Society surveys, reaching similar conclusions: Asian and British Asian groups are consistently less likely to volunteer, even after adjustment for socioeconomic factors. They also find that within minority groups, gender and age were significant barriers, with women and those in older age categories being under-represented in the volunteering population. They argued that the differences were not explicable, as has sometimes been suggested, by a different cultural understanding of formal and informal volunteering and therefore a different balance between the two in the case of these ethnic groups (Jump Projects, 2019: 34).

Associations between health status and volunteering are not always consistent across studies. Bennett (2013) finds a positive association between individuals' assessments of their general health and volunteering, whereas Li (2015) uses responses to a question on long-term illness in his analysis of the same data and finds no association. I found a positive association between self-assessed ill-health and informal volunteering but not with formal volunteering.

Religious affiliation and involvement forms social connections, promotes behavioural expectations and offers channels through which individuals may engage. Current surveys capture whether people *identify* with a particular religion but does not explore whether they are actively *practising* their faith, as has been done in previous surveys of this kind. In my own work (Table 3.1), religious people, whether they are Christian or from other faiths, are more likely to engage in either formal or informal volunteering, or in both, though this was not the finding of Bennett (2013) or Li (2015). While religious attendance promotes volunteering to some degree, the effect differs across religions, being significant mainly for Anglicans and other Protestants, with weaker effects among other Christian denominations and none for Muslims; it is important to note that these patterns are likely to reflect the different ways different religions express prosocial norms (Aksoy and Wiertz, 2023). So while there may be a volunteering dividend from those who actively practise their religion, in substantive terms, given the declining proportion of the population who are regularly taking part in worship, the impact is likely to be small.

Across these studies, though the mix of independent variables differs somewhat, we find evidence of strong educational and socioeconomic gradients in participation. Educational qualifications are consistently the strongest predictor of engagement in formal volunteering, as shown by Bennett (2013; see also Table 3.1); education did not feature in Li (2015) or Mohan et al. (2006). For the period 2017–22, I find a strong effect of increasing levels of education on informal volunteering, though not as strong as the effect for formal volunteering. This appears to contradict the argument of Williams (2003) that informal volunteering is a less stratified activity than formal volunteering and one that is very much associated with working-class communities. However, that argument was made on the basis of comparative levels of formal and informal volunteering in communities and not on the basis of a detailed statistical analysis of individual-level variations. The finding here is also in some measure in disagreement with Egerton and Mullan (2008), who found that informal volunteering was not strongly associated with educational qualifications (if anything, it was negatively associated with increasing levels of education). A possible reason for that is differences between the sources used. Egerton and Mullan's (2008) work was based on the analysis of time use diaries. These were completed by individuals and the information from them was then classified by researchers. In the Community Life Survey, individuals are presented with a range of options from which to choose. The rate of informal volunteering tends to be somewhat higher than that of formal volunteering, but in the data used for Egerton and Mullan's (2008) study, approximately four times as many people engaged in informal volunteering as formal. This may imply that direct comparisons between the surveys are not valid.

There is also consistent evidence that the likelihood of engagement in formal volunteering increases as you move upwards across socioeconomic strata. Li (2015: 52) found a particularly high likelihood of participation for routine and semi-routine workers, which he argued was because these groups were often in occupations that brought them into contact with people in their own immediate communities, thereby exposing them to opportunities to engage. In the case of the higher socioeconomic strata the pattern is as expected: these groups (intermediate/higher administrative and professional workers) would typically be regarded as highly desirable volunteers by virtue of their particular skills. The socioeconomic categories available in all these survey datasets are broad ones, and recent work has sought to prise open the 'black box' of volunteering further by using occupational data. Lambert and Rutherford (2020) identify numerous occupational groups where, after adjustment for a large number of individual characteristics, there remains evidence of a greater-than-average propensity to volunteer. Their work represents an advance on the broad-brush socioeconomic classifications used in many studies; it points to various professional occupations such as finance and education in which participation in volunteering is particularly high.

Considering only informal volunteering separately, the Community Life Survey (for 2017–22) also shows some evidence of a class gradient in which, in common with Li's work, small employers and self-employed workers are more likely than any other group to carry out informal volunteering. This somewhat runs counter to Dean's (2022) claim that inequalities in participation are less evident for informal volunteering.

Household income is, by and large, not associated with participation in formal volunteering, except at the upper end of the income distribution in the Community Life Survey analysis, where those in the top two income bands are more likely to engage in formal volunteering. Household income has small negative effects on informal volunteering; compared to the lowest income band, the likelihood of informal volunteering is reduced for other income bands, but the effects are not consistent (i.e. they don't increase consistently with income). People at this point in the distribution are significantly less likely to engage in informal volunteering. Owner occupation is associated with increased levels of formal and informal volunteering, though substantively it is of less significance than many other variables. Owner occupiers are significantly less likely than those in rented accommodation to be engaged in no volunteering at all.

As to temporal changes, my own work and that of Li (2015) enable changes to be considered between waves of the same survey. Li clearly shows that all years prior to 2010–11 – which was the first year of the Coalition government, whose Big Society policies envisioned rising public enthusiasm for volunteering – had significantly *higher* rates of volunteering. Interruptions to the survey time series thereafter, combined with changes in sample size and survey method, limit the possibilities for repeating Li's work. However, for the five waves of the Community Life Survey from 2017–18 to 2021–2, rates of formal volunteering were significantly lower than the base year (2017–18) in 2018–19 and especially in the subsequent two waves. Informal volunteering was significantly higher than for the base year in 2020–1 but dropped below it again in 2021–2. Thus, while we have some evidence of a short-term increase in informal volunteering for part of the COVID-19 period, this was insufficient to counteract the overall declining trend (see also Chapters 2 and 13).

There is a relatively consistent message from this body of research. Despite differences in methods and choice of independent variables for the analysis of volunteering, common features are the socioeconomic differences in volunteering, the influence of the presence of children (at least at some points in people's lives), the relative absence of income related differences, marital status and the statistically significant differences between men and women. Not all studies included educational qualifications but it proved to be a highly significant predictor of both formal and informal volunteering. Somewhat in contrast to earlier studies there is also scant evidence of a class dimension to informal volunteering. There are age-related differences and some evidence of change over time, with the youngest age groups now appearing to have the highest levels of volunteering, in contrast to the surveys from the late 1980s. Data on ethnicity are not always comparable across surveys, but generally people identifying themselves as being from Asian ethnic groups are less likely to engage in volunteering than the rest of the population, while there is some evidence that Black respondents are more likely to be involved in formal and informal volunteering. In short, there is considerable continuity: key predictors, principally education, social class, and age, remain influential over some 30 years – from the GHS of the late 1980s through to the Community Life Surveys of the 2020s.

Diversity of organisations

Formal volunteering is an activity that takes place through an organisational context, and voluntary organisations vary substantially regarding types of activities and purpose and their degrees of professionalisation, size and formalisation. The great majority of voluntary organisations are small, relatively informal in structure and entirely run by volunteers (estimates from robust national surveys of England suggest that only one-third of organisations employ any staff at all). In contrast, much of the economic weight of the voluntary sector is concentrated in relatively small numbers of organisations with considerable financial resources, employing numerous paid staff and mobilising volunteers, often in specialised roles. As a result, different types of organisation will have different requirements for the competence and skills of volunteers, implying that people with different levels of human, social and cultural capital will be sought out. For example, Meyer and Rameder (2022) found that inequalities in occupational status were highly visible in volunteering in the fields of sports and politics, whereas inequalities in educational status were more important within the fields of religion and social services.

Rather than speaking of volunteers as a general and homogeneous category it is thus more informative to look at volunteering within organisations or types of organisation, as can be illustrated with examples from case studies. Harflett's (2014) work on National Trust volunteers shows that they are not typical of the UK's population, nor even of the subset of the population that engages in volunteering. Two-thirds had higher-education qualifications (compared to one-third of the population at the time of her study), only 1 per cent did not describe themselves as white (compared to 14 per cent of the population) and 84 per cent were aged at least 55, compared to 35 per cent in the population of England and Wales. One reason for these differences is that many of the Trust's properties are in areas that are not themselves very diverse in socioeconomic or demographic terms. An earlier (Holmes, 2003) study of volunteers in a broader group of heritage organisations in the UK found a very similar age breakdown but the gender breakdown of the sample – 60 per cent male, 40 per cent female – was different, reflecting the prominence of transport heritage museums and attractions in the study. An elderly and female demographic characterised charity shop volunteers, over four-fifths of whom were women, with two-thirds aged over 60 (Maddrell, 2000), while qualitative work on Leagues of Friends of hospitals found that committees and active members had often been involved for several decades (Ellis Paine et al., 2019) and were therefore rather older than the general population.

In contrast, O'Toole and Grey's (2016) respondents in a study of Royal National Lifeboat Institution (RNLI) rescue volunteers were largely male, who were recruited through an extensive, if informal, vetting process which assessed the character and aptitude of potential recruits. While volunteers for lifeboat crews only account for around 15 per cent of the RNLI volunteers, 92 per cent of volunteer boat crew were men. O'Toole and Grey's work (see also O'Toole and Calvard, 2020) also emphasised community expectations about supporting the lifeboats, raising questions about how 'voluntary' the activity really was, as well as the dense network of social and kinship relations that underpinned participation ('we are like a band of brothers'). With these sorts of expectations, volunteering was also likely to be transmitted between generations of the same families.

Many organisations are located primarily in communities which are not themselves very diverse. In a large national survey, two-thirds of charities and social enterprises in England reported that they operated at the 'neighbourhood' scale and there were three times as many such organisations in the most prosperous communities as in the most disadvantaged ones (Clifford, 2012). The neighbourhood focus may thus restrict the pool from which volunteers can be drawn, and unless there is much population turnover in the community, the volunteer force may then age in place. As an interviewee from one organisation admitted, 'we started with brown hair, but there's none of us got it now and there doesn't seem to be anybody coming up behind us'

(Ellis Paine, 2015). Volunteers are therefore highly likely to reflect local demographics. This is well illustrated by a study of voluntary organisations in contrasting social and economic circumstances (a deindustrialised port in northern England, a small rural town in Wales and a regenerated neighbourhood in London). The authors argued that voluntary organisations are 'produced in place' through combinations of local economic and social histories with contemporary demographics and emerging opportunity structures (such as funding streams). The organisational demographics were very different across their case studies – highly educated young professionals at a food charity in London, environmental volunteers in rural Wales who had moved to the locality (at various stages of their lives, but they were generally older) to live out their environmental values, and young people with fewer educational qualifications at the port-based social enterprise in northern England, who hoped to use volunteering as a way into paid employment (Halford et al., 2015).

The combination of locality and organisational characteristics are what generates variations in the socioeconomic make-up of the volunteering population, and the limited number of studies of types of organisation (or of individual organisations) bear that out, providing as they do accounts of the structuration of routes into volunteering opportunities.

Diversity of roles within organisations

If volunteering is a form of work which just happens to be unpaid, to what extent can we identify divisions of labour and the social relationships involved from within extant data on volunteering? Wilson (2000: 233) warns against using ad hoc 'folk' taxonomies of volunteering (e.g. 'school-related', 'helping the elderly') which are not 'sociologically useful'. This is valid as a general comment since public discussion on volunteering speaks of it as if it were a unified, homogeneous phenomenon. Resource-based approaches to inequalities in volunteering need to complement work on the antecedents of engagement (i.e. individual characteristics of volunteers in general) with accounts of inequalities in the structural positions that volunteers occupy within organisations. In other words, they need to explore 'stratification' or 'job segregation' in volunteer work (Musick and Wilson, 2008). This is not straightforward because of the general lack of survey data on these aspects of voluntary action.

As with any other formalised organisation, there is a division of labour in the voluntary sector. People are recruited for certain roles because they possess certain qualifications or skills necessary to the execution of particular functions. In the UK, for instance, recruitment advertisements for trustee board positions regularly specify expertise in finance, human resources or property management, in recognition of the substantial resources being managed and of the requirements of regulators to prepare accounts to appropriate standards. Meyer and Rameder (2022) therefore argue that privileged citizens also occupy the most important positions within associations and, conversely, volunteers from disadvantaged groups confront exclusionary organisational mechanisms that confine them to marginal or routine roles.

While studies of individual organisations point to some of these particularities (see previous section), national survey data rarely permit identification of organisational types, illumination of the position of volunteers in the hierarchy of their organisation (e.g. whether or not they have managerial responsibilities) or insight into whether volunteer work is complex or repetitive (Sanghera, 2018: 310).

To develop research on this topic, one possibility is to consider socioeconomic diversity in specific types of voluntary activities undertaken by volunteers, and I give one specific example here: the role of charity trustees. Second, survey data provide some insights into the vertical stratification of the range of tasks that people carry out when they volunteer – from more closely supervised, repetitive, low-skilled roles, on the one hand, to those which involve considerable autonomy and decision making, are varied and high-skilled, and which may entail high levels of social and cultural capital.

Trustees are a good place to start. Unpaid trustees play key roles in the governance of UK charities, taking on what can be considerable responsibilities for the resources, activities, management and reputation of these organisations. Inequalities in their demographics are therefore relevant to wider questions of how inequality is reproduced in British society. Some 800,000 trustee positions exist in England and Wales, although some individuals hold multiple trusteeships so the actual number of trustees at any one point in time is somewhat smaller. Trustees are far from being representative of the general population or even of the volunteer population. Lee et al. (2017) showed that approximately 56 per cent of volunteers were women and 44 per cent men; the position is more than reversed for trustees, 64 per cent of whom are men, while 71 per cent of chairs of trustee boards are male (see Figure 3.1). In terms of education, 30 per cent of trustees in Lee et al.'s work had a postgraduate degree with 60 per cent having a professional qualification – perhaps the latter is no surprise, given that trustees are often sought out specifically for professional expertise in finance, human resources or law. Overall, the

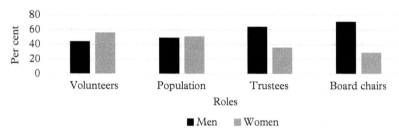

Figure 3.1 Gender breakdown of roles in the voluntary sector.
Source: trustees/board chairs – Lee et al. (2017); volunteers – author's calculations, Community Life Survey (2016–17).

report concluded that trustees lacked diversity in terms of age, gender, socioeconomic status and ethnicity.

Clifford (2023) was able to delve further into the pattern of trusteeships by looking at the types of organisation for which women were more likely to be trustees. In almost every field of activity women were in the minority, with the exception of village halls and PTAs, where five-sixths of trustees were women. Furthermore, women were substantially under-represented in the largest organisations, comprising 40 per cent of trustees, and only 30 per cent of chairs of trustees, for charities with incomes greater than £10 million.

Trustees have a very specific role in the voluntary sector, but some UK survey data on volunteering offer detail on the nature of a broader range of tasks involved in voluntary organisations. Harris (1996: 57) classified volunteer tasks into 'governance' roles (e.g. a member of a board), 'operational' roles (e.g. involvement in the provision of services) and 'support' roles (e.g. fundraising or providing administrative support). We can replicate this to some degree using UK survey data. The Community Life Survey asks about roles which can be broadly related to governance (leading a group or committee membership, getting others involved, organising or helping to run an activity, representing people and campaigning), operational tasks (visiting people, befriending them, offering advice or counselling, 'other practical' forms of help and transport) and 'support' roles (e.g. raising or handling money or providing secretarial and administrative services). The composition of each of these roles was analysed using logistic regression, treating each role as a binary (yes/no) variable depending on whether or not a respondent carried out such a role. Figures in the table greater than zero indicate an increased likelihood of carrying out that activity compared to a base category of respondents. Asterisks

Diversity and inequality in voluntary action 71

indicate the probability that the result is significant (e.g. two asterisks mean there is less than 1 per cent probability that this is a chance result). Among the roles included in the survey were 'leading a group or being a member of a committee', 'visiting people', 'befriending or mentoring people', 'giving advice, information or counselling' and 'secretarial, administrative or clerical assistance', among others. Table 3.2 gives illustrative examples of the demographic and socioeconomic characteristics of people carrying out a subset of these roles.

If we begin with 'visiting people', we find no differences in the likelihood of such activity according to age, socioeconomic status or qualifications. Household income (though not shown in Table 3.2) makes little difference except that at the upper end of the income distribution individuals are much less likely than others to carry out this form of help. Whether you are married or in a partnership makes a positive difference to the chances of you carrying out this activity, as is also the case for caring responsibilities. The activity of 'visiting people' is highly gendered: women are far more likely than men to take part. So this appears to be a more equal site of participation than is the case for other (broadly administrative) roles such as 'leading a group/serving on a committee' or 'secretarial, administrative or clerical' support (both shown in Table 3.2) and 'giving advice, information or counselling'. In such roles there are strong gradients that are related to educational qualifications. Once controls are in place for education, other individual characteristics such as socioeconomic status and income have little impact generally. In contrast to their lower likelihood of 'visiting people', men are more likely than women to be engaged in leading a group or being on a committee, in providing advice or information, in representing others and in campaigning; women are more likely than men to be involved in organising or helping to run an event and in raising or handling money. The influence of religion and ethnicity is seen in some categories of unpaid help. The religious dimension is very strong in relation to 'visiting people', and also (not shown) in 'befriending and mentoring' and 'giving advice and information'. Those identifying as being of Asian ethnicity are generally less likely to be engaged in these particular roles but those from Black ethnic groups are overrepresented.

With regard to age, younger age groups are more likely to be involved in 'befriending or mentoring' but substantially less likely to be involved in 'raising or handling money', both of which may point to distinctive patterns of activities (mentoring has featured only recently in the range of options offered in the survey). Conversely, age is highly significant in relation to secretarial and administrative

Table 3.2 Analysis of characteristics of people occupying illustrative types of volunteer roles, England, 2017–22

	Leading a group/ committee member	Visiting people	Secretarial, administrative, clerical	Providing transport/ driving
Sex (ref: men)				
Women	−0.11*	0.28***	0.21***	−0.46***
Socioeconomic status (ref: never worked/ long-term unemployed)				
Semi-routine/routine occupations	−0.28	−0.02	−0.22	0.99**
Lower supervisory/ technical roles	−0.48*	−0.28	−0.75*	1.02**
Small employers/own account workers	−0.25	0.16	−0.36	1.46***
Intermediate	−0.29	−0.11	0.16	0.98**
Higher administrative/ professional workers	−0.00	0.07	0.12	1.07**
Age group (ref: 16–19)				
20–24	0.25	−0.41	0.95	−0.28
25–34	0.20	−0.42	1.08	−0.31
35–49	0.32	−0.31	1.49*	−0.03
50–64	0.67*	−0.11	1.67*	0.29
65–74	1.19***	0.10	2.21**	0.50
Qualifications (ref: none)				
GCSE	0.50***	0.15	1.01***	0.51**
A-level or equivalent	0.72***	0.04	1.26***	0.72***
Higher education or equivalent	1.20***	0.27	1.48***	0.69***
Religion (ref: none)				
Christian	0.30***	0.47***	0.25***	0.29***
Other	0.25*	0.74***	0.13	0.37**
Caring responsibilities (ref: none)				
Yes	0.05	0.63***	−0.04	0.27***
Children in household (ref: none)				
Yes	0.07	−0.02	−0.04	0.47***
Ethnicity (ref: White)				
Asian	−0.74***	0.27*	−0.45*	−0.20
Black	−0.09	0.48***	−0.09	0.01
Mixed/other	−0.02	0.19	−0.05	−0.04

* $p < 0.05$, ** $p < 0.01$, *** $p < 0.001$

roles and leading groups or being a committee member. Something of an exception to the above remarks is 'providing transport or driving', where men are clearly more likely to be engaged than women. In contrast to the base socioeconomic category ('never worked/long-term unemployed'), all other socioeconomic groups are significantly more likely to be involved in this activity, and those from households with children, and those with caring responsibilities, are also much more likely to be providing transport.

To summarise, aggregate generalisations about the volunteering population take us only so far. We need to break these down further to gain insight into specific roles. When we do this, there remain strong dimensions of stratification along age, socioeconomic, educational religious and ethnic lines, with some roles clearly being the preserve of small subsets of the population. The disjuncture shown in Figure 3.1 is a good example of this, but as we have also seen, education is clearly key as a route into many roles within the sector. All of this casts doubt on whether the voluntary sector can be seen as an open and equal field for participation. The gaps are clear, but it is less clear whether they are changing over time.

Conclusions

It is sometimes supposed that socioeconomic factors are less influential on participation in an individualised, reflexive era than was formerly the case (Hustinx and Lammertyn, 2003), but the analyses reviewed here indicated substantial inequalities in volunteering. They certainly raise questions as to whether the 'voluntary spirit' has been ingested equally across the population. Observing that the volunteering population is socioeconomically stratified is not new, but the inequalities demonstrated here are significant, persistent and (to a greater degree than suggested by previous research) evident in both formal and informal voluntary action. These inequalities are reproduced in the roles held by volunteers, notably with regard to governance roles and specifically trusteeships of charities. Here the evidence suggests a very strong representation of people from higher socioeconomic strata with high levels of educational qualifications. In contrast, when we consider activities such as simply visiting people, we find that these socioeconomic gradients are not evident. Inevitably, there are limits to what can be said using survey data about particular forms of 'capital' deployed by volunteers, which is where a relatively small literature on organisation-level stratification provides useful insights. We see not just the demographic overrepresentation of certain groups but also the ways in which particular types of capital are valued in certain roles (some survey data also contribute here, flagging particular occupational groups who appear more likely to be engaged in volunteering, even after a range of socioeconomic controls have been applied).

Beyond socioeconomic and basic demographic categories, there are limitations to large-scale survey analysis, particularly around ethnicity. The largest specialist survey on volunteering (the Community Life Survey) only breaks data down into four categories (white British, Asian, Black and other), and there is no booster sample for minority groups as used to be the case in its predecessor, the Citizenship Survey (2001–11). So this enables only the most broad-brush conclusions to be drawn.

Here, qualitative and biographical research offers insights into the make-up of the volunteering population in particular organisations; there are still relatively few such studies, but they point to the importance of forms of capital other than socioeconomic ones through which people come to occupy specific roles and to the importance of the context (notably, type of place) in which organisations operate.

These inequalities in the volunteering population receive very little attention from policymakers. This issue has been stressed in independent inquiries into the state of the voluntary sector (e.g. Civil Society Futures, 2018: 59). That inquiry perceived the socioeconomic and demographic imbalances in participation, and specifically in governance roles, as part of wider structures of inequality that needed addressing. However, reports of parliamentary inquiries into charities (House of Lords, 2017) and civic participation (House of Lords, 2018) have largely not engaged with these questions.

This evidence points to the limitations of seeing volunteering as an undifferentiated activity, open to all and from which all may benefit. If volunteering is to be an activity that is open to all, the review of analyses of British survey data in this chapter suggests that little has changed over many years. These inequalities are also important because they affect access to the benefits that volunteering might provide (Chapters 7–10). Individual organisations may be able to implement small-scale initiatives to try and increase the diversity of their volunteers (see Van Overbeeke et al., 2022), but in the absence of wider public policies designed to limit inequalities, such strategies are likely to achieve only marginal gains.

4

Core and periphery

The UK has a relatively high and stable rate of engagement in voluntary activity, but most analyses focus on the headline figures about the rate of engagement (proportion of the population involved), while little has been said about the level of actual effort or contribution made (money donated, hours of volunteering undertaken) or about the overlaps between those aspects of prosocial behaviours (but see Low et al., 2007). This chapter illustrates the distribution of voluntary effort across the population and identifies a 'core' of individuals who make the largest contributions. Complementing this, there is also a discussion of what evidence there is for total non-engagement.

Reed and Selbee's (2001) influential Canadian study characterised the 'civic core' as a subset of the population who collectively provided two-thirds of volunteering, charitable giving and participation in civic associations. A 'primary core', containing 6 per cent of Canadian adults, accounted for between one-third and two-fifths of all civic engagement, while a 'secondary core', around three-tenths of the population, was responsible for some four-fifths of the total. They acknowledged that there were no theoretical or empirical bases for expecting any particular distribution of these behaviours (2001: 761) and that the choice of two-thirds of total effort was an arbitrary one. They nevertheless contended that the civic core was a 'strategic social resource' and a 'fundamental component of the social structure' (2001: 761, 776).

Much research on voluntary activity has emphasised that rates of engagement are socioeconomically stratified; there is also evidence of social gradients in levels of engagement. In general, prosperous, educated and employed individuals are not only more likely to volunteer or donate money but they are also likely to contribute more to the collective effort (Wilson, 2000; 2012; Forbes and Zampelli, 2013). These findings are all broadly consistent with the civic voluntarism model of Verba et al. (1995): individuals possessed of time, money and cultural and social capital are likely to be those who are asked to become involved in voluntary organisations.

Building on previous work (Mohan and Bulloch, 2012), I identify the characteristics and distribution of primary contributors to formal and informal volunteering and charitable giving, separately and in combination. The converse of a core is a periphery, so for a complete contrast, the second section of the chapter flips the narrative and concentrates on the extent to which there is evidence of no engagement in these behaviours whatsoever. As with investigations into other aspects of volunteering, what we find depends on where we look: there is less evidence of non-engagement than appears at first sight.

The civic core: data and analysis

Reed and Selbee (2001) defined the civic core in terms of the smallest grouping of the population who, collectively, accounted for two-thirds of all efforts in a particular sphere of activity. Thus, for formal volunteering, this was based on the sum of hours of unpaid help given; for charitable giving it was based on the total funds given to charity; for civic engagement effort was defined in terms of the numbers of memberships each individual had of various types of civic organisation.

These measures can be replicated for England using extant survey data but measuring contributions to associational life in terms of a count of types of organisation does not indicate anything about the extent of involvement in those associations. I therefore modified the approach of Reed and Selbee, dropping their measure of civic engagement, and substituting a measure of the time committed to informal volunteering. There are good reasons for doing so. As noted elsewhere (Chapters 1 and 3), there are concerns that informal volunteering is relegated to a marginal place in discussions of voluntary activity, and there are also arguments that it should be considered alongside formal volunteering and unpaid care as a behaviour which can play an important role in communities. In the Community Life Survey for England, respondents are asked how many hours they spent giving unpaid help to voluntary groups and organisations (formal volunteering) and in giving unpaid help informally in community settings (informal volunteering) as well as how much money they have given to charity in the past four weeks.

The data on volunteering (whether formal or informal) is an estimate of the numbers of hours individuals have committed to the activity over the preceding four weeks. For charitable giving, respondents are asked to estimate the sum of any donations made in the previous four weeks. A small number of large values are truncated – for instance, charitable giving is capped at £300, or £75 per week. The survey runs throughout the year so seasonal effects should not be an issue. There are some reports of very large amounts of volunteering. One respondent claimed the equivalent of approximately 84 hours per week. Since none of the reports were practically impossible (e.g. reporting the equivalent of more than 24 hours of volunteering in a day), and because of the focus on those providing the highest contributions, there was a substantive argument for retaining such cases.

Following Reed and Selbee's approach, ordering respondents in descending order of their contributions allows for the identification of those individuals who have contributed most of the collective effort. A respondent is considered to be a member of the core on a dimension of behaviour if they form part of the smallest grouping in the population to collectively provide two-thirds of the total effort. As an illustration, consider the volunteering core in 2016–17 (more recent data from the same source do not provide the level of detail on effort contributed to permit this analysis). Across the 3,784 respondents (36.9 per cent) who reported an amount of volunteering in the past four weeks, the total number of reported hours of volunteering was 29,606. Two-thirds of these hours were accounted for by 980 people (9.6 per cent of respondents). The threshold value for membership of this core group would be 10 or more hours volunteering in the previous four weeks. Calculated in a similar way, one would have to have given £30 or more to charity in order to be in the charitable giving core, while membership of the core for informal volunteering would have required at least six hours of volunteering in the previous four weeks.

While 37 per cent of the population engaged in formal volunteering, 9.6 per cent of them accounted for two-thirds of the total effort. For informal volunteering, 46.7 per cent participate in this activity but 12.9 per cent deliver two-thirds of the total number of hours, while for charitable giving 13.9 per cent of the population account for two-thirds of total donations. This is not unexpected – charitable giving is more widespread than the other two behaviours, and the great majority of charitable donations are small (the surveys underestimate the concentration of charitable giving because they cannot capture rare, but very large, donations).

Following previous terminology and an earlier UK study (Mohan and Bulloch, 2012), I divide the core into a primary and secondary core. I contrast those core groups with groups comprising individuals who are engaged in prosocial behaviours, though to a level that doesn't reach the threshold of 'core' membership (the engaged non-core), and a group that, according to survey data, are not involved at all in any of the three dimensions of behaviour (the non-engaged). The results are summarised in Table 4.1. The wider primary core is composed of individuals who contribute to a core degree in two out of the three dimensions of behaviour. The primary core holds 6.4 per cent of the population of England and Wales. This group accounts for 38 per cent of formal volunteering and 24 per cent of informal volunteering and charitable giving. A very small subset – 1 per cent of the population – participate in all three of the dimensions of formal engagement to a core degree. They account for 9.6 per cent of all the volunteering hours given, 6 per cent of funds donated to charity and 6 per cent of informal volunteering. Though not discussed here, individuals have diverse ways of making contributions – some members of the primary core are contributing at a high level in two fields of activity but hardly at all in the third.

The secondary core holds 22.4 per cent of the population. This is the subset of people that reach the threshold for membership of the core on only one of the three dimensions of prosocial behaviour. There are 4.6 per cent of the total population in the formal volunteering core, as compared to 8.3 per cent for the informal volunteering core and 9.5 per cent per cent in the charitable giving core. Aggregating the primary and secondary cores together, the full core comprises 28.8 per cent of the population and it provides 78 per cent of all volunteering, 75 per cent of all money given to charity and 74 per cent of participation in informal volunteering. The remaining contribution to these behaviours is provided by the engaged non-core, making up 56 per cent of the population. They may be engaged in any or all of the three activities examined but in no case does their involvement exceed the level that would lead us to classify them as being in the civic core. The remainder of respondents, 15.2 per cent, are not engaged at all in any of these dimensions of behaviour.

As in Reed and Selbee's study, then, behind the headline rates of engagement there lies a wide disparity in levels of participation across the three types of engagement. Reed and Selbee (2001) went on to consider whether different social groups were contributing in proportion to their share of the population. In the analysis presented here, the 1 per cent who are in the core on all three areas of participation provide 9.6 per cent of the total formal volunteering effort. That is obviously disproportionate, being 10 times greater than would be the case if volunteering were to be distributed entirely evenly across the population. Likewise, the 6.4 per cent of the populace who comprise the primary core account for 38 per cent of the total voluntary effort in England, a sixfold disparity.

Table 4.1 Contributions of groups to voluntary effort, England, 2016–17

	Population	Formal volunteering (% of total hours)	Informal volunteering (% of total hours)	Charitable giving (% of total donations)
Non-engaged (on any of these activities)	15.2	0	0	0
Engaged, but non-core	56.0	32.3	26.0	24.5
Secondary core	22.4	40.3	50.2	51.6
Of which:				
Just informal volunteering	9.5	6.2	44.1	4.8
Just giving	8.3	4.3	3.8	44.2
Just formal volunteering	4.6	29.8	2.3	2.6
Primary core	6.4	38.3	23.8	23.8
Of which:				
Giving and formal volunteering	1.9	13.8	10.7	1.3
Giving and informal volunteering	1.4	1.5	5.9	7.0
Formal and informal volunteering	2.1	13.4	1.2	9.6
All three	1.0	9.6	6.0	5.9

Source: Author's calculations from Community Life Survey for England, 2016–17

Is it helpful, however, to propose that contributions to voluntary initiative ought to be 'proportionate'? There are no normative guidelines as to how much engagement we ought to expect from citizens. Should we expect more from the wealthy, since they have the financial resources to contribute, or from the retired, since they have time on their hands? These groups may be regarded as having made contributions either through higher rates of income tax, through a lifetime of working and raising children, or through their working lives. The implication that some groups are contributing less than 'their share' is potentially very problematic, as is the idea that everyone can automatically be expected to do more (see Chapters 11 and 13).

The unequal distribution of voluntary action in England raises the question of whether the members of the different groups we have identified differ from one another. In Table 4.2, the characteristics of three groups of people are presented according to their level of engagement in volunteering and charitable giving. For simplicity, the primary and secondary civic cores are combined here and placed alongside those who are not engaged at all and those who engage at some level in volunteering and giving, but below the threshold of the civic core.

Men are clearly less likely than women to feature in the civic core; well over half of the combined primary and secondary core are female. Membership of the core is skewed towards those aged above 50, compared to younger age groups, where individuals have pressures on their time that limit their level of engagement. There is no obvious pattern according to ethnicity. Education matters: approaching three-fifths of the primary and secondary cores have higher-education qualifications, compared to fewer than one-third for the groups that are not engaged in voluntary activity at all. Socioeconomic status seems strongly associated with core membership; over half of the core are from managerial and professional strata compared to under a third for those who are not engaged at all.

These characteristics interact (Figure 4.1). Some two-fifths of respondents with degrees aged over 50 are part of the primary or

Table 4.2 Characteristics of the civic core and those who are not engaged in volunteering or charitable giving

	Share of:			
	Not engaged in volunteering/ giving	Engaged in volunteering/ giving, but below 'core' threshold	Primary or secondary core	Share of population
Men	58.9	48.1	45.1	49.0
Women	41.1	51.9	54.8	51.0
	Age group			
16–29	32.2	21.9	17.1	22.3
30–39	17.7	16.9	14.0	16.2
40–49	13.1	18.5	16.0	17.0
50–64	20.4	22.2	23.7	22.6
65+	16.5	20.0	29.1	21.9
	Ethnicity			
White	86.1	86.7	86.1	86.5
Asian	8.1	6.6	7.3	7.1
Black	2.4	3.4	3.4	3.2
Mixed/other	3.4	3.2	3.2	3.2

	Share of:			
	Not engaged in volunteering/ giving	Engaged in volunteering/ giving, but below 'core' threshold	Primary or secondary core	Share of population
	Highest educational qualifications			
Higher education	32.5	46.9	57.2	47.6
Post-16	23.0	20.8	17.2	20.1
Secondary/no qualifications	44.6	32.3	25.5	32.3
	Socio-economic classification			
Higher managerial, admin and professional	31.0	46.4	56.5	47.1
Intermediate occupations	18.0	21.2	17.7	19.8
Small employers/ own account professionals	5.4	5.4	4.0	4.2
Lower supervisory and technical occupations	7.8	4.2	2.7	4.3
Semi-routine and routine occupations	27.8	20.4	15.6	20.1
Never worked/ long-term unemployed	10.0	3.7	3.5	4.6

Note: Figures are column percentages within each characteristic – thus, of the non-engaged group, 44.6 per cent have secondary-level or no qualifications, 23.0 per cent have post-16 qualifications and 32.5 per cent have higher-education qualifications.
Source: Author's calculations, Community Life Survey, 2016–17.

secondary core, with the proportion exceeding 50 per cent for women aged over 65 with higher-education qualifications; this picture is slightly obscured by the absence of reliable data on education qualifications for those over 70. What this points to is the challenge of persuading those who are already highly engaged to do even more.

Furthermore, there are also questions of geography: members of the civic core are not randomly distributed. Comparing regions, the south-west of England has the highest proportion of its population in the civic core (34 per cent), while the north-east has the lowest proportion (24 per cent).

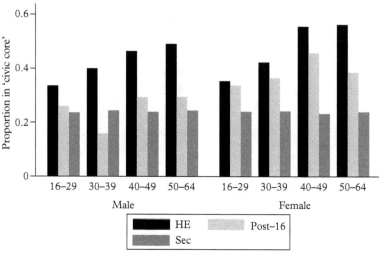

Figure 4.1 Civic core by qualifications, age and sex. Source: Author's calculations from Community Life Survey (2016–17).

The survey data contained deciles of the English Index of Material Deprivation (IMD), which show that around one-quarter of respondents who live in the most disadvantaged parts of England are in the core, but the proportion rises to around 35 per cent in the most prosperous decile of areas. Greater variation is evident when we cross-tabulate region and decile of deprivation, with some areas within regions such as south-west and south-east England having over two-fifths of their residents being part of the civic core. However, caution is advisable with these cross-tabulations, as there are small numbers of survey respondents in some areas (e.g. some regions of England have few communities that are in the most prosperous decile in the country). The figures that we do have still point to the contrasts that exist between communities. The converse patterns are evident for non-engagement; nearly 20 per cent of the residents of the most disadvantaged decile of England are not engaged at all in any of the activities examined here, compared to 10 per cent in the most well-off places. Causal interpretation of geographical patterns requires some caution. First, deprivation is measured at the residential locations of respondents and so we cannot tell whether or not individuals' actions or donations are oriented towards the neighbourhoods where they live. While we know that a larger share of the population of prosperous areas are in the civic core, they could still be volunteering in disadvantaged places, but the data cannot throw light on that.

Summing up this discussion, the value of the idea of a civic 'core' is in drawing attention to the skewed nature of participation, with all three dimensions of behaviour being characterised by reliance on relatively small subsets of the population. Socioeconomic patterning of the membership of the core group is a notable feature, again suggesting that those possessed of resources, of various kinds, not only are more likely to participate but are also more likely to contribute a greater share of the total effort.

Though not shown here, it can also be suggested that the civic core is a fairly stable feature of voluntary action. An earlier version of this analysis (Mohan and Bulloch, 2012) did not include informal volunteering but found broadly similar distributions for charitable giving and formal volunteering (direct comparison is not possible because less detail is available in the survey data for 2016–17 about the hours of volunteering and amounts given to charity). That earlier analysis also found similar spatial gradients between regions and geographical areas. This raises the point that the civic core constitutes a significant proportion of the adult population in some communities and that they are already heavily engaged. If more is to be expected of communities, there are places where an existing high level of engagement constrains what additional effort may be forthcoming.

The periphery: non-engagement in volunteering

The decline of citizen participation in voluntary action has been lamented, and key sector stakeholders, influential enquiries and policy pronouncements have all emphasised the desirability of giving those who are apparently not engaged in volunteering opportunities to do so. By implication, there is a problem of non-engagement.

The analysis of the civic core points to clear differences between that core and those who, on the basis of the measures available in the survey used to analyse it, are not engaged at all. If we can clearly identify the non-engaged, it would be useful to know whether they constitute a highly distinctive subset of the population, or whether there is little that demarcates them from those who are civically active. There is a literature on 'volunteerability' (Haski-Leventhal et al., 2018) which points to subsets of the population who in principle might be drawn into volunteering, but – in the UK at least – we know little about how large this group might be or about the characteristics of those involved.

In this section I draw on a wider body of evidence to quantify the *extent of non-engagement* in voluntary action, using cross-sectional and longitudinal survey data by considering not just volunteering itself but also combinations of individual behaviours (participating in associations, volunteering through organisations, informal volunteering in communities, giving to charity) and variations therein over the course of individual lifetimes. I then illustrate some of the underlying covariates of non-engagement, such as levels of education and age. Longitudinal sources offer further insights into whether individuals have intermittent patterns of participation over time. I also turn to qualitative research into people's understandings of non-engagement. This enables consideration of how voluntary action does (or does not) fit easily within people's life-courses, and how circumstances may disrupt trajectories of engagement or, alternatively, provide new opportunities for becoming involved. All of this points to a more complicated – yet arguably more optimistic – picture of non-engagement than has perhaps hitherto been available.

The extent of nonparticipation

The scale of nonparticipation is hard to estimate, one reason being the range of surveys in which questions are asked that bear on (or could be relevant to) the topic. The focus of these can be very narrow, such as specific dimensions of civic engagement; others are very broad, investigating many topics such as formal and informal volunteering, donations of money to charity and associational membership. As a result, the non-engaged are sometimes in a minority, sometimes not, depending on what is measured and with what degree of detail. I draw on two decades of survey data about informal and formal volunteering, and charitable giving, drawn from the Citizenship Survey and its successor, the Community Life Survey, for 2001 onwards. The focus on multiple dimensions of engagement is because of the possibility that individuals are substituting activity in one domain for activity in another (e.g. replacing the giving of time with donations of money). On individual dimensions of engagement, there is usually a non-engaged majority – for example, currently over 60 per cent of the adult population report that they do not do formal volunteering. In contrast, only some 25–30 per cent do not give to charity. Across the board, around one-fifth or fewer respondents to these robust annual surveys have, in recent times, reported neither volunteering (whether formal or informal) nor charitable giving.

Thus non-engagement is small, and if we were to consider unpaid caring in addition (and remember that its value is over five times that of volunteering, see Chapter 2 and Petrillo and Bennett (2023)), then the effect would be to reduce the proportion who are not engaged by a further 3–4 per cent (although around one-tenth of respondents indicate that they carry out unpaid care in some capacity, more than half of these are also volunteering too).

The level of non-engagement is much higher in some subsets of the population. Figure 4.2 demonstrates this: for those aged 18–69 and who have higher-education qualifications, the proportion who do no volunteering (formal or informal) nor give money to charity is generally less than 10 per cent, whereas for those who have left school with only secondary-level qualifications the proportion is at least double that.

On the basis of these data we might conclude that there is really not a generalised problem of non-engagement, though if we were to focus on specific, individual dimensions of engagement, such as formal volunteering, we would find that a majority of the population are not engaged.

The numbers would shrink further if we asked not about non-engagement at one point in time but instead posed the question: what proportion of people do not engage at all *during their lives*? As shown in Chapter 6, when the same people are tracked through successive waves of longitudinal surveys, the baseline proportion engaged in volunteering is half the proportion of the population that engages in it on more than one occasion over a series of years. Cross-sectional surveys provide snapshots of involvement but underestimate lifetime engagement.

The study which has asked people about volunteering and civic engagement over the longest timespan of people's lives is the National Child Development Study (NCDS), which follows all babies born in one selected week in 1958 in England, Scotland and Wales (Power and Elliott, 2006). Through 12 waves of data collection, information has been assembled on the number and type of groups and organisations of which individuals have been members, the frequency of participation in group activities and (though not in every wave) whether they undertake voluntary work. Approximately 6,450 people took part in every adulthood data collection wave up to 2008, following cohort members at the ages of 23, 33, 41, 46 and 50. I draw on a comprehensive investigation (Brookfield et al., 2014; 2018a; 2018b) of the volunteering and civic engagement of several thousand individuals tracked during a period of 27 years of their lives when they were aged between 23 and 50.

86 Contours

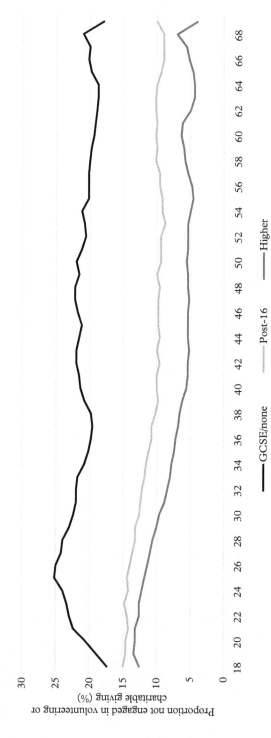

Figure 4.2 Age, education and non-engagement, ages 18–69. Source: Author's calculations from Citizenship Survey/Community Life Survey data (2001–16). Note that subsequent surveys no longer provide age as a continuous variable, reducing the granularity of the data. Figures are five-year moving averages.

The survey data provided an overview of lifelong participation and its converse: nonparticipation. The lifelong participants had recorded associational activities at all survey waves since 1981 and volunteering on the two occasions questions were asked directly about it, in 1981 and 2008, when cohort members were aged 23 and 50 respectively. Conversely, the survey data identified 974 members as lifelong nonparticipants. These individuals (approximately 15 per cent of those participating at every wave) reported nonparticipation in group activities, volunteering, clubs and groups and non-attendance at religious services throughout their adult lives. This may appear to be a relatively low level of non-engagement, but Brookfield et al. (2018b) suggested that even so, it was an *overestimate* of 'true' nonparticipation because there was evidence that, at various points through these individuals' lives, they had been involved in one or more of these activities but had not reported them in surveys (possibly because they weren't actually involved at the time of the surveys but had instead been engaged at some point between survey waves – recall that these take place at wide intervals).

The evidence for this came from the Social Participation and Identity Study (SPIS), which was carried out through interviews with 220 NCDS cohort members in 2008 (Elliott et al., 2010). Interviews explored the nature and extent of cohort members' participation behaviours, the motivations for participating, how participation fitted into an individual's life, patterns and changes in participation behaviours and the reasons behind any changes. Brookfield et al. (2018a) identified, using the NCDS survey data, individuals whose responses indicated either lifelong nonparticipation or lifelong participation, as well as patterns of frequent participation in between these two extremes. They drew on the transcripts for 50 interviewees, chosen to reflect these extremes of the participation distribution as well as those in between. Most of those identified as lifelong nonparticipants by the survey data described a range of occasional activities which clearly corresponded to conventional definitions of voluntary action. These included helping with groups and organisations, usually on an ad hoc basis and usually ones associated with their children. Having selected 21 'lifelong nonparticipants', Brookfield et al. (2018a) concluded that only six of these emerged as 'true' lifelong nonparticipants, which is therefore very much a minority disposition (Brookfield et al., 2018a). Lindsey and Mohan (2018: 78) also record similar examples of individuals writing for Mass Observation who declared that they were not volunteers when prompted to write about voluntary action, yet evidence from other responses they had submitted demonstrated long and substantial involvement in organisations.

What can we say, then, about the characteristics of nonparticipants? An absence of participation has long been associated with certain socioeconomic and demographic traits (Verba et al., 1995; Pattie et al., 2004). In one of a small number of published works that address the topic, Sundeen et al. (2007) adopted a resource-based approach in seeking to understand the reasons given by individuals for their non-engagement. When individuals are asked about why they *haven't* volunteered, they give three types of rationalisation. First, there are reasons relating to the resources which they possess: a lack of time or money; perceptions that they lack relevant skills or experience; and the costs and constraints of engagement such as childcare or transport. Second, there are reasons relating to their social networks and social capital – particularly that they have not been asked, which is a function of their social networks. Third, cultural capital and resources: their beliefs, attitudes or values are not a good fit with the opportunities available to them, leading individuals to cite a lack of interest.

These economic, social and cultural resources are not randomly distributed, a conclusion echoed by other studies (Plagnol and Huppert, 2010; Brodie et al., 2011). But the reasons given by respondents for non-engagement will vary. In Sundeen et al.'s (2007) work, respondents citing time pressures were found to differ from those who referenced a lack of interest, the latter being much more likely to lack resources and to be occupying subordinate socioeconomic statuses and roles.

Representative national survey data for England echo Sundeen et al.'s (2007) findings. Considering only those who do not volunteer, respondents to the Citizenship Survey were presented with a menu of 17 potential answers to a question about barriers to volunteering. Work commitments (56 per cent) were followed by caring and family commitments of various kinds (40 per cent) and 'having other things to do with my spare time' (24 per cent) (respondents could choose more than one possible response). Confirming Sundeen et al. (2007), over 70 per cent of those with higher-education qualifications who did not volunteer said that they did not do so because of work commitments. In contrast, for those with caring responsibilities the educational gradient was in the other direction (Lindsey and Mohan, 2018: chapter 6); those who had lower educational qualifications were more likely to cite caring responsibilities as a reason why they were not engaged in voluntary action.

In Brookfield et al.'s (2018a) work, lifelong nonparticipation had distinctive demographic traits, being strongly associated with lower educational attainment; frequent and lifelong participants were more likely to possess higher-education qualifications than were lifelong nonparticipants while the majority of nonparticipants held qualifications at NVQ level 2 or below (that is GCSE-level qualifications taken at age 16). Poor health was also implicated. Self-reports of poor health at the age of 50 were much more common among lifelong nonparticipants compared to persistent participants; over two-thirds of nonparticipants had scores, on an established scale used to assess psychological well-being, above a threshold used to measure risk of psychological distress. Other aspects of socioeconomic differentiation did not appear to be specifically associated with lifelong nonparticipation, though median weekly take-home income was substantially greater for the lifelong participants compared to the nonparticipants (Brookfield et al., 2018a).

Qualitative accounts about non-engagement from individuals

What accounts are given by individuals of non-engagement? We have seen that survey data about barriers to volunteering can provide some insights, but we cannot differentiate a respondent who genuinely has no interest in becoming engaged in their community, and who responds to a question about barriers to volunteering by choosing what looks like the most socially desirable response, from someone who has completely rigid constraints on their time which therefore prevent them from becoming involved.

Available qualitative accounts strongly emphasised substantial competing pressures from work commitments and caring responsibilities. In the SPIS interview transcripts, work commitments, specifically long or unsociable working hours, shift patterns and lengthy commutes, as well as work-related tiredness, were put forward. The prominence of work constraints was interesting, according to Brookfield et al. (2018a), because the work patterns and histories of nonparticipants did not appear to set them apart from other cohort members who were also more active social participants. The issue might therefore be the *experience* of time pressures – some individuals, perhaps because of resources or personality, found pressures much harder to manage (Brookfield et al., 2018a: 8). In common with previous findings (Brodie et al., 2011; Lindsey and Mohan, 2018: 173–5, 210–11), caring duties, which encompassed caring for children, older parents, and even pets, were presented as longstanding and binding constraints which had evolved over cohort members' lives. From the responses given, the combination of work and caring appear to squeeze out opportunities for participation and responses of this kind were more common than what might be termed person-related factors such as individual preferences (e.g. someone with a predilection for avoiding participation in organised groups). Where such influences were mentioned, they included a preference to spend time at home, a lack of interest in participation (and very occasionally an active dislike of clubs and groups), health problems, sometimes associated by cohort members with the ageing process (see also Brodie et al., 2011), and occasional specific references to mental health (Lindsey and Mohan, 2018: 173–5).

An important finding of Brookfield et al.'s work is that some individuals were identified by survey data as lifelong nonparticipants, but their qualitative interview transcripts show that in fact they had had some experiences of community participation. The informal, past and ad hoc involvements of the lifelong 'nonparticipants' whose SPIS interviews indicated that they had some participation experience appeared to be motivated by self-interest; the prospect of direct or indirect personal gain usually prompted participation. Examples of self-interested motivations could include participation in leisure, through the medium of a gym subscription; establishing a homeowners' association to save money on leasehold fees; paying a subscription to sports clubs in order to play for a team; or becoming members of heritage organisations. Some had, however, helped out in organisations and activities associated with their children, though participation in these activities and groups ended when their children's involvement ceased. For some commentators, this type of instrumental participation has been seen as replacing traditional, close-knit social ties built on principles of mutual support and cooperation (Putnam, 2000). If, strictly speaking, these people could not be classed as nonparticipants, those involved were participating in a somewhat transactional fashion. By and large, these 'nonparticipants' did not engage in groups or activities that benefited people beyond their immediate circle; unpaid help given to unknown others was uncommon.

Conclusions

This chapter has drawn together findings on two contrasting groups: those who constitute the 'civic core', providing a disproportionate share of volunteering and other forms of civic engagement; and those for whom there appeared to be no clear evidence of any involvement in voluntary action.

The idea of voluntary action in communities being led by a small group of committed and skilled individuals is a familiar one from the history of voluntary action (Beveridge, 1948). There is certainly strong evidence that a relatively small minority which provides the bulk of volunteering and charitable giving remains important. It is striking to note that the phenomenon of disproportionality is as evident in England as it was in Reed and Selbee's original study of the topic: around three-tenths of the adult population account for over three-quarters of the varying commitments analysed. As with the likelihood of engagement, the level of engagement is also socially stratified. Within some demographic subgroups of the population (educated women aged above 50), around three-fifths are members of the core on at least one dimension of activity. Our findings are consistent with the existing literature on prosocial behaviours, which has emphasised a number of individual characteristics that have been shown to be associated with levels of activity as well as rates of activity.

What about a periphery? Here, the evidence is less clear-cut. Cross-sectional studies suggest that nonparticipation in both formal and informal volunteering is very much a minority disposition, while longitudinal studies which track individuals over significant portions of their lives suggest that there are really very small proportions of the adult population who can be regarded as genuine lifelong non-participants. Arguably, there is no reasonable way in which we could confidently characterise an individual as being permanently disengaged. Participation, however informal and ad hoc, at some point in nearly everyone's lives, appeared by far the dominant condition. Where it can be definitely identified, nonparticipation appears more strongly associated with lower levels of income, poorer health and lower levels of educational attainment; in this regard, the analysis echoes prior scholarship (Sundeen et al., 2007). Adverse labour market experiences, and levels of community disadvantage, also seem to play a part in processes of disengagement, as is also revealed by discussions of the consequences of economic change for disengagement (Chapter 11). With this in mind, policymakers and stakeholders should focus on the issues that are reported as barriers such as working arrangements or the availability of childcare.

What, then, are the prospects for an expansion of the civic core? The think-tank ResPublica suggested that we need to double the size of the core (Wilson and Leach, 2011). This is superficially attractive, although it is obviously impossible for some subsets of the population where over half already engage at the requisite level. More fundamentally, the idea of expanding the core is a moving target. The way the degree of concentration of effort is measured influences the results. If reports of charitable giving were not capped at £300 in the survey data analysed here, the reporting of amounts above that threshold would decrease the size of the charitable giving 'core', because a smaller number of individuals would account for a larger share of the total funds donated. Discussions about the 'core' also draw us into the normative terrain of 'proportionality': the implication is whether or not subsets of the population are doing 'their share' or not. From a policy perspective, this is potentially contentious. Suggesting that particular groups are 'poor' contributors and need to make more effort (whether by becoming engaged at all or by doing more) is judgemental, politically problematic and potentially inaccurate, if it is based on evidence that does not capture all of the ways in which people engage in their communities. It is often a complex combination of structural factors that either enable or prevent individuals from engaging (Musick and Wilson, 2008).

A focus on getting people to engage in volunteering to begin with, or on raising their level of engagement to that of the 'core', ignores the diverse reality of people's lives. When discussing non-engagement, qualitative research usually finds that there are good reasons for it. The idea of the 'total social organisation of labour' (Glucksmann, 2005) draws attention to the multiple combinations of paid and unpaid work, formal and informal voluntary activity, and unpaid caring that citizens undertake. The general lesson for policy is that undifferentiated appeals for people to do more in their communities need to be tempered by an acknowledgement of individual circumstances and different ways of contributing to society. Individuals make decisions to engage but they do so under conditions not of their own choosing, and states can make choices about economic management and welfare provision which can influence those conditions.

Finally, a particular challenge for policy arising from this analysis is that there are very strong geographical gradients in the distribution of the core. These groups tend to be concentrated in the most prosperous locations. This is largely a consequence of socioeconomic segregation, but it matters if communities are going to be called upon to play a greater role in meeting social needs. Since the most prosperous communities also turn out to be those where we find the people who contribute most, should we assume that those communities will also benefit most? With these and other related questions in mind, we now turn to the issue of community-level variations in voluntary action.

5

Community-level variations in voluntary action: places don't volunteer, people do

Introduction

Introducing his report to the then Prime Minister Boris Johnson on the theme of 'levelling up our communities' in July 2020, Danny Kruger MP cited the wave of volunteer support during the COVID-19 pandemic as evidence of an appetite for reforms in social policy which would place communities at the heart of a 'more plural, local, bottom-up system' (Kruger, 2020: 7). An omission from his report was a discussion of community-level variations in voluntary action – arguably a striking omission given that 'levelling up' is a shorthand for policies designed to reduce economic and social inequalities between and within the UK's regions. A subsequent government White Paper (DLUHC, 2022) gave considerable detail about community-level variations in economic statistics, education qualifications and life expectancy, and life satisfaction. While making frequent references to social capital and voluntary action, like the Kruger report, this report was also silent on spatial variations in volunteering rates. These vary substantially between the most disadvantaged and most prosperous parts of England – put another way, these patterns are far more unequal than many of the disparities which featured in the White Paper.

There hasn't been much debate about these variations, but since spatial inequality is likely to endure as a challenge for social policy in the UK, what can be said about the drivers of community-level variations in volunteering? Coverage of voluntary action occasionally features accounts of ostensibly exceptional, locally based projects. One example is the 'participatory city' initiative, seeking to mobilise voluntary effort in the London Borough of Barking and Dagenham. It was claimed that this had generated some 28,000 additional hours of voluntary effort in the borough (Britton et al., 2023; Shaw, 2021) (though the achievements of this initiative have been disputed, as it also relied on substantial private and foundation grants leveraged by substantial public money, see Mahony and Northrop, 2020). Without wishing to decry the efforts of those involved, that number of volunteers represented approximately 1,000 extra volunteers in a borough with a population of around 210,000 (assuming that the recruits donate the median hours of voluntary effort each month as reported in reliable national surveys).

Data on variations in volunteering levels can be trumpeted as a badge of community innovation and virtue but can also prompt stigmatising rhetoric which lays the blame for disadvantage at the apparent failure of communities to meet their own needs through voluntary action. This matters, because public policies have been predicated on a prominent role for voluntary action which has been justified on the grounds that communities are best placed to identify and meet immediate local needs. There is a widespread acceptance that current and likely future scenarios for public service provision will continue to require communities to step forwards. Therefore, we need a better understanding of variations between communities in the likelihood that such responses will be forthcoming.

Identification of community-level variations dates at least to the 1978 Wolfenden Report, the key post-war investigation of the voluntary sector, which argued that 'some social and geographical contexts seem to provide a much more fertile soil for voluntary action than others' (Wolfenden Committee, 1978: 58). However, the research team lacked the data that would have allowed them to evaluate this proposition. When regional differences in volunteering were first revealed in survey data, it was thought that rates of volunteering varying from 17 to 31 per cent seemed unlikely to be explicable solely by variations in the composition of those living in different areas. But due to small sample sizes for subnational units, researchers were reluctant to assert that there were regional effects on engagement (Mohan et al., 2006: 267–70).

The first policy focus on community-level variations was in the Blair government's wider programmes of economic and social renewal. Participation and engagement of communities were a specific requirement of urban renewal initiatives such as the New Deal for Communities. Local authorities were expected to play their part, too, in supporting the government's desire to increase the national rate of volunteering, and local volunteering rates became one of a basket of performance indicators against which local authorities might be assessed. The Coalition government of David Cameron (2010–15) disavowed such targetry, but inevitably its Big Society policies, with their combination of voluntarism and localism, invited community-level comparisons. English local authorities were ranked in terms of their 'community wealth' or their degree of preparedness for the 'Big Society' (Sutcliffe and Holt, 2011). One such analysis displayed an impressive degree of confidence in its precision, offering a 'Big Society metric' which was calculated to nine decimal places (!) (Keohane et al., 2011: 110–15).

In the subsequent decade, despite many investigations into the strengths of voluntary action, there has been little acknowledgement of the persistent gradients between communities in volunteering. The Centre for Social Justice's report *Something's Got to Give* noted the importance of increasing volunteering rates in disadvantaged areas (CSJ, 2013: 80–1) but did not analyse the substantial community-level variations evident from survey data. Subsequent inquiries have paid relatively little attention to the issue, apart from some references in a House of Lords (2018) report regarding efforts to ensure that engagement opportunities for young people were available in disadvantaged areas. In the Levelling Up White Paper, as noted, variations in volunteering rates are not discussed, though there are references to efforts to increase opportunities for youth volunteering and to target some funds on places with low social capital (DLUHC, 2022: 212–14).

From a policy perspective, with the current emphasis on social capital as a key element in community renewal, we need to understand the extent to which geographic context influences volunteering and the mechanisms through which it might do so. In this chapter I first of all explain why there might be reasons to expect variations between communities in the proportions of their residents engaged in voluntary action. Then I describe the scale of the variations, initially by deploying large-scale datasets and cross-referencing volunteering rates against measures of socioeconomic characteristics. This is followed by an overview of the results of analyses which have sought to separate out genuinely *contextual* effects on volunteering – in other words, influences that are not simply a result of variations in the mix of individuals between communities.

Reasons to anticipate community-level variations in volunteering

Why might volunteering rates vary between communities? First, there are variations in the social mix of communities by age, class, ethnicity and gender (see Chapter 3; Musick and Wilson, 2008; Rochester et al., 2010: chapter 4; Wilson, 2000). Therefore, some variations between communities in volunteering will be attributable solely to the mix of individuals resident in different places.

Furthermore, volunteering largely takes place locally: most people become involved through social networks which are local in focus (e.g. school, church or other voluntary groups) or in response to solicitation from a local organisation (Musick and Wilson, 2008: 319). Most people travel short distances to volunteer and serve local organisations (the great majority of UK registered charities operate only within a single local authority (Clifford, 2012)). Participation is shaped by local issues and problems and also by local social networks which draw people into engagement. Musick and Wilson (2008: 323–41) also point out other community-level influences, including the uneven distribution of voluntary organisations, which reflects a combination of historic influences and contemporary conditions. Since uneven development means that the resources available to communities to support voluntary organisations are likely to depend on the local distribution of wealth, the spatial pattern of organisations is often inversely related to need (Wolch, 1990; Clifford, 2012; 2018). Such variations are persistent – the pattern of charitable organisations in England in 2011 was closely correlated to the pattern evident in 1971 (McDonnell et al., 2020; see also Sampson, 2012, for a similar argument from the USA). Researchers find a small but significant increase in the likelihood of voluntary action as the density of voluntary organisations rises (Rotolo and Wilson, 2012: 454; Lam et al., 2022; Mohan and Bennett, 2019).

How then do we account for community-level variations in volunteering? Self-selection into geographical areas means that some areas will be composed of people with more human, social and cultural capital resources that in turn increase the likelihood that they will volunteer (Wilson and Musick, 1997). In a statistical sense, controlling for this *compositional* influence will account for some area-level differences in volunteering. An analogy is that when comparing the relative health status of communities (e.g. their mortality rates), we routinely standardise for the age composition of the population. Second, if we are able to investigate the independent influence of *contextual* factors associated with certain characteristics of an area, over and above the aggregate properties of individuals resident there, we may be able to explain more of the variation in volunteering between areas. The level of disadvantage of an area may explain some of the variance – for example, because it provides fewer opportunities, and all citizens in a deprived area are affected by this context and are thus less likely to volunteer irrespective of their own socioeconomic status. The degree of ethnic heterogeneity or population turnover in a neighbourhood may also influence people's trust and willingness to engage with their co-residents (Sampson, 2012).

Measuring voluntary action locally

The UK possesses various data sources on community-level variations in volunteering. Social surveys usually do not have a sufficiently large sample size to generate precise local authority-level estimates. For England, survey data for named local authorities are available from the large-scale Place Surveys conducted in 2008–9. The usual source of socioeconomic data about communities and their residents is the decennial census. The possibility of including a question on volunteering was considered by the Office for National Statistics (ONS) in planning for the 2011 census, but it was concluded that there was insufficient user demand. However, a question was included in the Northern Ireland census for 2011, although it was not repeated in 2021. An alternative source for local information is administrative data – for instance, blood donorship rates provide a potential measure of local variation in prosocial behaviours. They were used in an earlier analysis (Mohan et al., 2004) but donation is a managed process, and opportunities to donate are not uniformly distributed, so blood donation rates are not an unproblematic measure of community dispositions. Sample survey data on voluntary action provides some spatial references, and the results of work with such data are considered in the section 'Patterns and trends of volunteering by region and deprivation'.

Place Surveys of England

The largest social survey to ask about volunteering was the one-off Place Survey, conducted for English local authorities in 2008. This survey was introduced as part of the Labour government's performance regime for public service reform, under which local authorities were assessed against a range of 'national indicators', one of which was 'participation in regular volunteering' (DCLG, 2008). Some 500,000 individual responses were gathered.

The Place Survey asked whether or not individuals engaged in the provision of 'unpaid help' to any group, club or organisation. It did not offer the extensive prompts characteristic of the NSV (Chapter 2). Nevertheless, it remains the only large-scale attempt to measure

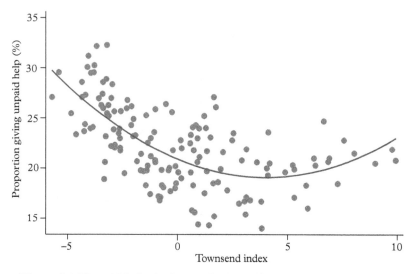

Figure 5.1 Unpaid help (volunteering) and Townsend Index of Deprivation, English local authorities, 2008. Source: author's calculations from Place Surveys (2008); census (unpaid care) (2011).

volunteering for local authorities in England. There were some variations in survey methodology between local authorities, prompting concerns as to the representativeness of responses, so analysis is restricted to those local authorities for which the confidence intervals on the estimate were less than +/− 3 per cent.[1]

Rates of engagement ranged from 14 to 36 per cent, an order of magnitude of 2.5, which is broadly comparable with the range in reported levels of formal volunteering for a cross-classification of region and decile of deprivation (McCulloch et al., 2012). These figures are plotted against the Townsend Index of Deprivation for 2011; a negative score on this index indicates a lower level of deprivation (Figure 5.1). A simple trend line is fitted; as deprivation increases, the level of volunteering drops steadily but then flattens out, rising

---

[1] Unfortunately, these surveys were the responsibility of individual local authorities, and variations in the survey methods used give rise to patterns of response which may not be comparable across local authorities – hence the pragmatic focus on local authorities with estimates within these confidence intervals.

again in the most deprived areas. All those with a Townsend Index greater than 5 are London Boroughs. Their volunteering rate is low but it does not continue to decline – possibly because of other features of their demography not captured here. Nevertheless, the contrast between the more prosperous and most deprived areas is clear enough.

Census data

Only in 2011 was a question on volunteering included in the UK census, and then only in Northern Ireland. It asked, rather generally, without any more contextual guidance: 'In the past year, have you helped with, or carried out any voluntary work without pay?' However, by definition (since it was asked of every adult in Northern Ireland, and there is very high compliance with the UK's census) it had the largest number of responses of any UK attempt to ask about volunteering (231,851 volunteers were recorded, out of a population of 1.43 million aged 16 and over). Variations between local authorities were small, from 14 to 17 per cent, but this is within a small area of the UK without much variation in prosperity at local authority level. A small-area analysis shows volunteering rates ranging from below 5 per cent, typically in the most disadvantaged parts of west Belfast, to over 20 per cent in the most prosperous, generally rural, communities. When we cross-reference this against socioeconomic statistics such as unemployment, we find a clear gradient in which volunteering rates declined as levels of local area deprivation in the community increased (Figure 5.2).

These illustrations point to the strong ecological (area-level) association between disadvantage and levels of engagement in voluntary action. Though not discussed in detail here, the same was true for blood donation, using local authority-level data for 2011 from the National Blood Service. Restricting analysis to 324 local authorities in England in which there were at least 1,000 active donors (a total of 1.3 million across the local authorities combined), donorship rates ranged from practically zero to 5 per cent of the adult population (mean 27 per cent, standard deviation 0.8). As with the Place Surveys, there is a strong negative relationship between donorship rates and deprivation (a correlation of −0.71). Other analyses highlight the relatively low rate of donation in London, urban–rural differences and variations in the opportunity to donate (Lattimore et al., 2015). Mohan et al. (2004) showed that various prosperous rural and suburban places appeared much more likely than others to generate high donorship rates, even after allowing for local demographics.

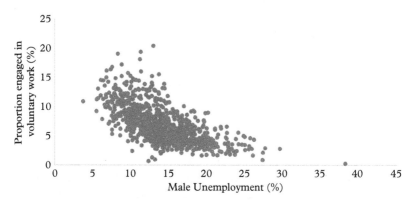

Figure 5.2 Volunteering and male unemployment rates, Super Output Areas, Northern Ireland, 2011. Source: author's calculations from 2011 census.

Donorship rates will reflect administrative processes – decisions taken by the blood collection service to locate its collection centres. As such, while the associations with social disadvantage are striking, there are limits to what can be said about community-level variations without more granular, individual-level data on how individuals behave in different contexts. Nevertheless, these contrasting sources for local measurements of volunteering, conducted in different ways and in two different parts of the UK, display a consistent picture of a strong negative relationship between volunteering rates and community socioeconomic disadvantage.

Patterns and trends of volunteering by region and deprivation

These local authority measures are snapshots at one point in time. What can be said about change or stability in the patterns over a period of years? Survey data usually contain geographical references which allow some disaggregation of volunteering statistics. In England, the Citizenship Survey (2001–11) and most waves of the Community Life Survey (2012–) allow a cross tabulation of region and level of deprivation in the area of residence of respondents. The latter is the IMD, a composite socioeconomic index that is split into deciles or quintiles according to the national distribution of observations on it. This gives a classification with 90 (or 45) cells (i.e. nine regions (of England) cross-classified against 10 deciles of the IMD (or five quintiles)). Alternatively, analysis can be presented for deciles or quintiles of deprivation on a national basis.

In all regions of England, we find substantial variations within the units defined by this classification. This can be seen in Figure 5.3, which contrasts the 90th and 10th percentiles of the distribution of annual rates of formal volunteering over time.

The gap between rates across these units is substantial – for example ranging between 50 per cent to under 25 per cent in the 2000s and, at the end of the time period, between 35 and 15 per cent.

Analysis of comparisons between quintiles of the distribution of deprivation shows a very similar pattern. There is a clear distinction between the most prosperous areas, where formal volunteering rates on an annual basis have been 50 per cent or even higher, and the most disadvantaged areas, where rates are often around 20 per cent, if that. Figure 5.4 shows the rates of engagement in formal and informal volunteering for the period from 2007 to 2022. It contrasts the most prosperous communities (as measured by quintiles of the index of deprivation) and the least prosperous.

Because there were changes to the indices of deprivation over this period, some areas will have moved into different parts of the distribution of deprivation. This limits the ability to compare local variations in volunteering rates over time, but the representation of the data here simply seeks to show the gap in rates of volunteering, so it does not rely on comparing absolutely identical spatial units.

The key features are that for these relatively large aggregations of places – covering one-fifth of the population in the country – formal volunteering through organisations is nearly twice as common in the most prosperous locations. More than half of adults in the most prosperous quintile of the country were engaged in this way in the early 2000s, compared to 30 per cent or fewer in the most deprived quintile. Indeed, in some areas of the country, estimates of formal volunteering at this time would have had a little over three-fifths engaged in this activity. The gap has persisted over time, throughout the 17-year period for which the data are available, so it is a fairly stable feature. Informal volunteering has a narrower gap – because it isn't an activity that requires so much in the way of economic, social and cultural capital, nor necessarily the presence of a strong organisational base, we would expect more people to be able to engage in it generally. Typically, informal volunteering rates in the most disadvantaged areas are between two-thirds and three-quarters of those in the most prosperous quintile of neighbourhoods. So there is some evidence that informal volunteering is more evident in disadvantaged

102 Contours

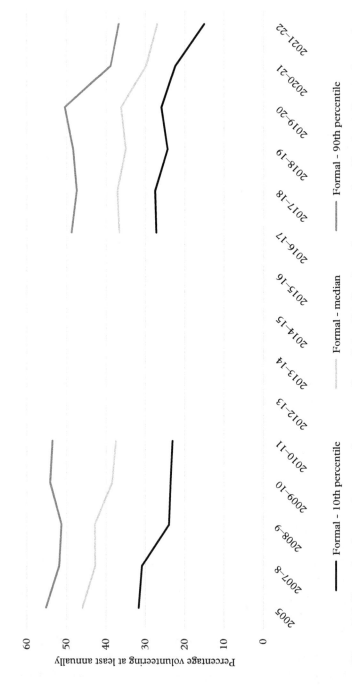

Figure 5.3 Formal volunteering rates for percentiles of the distribution of a cross-classification of areas by region and deprivation, 2005–22. Source: author's calculations from Citizenship Survey and Community Life Survey. Note: data omitted for 2012–13 to 2015–16 due to small sample sizes.

Community-level variations in voluntary action 103

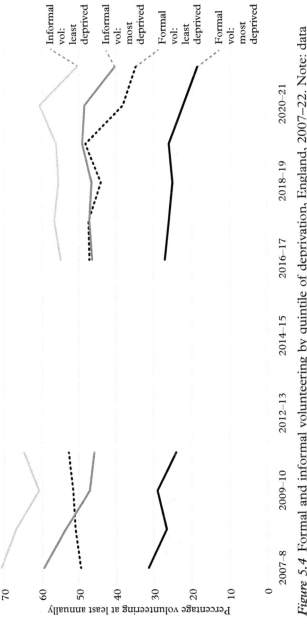

Figure 5.4 Formal and informal volunteering by quintile of deprivation, England, 2007–22. Note: data omitted for 2012–13 to 2015–16 due to small sample sizes.

neighbourhoods than formal volunteering, but it remains the case that there are higher rates of informal volunteering in prosperous areas than there are in deprived ones.

These are aggregate figures, but their importance is in illuminating the scale of community-level variations and their relationship with disadvantage. Moreover, the gaps are ones which endure. The question which then follows is whether the differences indicate the presence of a genuine contextual effect rather than being merely the outcome of compositional differences in the mix of populations between communities.

Multi-level studies of volunteering

There are strong and persistent community-level variations in volunteering, but to what extent are those due to differences in the mix of individuals between places, as opposed to being the result of specific characteristics of places? The overall likelihood that an individual will act as a volunteer in their local community will partly reflect individual characteristics (age, gender, ethnicity, material circumstances) and it will also reflect ecological or contextual influences. Analyses therefore need to capture both individual and area effects simultaneously and analyse interactions between the two. For example, there may be place effects which serve to depress or raise the probability of volunteering that we would otherwise have expected on the basis of an individual's personal characteristics.

This requires a particular type of analytical strategy – multi-level modelling, which takes account of effects at an individual level (personal characteristics of survey respondents) and at an area level (e.g. contextual features of the neighbourhoods or locations in which the respondents are located). To do this, survey data are required that contain data both on individuals and on the characteristics of the places in which those individuals live. One of the largest surveys of voluntary action – the GHSs of 1987 and 1992 – presented data for at most 22 spatial units (11 regions, disaggregated into metropolitan and non-metropolitan areas). However, the socioeconomic statistics attached to the survey data also allow researchers to investigate associations between both individual and area characteristics and the likelihood of volunteering.

My colleagues and I (Mohan et al., 2006) utilised the 1987 and 1992 GHSs which included a combined 37,000 respondents. In addition to data on individual and household characteristics, country and region of residence were known; moreover, a clustered sampling design was used, selecting small areas (primary sampling units (PSUs)) for the survey fieldwork. The precise location of the PSUs was unknown, but by aggregating the survey data up to the PSU level we could produce information about the characteristics of the localities where the respondents lived. Thus we could estimate community-level characteristics, such as the proportion of residents who did not have access to a car. Our dataset contained information at three levels: individuals, the communities (PSUs) within which they lived and the region in which those PSUs were located. The multi-level modelling approach takes account of the variation attributable at each of these levels. We assessed the probability that individuals were what we defined as 'committed' volunteers – that is, people who said they volunteered approximately monthly.

Rates of volunteering in these surveys were somewhat lower than those found when the more intensive questioning characteristic of specialist surveys is deployed (Chapter 2), ranging from 9 per cent in the metropolitan areas of the northern region to 19 per cent in south-west England, and between 5 and 28 per cent across PSU areas. The first point to note is that the analysis indicated that 91.5 per cent of the variation between communities was a result of individual characteristics – with only 1.5 per cent of variation occurring because of regional effects and 7 per cent variation being at the local (PSU) level. The individual-level variation shows results that were consistent with established predictors of volunteering (age, gender, ethnicity, social class, housing tenure and economic activity were all significant). In terms of area characteristics, the only significant term was that associated with the percentage of people who were in social class I or II, which had a very small positive effect on individual volunteering. Once we took account of individual characteristics, the regional variation in rates of engagement was largely attributable to differences in the social class make-up of local neighbourhoods. A small amount of variation remained at the local scale, and was associated with neighbourhood social status, but its effect was small.

Some more recent surveys now permit the attachment to individual data of more information on socioeconomic conditions in the communities within which survey respondents live. For the 2008–9 Citizenship Survey of England and Wales, local authority-level data were attached, though precise locations were not disclosed to the researchers. The linkage to survey data of census-derived information provided an opportunity to explore three dimensions of community context that may have an influence on voluntary action (Bennett, 2013).

Residential stability: length of residence in a community is an established predictor of volunteering at the individual level, but could there be benefits from living in an area that has a high level of residential stability? In such communities, residents will have had longer to establish social ties and develop relationships with their neighbours, so that the collective efficacy of communities (Sampson, 2012) – their capacity to come together to respond to local issues – will be better developed. Conversely, high levels of population turnover could have negative effects on neighbourhoods, reducing social cohesion and making it harder for individuals to build up the networks through which they become involved in volunteering. The likelihood of volunteering increases where residents feel that they have established connections with people and place.

Social deprivation: arising from the strong evidence that there is a negative association at the area level between volunteering and disadvantage, can we detect effects on individuals of living in areas of disadvantage, over and above those that would be predicted by individual characteristics? Community-level disadvantage may have an influence on volunteering, perhaps by promoting certain values or providing fewer resources and therefore opportunities.

Ethnic heterogeneity: there has been a sustained debate about whether diversity breeds a lack of trust and, therefore, when translated into the sphere of voluntary action, whether it depresses volunteering rates. The suggestion here is that people 'hunker down' among those they consider to be like themselves, reducing the extent of involvement in causes that would otherwise benefit a greater range of citizens. Certainly, studies confirm a negative relationship between ethnic heterogeneity and volunteering (Musick and Wilson, 2008; Rotolo and Wilson, 2012) although there is also an argument that, in generating attitudes and influencing behaviours, it is deprivation, not diversity, that has more of an effect on trust.

The distribution of voluntary organisations: a key influence on volunteering is the opportunity to do so, but these opportunities vary between communities since the distribution of voluntary organisations is highly uneven. As well as reflecting present-day conditions, there is strong path dependency in the pattern, with many organisations reflecting a legacy of earlier social initiatives. A small number of studies have explored the effects of organisational distributions on the likelihood of volunteering (Mohan and Bennett, 2019; Lam et al., 2022).

The UK studies of the influence of socioeconomic context on volunteering have used data from the Citizenship Surveys of the late 2000s to which data for local authorities have been attached (Bennett,

2013; Mohan and Bennett, 2019). They show that residential stability – that is, relatively low levels of population turnover in a community – has a curvilinear relationship with volunteering. It appears that rates of volunteering are higher at low levels of residential stability, as well as at higher levels, while dropping in between. It is possible that people who are new to an area may use volunteering as a route into networks and friendships, especially if they are from mobile groups of the population such as students or young professionals. As to type of place, residence in an urban area, consistent with international findings, is consistently associated with lower levels of volunteering than in rural areas. Deprivation is associated with a reduction in the level of volunteering. Certainly individual-level factors are at play, but there is an additional negative effect on volunteering for those living in a deprived area regardless of their personal socioeconomic background. The effect of community-level deprivation is likely to operate through low levels of resources, weaker social networks and limited (bridging) connections to the wider society (McCulloch et al., 2012). There is also evidence that religious and ethnic segregation and diversity also have negative effects on the likelihood of volunteering, which also persist despite controls for deprivation and the urban/rural character of places. This suggests that it is not just a trade-off between deprivation and diversity that matters: both of these appear to have negative effects on the likelihood of engagement.

Finally, what effect does the distribution of voluntary organisations have? Publications from the Centre for Social Justice (2013), a Conservative think-tank, and recent government policy documents such as its Levelling Up White Paper (DLUHC, 2022) have pointed to low levels of social capital and volunteering in disadvantaged areas, the implication being that more needed to be done to establish charities in such locations, though with no suggestion of where resources might be found to enable that. The implied theory of change was that there were reserves of social capital that weren't being mobilised. Redistributing voluntary organisations is intrinsically difficult, for obvious reasons. But what exactly is the effect of the distribution of charities on volunteering? If we increase the numbers of organisations in a place, could that have a significant impact on the rate of volunteering?

In an analysis of the Citizenship Survey we were able to link the survey respondents to their area of residence, enabling us to assess contextual influences on volunteering such as deprivation or variations in the distribution of registered charities. Thus for the first time we were able to estimate local authority-level volunteering rates from survey data and cross-reference them against the distribution of charities (Mohan and Bennett, 2019).

There was a positive relationship between the ratio of charities to population in an area and the level of volunteering, being strongest for what we described as 'active, local, general charities', with a correlation coefficient of 0.32 (significant at the 0.1 per cent level). We drew on the Register of Charities for our data on charity distributions, defining an 'active' entity as one reporting a non-zero financial return around the time of the survey, and a 'local' charity as an entity reporting that it operated only within one local authority. Finally, the definition of a 'general charity', following work originated by ONS and developed by NCVO, seeks to capture entities that conform to the public's perception of a charity – thus excluding charities that provide benefits only to limited classes of the population or are not formally independent of government. We found a small but statistically significant positive relationship between the distribution of local charities and the likelihood of volunteering, which strengthened as the numbers of charities were restricted to 'active' and 'general' organisations. Measures of the distribution of organisations with a wider regional, national and international focus were not significantly associated with volunteering – presumably indicating that these organisations are not always carrying out activities locally. Measures of the economic weight of the voluntary sector (e.g. the median income of charities in a local authority) were unrelated to the likelihood of volunteering, which we might anticipate, since the majority of voluntary organisations are small and volunteer-run, with limited budgets and no employees.

Other contextual factors were influential – residents of urban areas were less likely to volunteer than their rural counterparts, while social deprivation had a negative influence on the probability of engagement, though the ethnic diversity of local authorities was unrelated to volunteering. The negative association with deprivation and the positive association with the distribution of local charities means that some areas are doubly disadvantaged – by material circumstances and by a relative absence of social infrastructure.

These pieces of evidence, collectively, provide a consistent message. The more disadvantaged the area in which the survey respondents live, the lower the proportion of residents engaged in voluntary action. Such negative associations could result from what are termed compositional effects (they result from concentrations in disadvantaged areas of people who are less likely to volunteer) or from contextual factors (there is something about spatially concentrated disadvantage that reduces the propensity to volunteer). Mostly, the answer is a compositional explanation – these patterns substantially reflect variations between places in the composition of the population, though there are some small community-level effects.

Conclusions

In studies of political geography it is sometimes said that places don't vote, people do – and the same could be said for volunteering. Once allowance is made for social composition – the mix of people living in different types of place – community-level variations in volunteering largely shrink or disappear. Strengths of associations between community-level measures of deprivation and volunteering rates are consistently found for several measures (census, local authority surveys) and are consistent over time within the same surveys (Citizenship Survey, Community Life Survey). There is a marginal positive effect of the distribution of registered charities on the likelihood of volunteering, but organisational distributions are highly stable over time; attempting to change those distributions, with the aim of increasing citizen engagement, will require persistence and significant investment.

Thus, care should be taken in using community-level measures of volunteering and in drawing inferences from them. Are they measuring preferences, the capacity to do more or reluctant enlistment into maintaining vital local resources where there is no alternative (e.g. sustaining libraries or running food banks)? Attitudinal studies (Chapter 11) and longitudinal qualitative work (Lindsey and Mohan, 2018), which provide insights into the lifetime volunteering journeys of individuals, clearly show awareness of economic, labour market and family constraints on the likelihood of engagement. Such pressures are particularly acute in disadvantaged areas. Therefore we should not automatically assume that what appears to be a low rate of volunteering implies a reserve of social capital that just needs mobilising. Nor should we infer that community-level variation in volunteering constitutes an index of social capital, which somehow exerts independent effects on a wide range of social outcomes. In effect these patterns are really just redescribing a combination of the historical inheritances of organisations and existing patterns of inequality. Finally, the measures of the distribution of volunteers used all relate to the residential location of the volunteers themselves. We cannot tell from these sources where their activities occur. However, since research tends to emphasise that volunteering is largely a local matter, it is reasonable to assume that most, though not all, of the volunteers resident in a given area are volunteering there. Conceivably, online forms of volunteering give voluntary organisations greater flexibility to recruit volunteers, but for that to effect a substantial change in the distribution of volunteers, the arguments of this chapter (and also Chapter 3) suggest that new groups of volunteers would need to be drawn in.

Are there policies that can influence community-level variations in volunteering? There have been arguments that institutional structures can make a difference to levels of participation and thereby influence the formation of social capital. There have been examples of deliberate localised efforts to stimulate volunteering, such as the neighbourhood renewal programmes of New Labour (Lawless et al., 2010; the actual effect on participation was limited) or grassroots initiatives of the various National Lottery funds. Moores (2014) has therefore argued that the relationship between state intervention and voluntary action has often been a synergistic one. The voluntary sector's response here has often been to argue for the importance of infrastructural investment on the basis that volunteers need to be mobilised. The challenge for this argument is that while such investment was increased substantially during the period of Labour government (1997–2010) and dropped back again under later administrations (Kane and Cohen, 2023), volunteering levels have flatlined (Chapter 2). Beveridge argued that the 'spirit of service ... bloweth where it will', but the evidence here seems to be that its ability to do so is considerably greater in those communities in which individuals possess a basic level of security, from which they are then able to contribute in a voluntary capacity.

6

Circumstances, habits and trajectories: journeys into and through volunteering

Introduction

Discussions about voluntary action are often conducted in terms of the proportion of citizens engaged in it, based on snapshots at one point in time from cross-sectional surveys. These underestimate the voluntary contributions that people make during their lifetimes. Someone may not be recorded as an active volunteer at one point in time but we cannot judge whether this means they have never engaged at all or temporarily ceased to do so (McPherson, 1981; Rotolo, 2000). Nor does it mean that these individuals won't engage in future. Scholars have used longitudinal surveys to demonstrate that underneath an apparently stable aggregate level of volunteering, the pattern is one in which individuals move into and out of voluntary commitments at various points in their lives. Undifferentiated appeals for us all to do more are not especially helpful; we need an understanding of the place of volunteering in people's lives, the barriers to engagement, the reasons why once-active citizens withdraw from it and the underpinnings of what have been termed 'habits of the heart' (Bellah et al., 1985). What differentiates regular and consistent participants from those engaged only intermittently? One approach, used by the Jubilee Centre, was to ask young people who had already participated in 'social action', broadly defined, whether they would intend to do so again in the future (Taylor-Collins et al., 2019). It's not surprising that the individuals involved were highly likely to express an interest in doing so – they had been recruited mainly through organisations involved in delivering programmes for young people and more than half had participated in the high-profile, well-funded National Citizen Service (NCS) programme. But an indication of intent to engage in the future hardly counts as the internalisation of a 'habit of service'. It may be more helpful to distinguish the *circumstances* that influence the choices of individuals than to postulate that there is an identifiable facet of character or personality that can be represented as the key to a volunteering 'habit' (Lambert and Rutherford, 2020).

How would we account for individual volunteering trajectories? Individuals experience transitions in their roles, statuses and resources, such as entering into long-term relationships, having children, changing jobs, acquiring qualifications, taking on caring responsibilities or experiencing long-term illness. Such changes are likely to influence a person's involvement in voluntary associations. They might cause individuals to re-evaluate their priorities, provide them with more (or fewer) of the resources that sustain participation (Musick and Wilson, 2008; Brady et al., 1995) or contribute to changes in their values and attitudes which may prompt them to become engaged (or not). The aggregate rate of volunteering will therefore reflect the outcomes of these processes for the population over time. A well-established literature points particularly to the influence of family and household circumstances and commitments, some labour market transitions, including retirement, and the acquisition of education (Butrica et al., 2009; Lancee and Radl, 2014; Oesterle et al., 2004; Thoits and Hewitt, 2001; Wilson and Musick, 1997; Musick and Wilson, 2008: 221–3). Resources are important too – people require time, money, skills, social networks, health and other resources for active involvement (Musick and Wilson, 2008; Brady et al., 1995) – and changes in those resources can affect an individual's volunteering behaviour. The requisite resources are not just economic – they also include social and cultural capital; moreover, they are unevenly distributed.

The knowledge of individual longitudinal patterns of volunteering also provides a more nuanced understanding of socioeconomic differences in volunteering because we obtain more information about changes in the circumstances of individuals that contribute to their ability to become engaged and to sustain that engagement. For example, working-class individuals tend to have lower levels of civic engagement not just because they are less likely to join organisations but also because they are less likely to sustain involvement, since they are more likely to experience economic precarity (McPherson, 1981; Wilensky, 1961).

Here I review evidence from longitudinal UK studies (Pearson, 2016) in which people have been asked to record (sometimes contemporaneously, sometimes retrospectively) various dimensions of participation. These studies have facilitated sophisticated quantitative work on the influences of changing individual, household and personal circumstances on patterns of engagement. The chapter also considers several qualitative studies of how people describe the relationship between their changing life circumstances and trajectories of engagement in voluntary action.

In these studies, respondents are prompted to recall how they became involved in voluntary action, the organisations of which they were part, drivers of their participation and experiences of it. This research has sought to set the volunteering histories of adults against the background of life-course events and personal circumstances; typologies have been developed (e.g. variations on the theme of 'lifelong', 'serial' and 'trigger' volunteers) which recognise the 'contingency' of participation – in other words, whether individuals were engaged in volunteering continuously, intermittently or not at all depended largely on changes in personal circumstances (Sherrott, 1983; Roberts and Devine, 2004; Brodie et al., 2011; Hogg, 2016; Lindsey and Mohan, 2018). These studies relied on the ability of individuals to recall engagement, and trajectories of engagement, at some distance in time, which constituted a clear potential limitation (Hogg, 2016: 174). A longitudinal study using the resources of the Mass Observation Project (MOP) sought to overcome this constraint, drawing on responses from individuals who had been prompted to recall elements of civic engagement at intervals during their adult lives (Lindsey and Mohan, 2018). All these studies selected participants who were or had been active volunteers, but not all of those whose accounts were analysed were perennially engaged, and their experiences are therefore valuable for what they tell us about how circumstances influence individuals' moves into and out of engagement.

A better understanding of the characteristics of those with what has been termed a 'stable orientation' towards volunteering (Lancee and Radl, 2014) would be highly desirable from the point of view of both encouraging more people into volunteering and supporting the sustained engagement of those who commence it. The implications of this for practitioners and policymakers are considered in the concluding section.

Longitudinal perspectives on trajectories using survey data

Here, I summarise quantitative findings from longitudinal studies which demonstrate the extent of moves into and out of 'unpaid voluntary work' over various time periods by the same individuals. Then, I present evidence of the significant and enduring influence of socio-economic factors on sustained participation. Finally, I consider the evidence of the effects of key life transitions (such as retirement or engagement in unpaid care) on the extent of volunteering.

Characterising trajectories

The BHPS (from 1991) and its successor, the UK Household Longitudinal Survey (UKHLS, 2008–; also known as Understanding Society), have asked questions on volunteering behaviour on alternate years from 1996 (BHPS), offering 'doing unpaid voluntary work' as one of over a dozen possible responses to a question about what people do in their *leisure* time. In an earlier study my colleagues and I analysed responses to questions about volunteering asked on eight occasions between 1996 and 2011 (2011 being the first year of Understanding Society, which asked an almost identical question) (Lindsey and Mohan, 2018: chapter 7).

We constructed a sample of respondents from the BHPS/UKHLS comprising individuals who had responded in each wave of the survey to questions on volunteering behaviour, and who had reported volunteering at least once over several waves of the survey. While in any *one* wave we found that around 20 per cent of respondents stated that they had done *some* volunteering, some 40 per cent of respondents had volunteered *at least once* in this 15-year period. If measured in a lifetime context, this shows that a much higher proportion of the population has been a volunteer *at some stage in their lives* than is revealed by cross-sectional studies (cross-sectional surveys support this, for example by asking people who are not engaged at the time of the survey about whether they can recall earlier instances of volunteering) (Wheatley, 2017: chapter 3; Low et al., 2007: 64). If we therefore define volunteers as *those who have volunteered at some stage of their lives*, then the proportion with volunteering experience is obviously somewhat higher than previously acknowledged. A practical implication is to learn from volunteers about what would facilitate more continuous involvement and about the circumstances which have led to them ceasing to engage.

We can unpack this quantitative picture by considering transitions in volunteering status between waves of the survey and individual trajectories through it. First, a very small group (some 3 per cent of those who provide a clear answer to the question about unpaid work at every wave of the survey) continuously reported episodes of volunteering at *every* survey wave in the 1996–2011 time frame. We then looked at transitions between pairs of waves of the study (e.g. between 1996 and 1998). There is underlying stability in non-engagement: over 90 per cent of those individuals who do not report unpaid voluntary work at one wave of the survey also do so at the next; conversely, switching from non-volunteering to volunteering is therefore very much a minority pursuit. Given the underlying stability in non-volunteering, fewer than 10 per cent of those who did *not* report volunteering at one wave will say that they *are* doing so at the next wave. Of those engaged in volunteering at one point in time, between 58 and 66 per cent will report that they are volunteering at the next survey wave. Thus, if 20 per cent of respondents say that they are volunteering at one wave, then we would expect that between 11.6 and 13.2 per cent would also volunteer at the next wave. It also follows that around two-fifths of volunteers report that they *stop* volunteering over each of the two-year intervals at which this question is asked.

The proportion (up to two-fifths of respondents) who volunteer at one time point moving to a 'non-volunteering' status when they are next surveyed may seem high. Perhaps the very general question framing ('unpaid voluntary work'), and its placement in a suite of questions about leisure, means that people are less easily able to recall instances of volunteering. Alternatively, these findings may suggest that once an individual is on a particular trajectory, they are more likely to remain on it. We also found that few individuals transition from non-volunteering to volunteering between one wave of the survey and the next.

We split the data into two clusters of volunteering 'types'. Of the 2,151 cohort members who reported volunteering at least several times a year on at least one occasion between 1996 and 2011, we considered 71 per cent (n = 1,525) to be 'short-term' volunteers; in terms of frequency and intensity of volunteering, this high proportion of short-term volunteers contributed fewer than half of the episodes of voluntary action (46 per cent) undertaken by BHPS/Understanding Society participants in this time frame. The demographics of short-term volunteers had strong similarities with the general British population, whereas the long-term volunteers were more likely to be women over the age of 50.

To illustrate the variety of trajectories, I use an illustration from this earlier study (Figure 6.1). In any one column of the figure, corresponding to a wave of the survey, the dark bands are proportional to the numbers volunteering in that wave. Thus, in the top left-hand corner of the diagram, we see a grouping of respondents who do not volunteer at all initially, often for several successive waves, but then (proceeding from top to bottom) do so in the last wave, or in the penultimate wave, or in both of the last two waves, and so on.

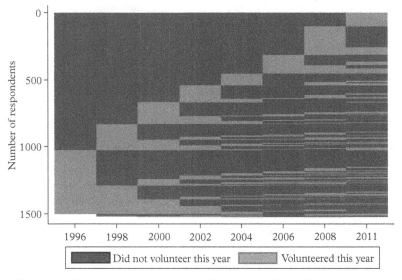

Figure 6.1 Sample of short-term volunteers' trajectories of volunteering, 1996–2011. Source: Lindsey and Mohan (2018).

Conversely, and reading up from the bottom of the diagram, there are individuals who volunteer consecutively in several waves but cease to do so thereafter.

The other cluster we identified (not shown here, see Lindsey and Mohan (2018: 159, figure 7.2) included a much smaller number of individuals (626) who had reported volunteering on average 5.9 (standard deviation = 1.6) out of a potential eight time points. In that cluster, the majority of trajectories suggested strong and consistent engagement over time; around one-sixth of these had reported volunteering at every single wave of the survey. Though small, this group contributed 54 per cent of the total episodes of volunteering activity reported in the survey across this time frame. Thus, *slightly fewer than one-third* of the longitudinal sample of volunteers contributed *over half* of the total *episodes* of voluntary activity (we do not have data on the amount of time contributed) reported by survey respondents. This resonates with the notion of a civic core, not least in terms of the socioeconomic make-up of the long-term volunteers, which is skewed towards the better-off, middle-class sections of society (Chapter 4).

Another analysis of the same data (Dawson et al., 2019) went further, by subdividing the volunteers by frequency of engagement. They showed that volunteering transitions rarely involve a move from non-volunteering straight to very regular engagement (or the converse); instead, individuals begin their journeys with less frequent involvement. More importantly, they argued that persistent volunteering behaviour is driven by two separate mechanisms. One is termed 'spurious' state dependence, which suggests that there are characteristic volunteering behaviours that are established early in life and which remain stable. The other is 'true' state dependence – the causal influence of prior volunteering behaviour on current behaviour, which is consistent with theories of social capital and with 'warm glow' accounts of prosocial behaviour (Andreoni, 1990). They argue that around one-third of persistence in volunteering behaviour can be attributed to 'true' state dependence; if so, they suggest, there is scope to expect that investment in volunteering opportunities (e.g. through formal programmes such as NCS) might produce an upward shift in the level of volunteering. However, as they also acknowledge, the likelihood of engagement in volunteering is heavily determined by socioeconomic influences and early life experiences, and there is a limit to which one might expect any adverse effects of such influences to be counteracted by policies designed to increase volunteering opportunities alone (Dawson et al., 2019: 1017).

This longitudinal evidence suggests that 'true' levels of engagement are underestimated; it illuminates the extent of variation in volunteering over time for individuals; and it points to socioeconomic gradients in the depth of involvement over time.

Socioeconomic circumstances and persistent engagement

If volunteering by individuals is a function of the resources and forms of capital on which they can draw, we would expect this to be particularly evident in relation to the ability of people to sustain engagement in volunteering over time. We might also expect that the resources of the households in which individuals grow up would also affect the likelihood of engagement. There is support for both these expectations.

The influence on adult civic engagement of socioeconomic circumstances at formative periods of people's lives is illustrated by the

NCDS, which tracks babies born in the UK in a selected week in 1958 at regular intervals. It provides strong evidence that those who gain experience of volunteering in early adulthood are more likely to volunteer later in life, though there is a socioeconomic sting in the tail. When aged 23 (in 1981), individuals were asked about their involvement in 'unpaid voluntary work' and the same question was also put to them in 2008 (aged 50). Vicki Bolton (2016) demonstrated that without any further adjustment for individual or household characteristics, an individual who reported volunteering at age 23 had 2.5 times higher odds of being a volunteer at age 50 than someone who did not volunteer at age 23. This is partly a result of the beneficial effects of early adult experiences of volunteering, but much of the relationship between volunteering at age 23 and volunteering at age 50 is accounted for by the interaction between social class and volunteering at age 23. Volunteers in young adulthood who came from families with skilled and professional social class backgrounds were more likely to go on to be volunteers at age 50 than those from unskilled and manual social classes (Bolton, 2016; see also Hietanen et al., 2016: 499; Evans, 2020).

There is other evidence on the socioeconomic background of those engaging in sustained volunteering. Research on perennial participants (those with repeated engagement in voluntary and civic affairs, as well as a range of social activities) tracked through successive waves of the NCDS found that three-quarters of this group were in possession of degrees when observed at age 50 (Brookfield et al., 2014; 2018a; 2018b). Sacco et al. (2021) showed that those approaching retirement and moving into multiple activity pathways that included volunteering (as well as a combination of paid work and caring) were more likely to be from upper socioeconomic strata. Frequent participants over a number of waves of the BHPS were more likely than nonparticipants to be better educated or from higher socioeconomic strata (Geyne-Rajme and Smith, 2011; Tabassum et al., 2016; Lindsey and Mohan, 2018) or from upper tiers of the occupational strata (Lambert and Rutherford, 2020). Socioeconomic disadvantage was also translated into lower levels of volunteering as people grew older through the differential effects of the process of ageing on health status. As Steptoe and Zaninetto (2020) put it, lower socioeconomic groups were likely to age more rapidly than higher groups (their study included a number of biomarkers to back this up), and this then had discernible effects on their engagement in volunteering. They used household wealth (excluding pension assets) as a measure of socioeconomic status, and in a country characterised by increasing inequalities in the wealth distribution, such as the UK, the substantial wealth-related differences in likelihood of volunteering ought to give pause for thought.

Key life-course transitions and their impact on engagement

Longitudinal studies can also illuminate key transitions in life and the presence of competing demands on time that may facilitate or inhibit involvement. We explore some aspects of this – the influence of economic change on engagement – as part of Chapter 11. Here, we focus on the available evidence from longitudinal surveys on the effects of retirement on volunteering, and on the extent to which caring responsibilities, paid work and voluntary action are related.

The belief that prosperous baby boomers would retire and make ample contributions to voluntary effort has featured regularly in policy and public debate. Evidence on the impacts of retirement on engagement includes the high (though variable in intensity of commitment) levels of participation in volunteering by those beyond retirement age (Wheatley, 2017: chapter 6; Bennett et al., 2012). However, longitudinal studies have demonstrated a positive impact of retirement. Smith demonstrated a 25 per cent increase in involvement in 'voluntary service' groups after retirement, using longitudinal BHPS data (S. Smith, 2010). Eibich et al. (2022) use English Longitudinal Survey of Ageing (ELSA) data for England to demonstrate that there was a substantial (10–20 percentage points) increase in volunteering by individuals after retirement compared with their engagement prior to it, a result broadly consistent for two other longitudinal datasets (from Ireland and the USA) used in their work. The effects of retirement were stronger for men. The authors suggest that the results are compatible with a view of volunteering as role substitution – on retirement, many people are seeking a substitute for the routine and companionship of paid work.

To what extent might the growing burden on families of unpaid care for relatives mean that individuals become *less* likely to prioritise voluntary action? There are widespread concerns about the adequacy of provision of social care for the elderly, and therefore widespread expectations that more will be expected of families. Qualitative work (see below) confirms the salience of such concerns. We know that when people are contemplating retirement, family commitments rank higher than volunteering in their preferences (Chapter 11).

Are caring and volunteering in conflict or in harmony? Somewhat counter-intuitively, Wheatley finds that the provision of unpaid care was associated with *greater* volunteering at *low* levels of involvement in caring, and also at the highest levels – in other words, those who are providing the most unpaid care are also *most* likely to volunteer. Wheatley argues that this is possibly because those involved are themselves older, and thus less likely to be in the paid workforce, so they have more time to offer as a volunteer (Wheatley, 2017: 141, table 6.3). This points to the way in which combinations of caring, paid work and volunteering vary across individuals. O'Reilly et al. (2017a) suggest that volunteering is often perceived in a positive light, whereas unpaid care carries more obligations and is seen as burdensome and likely to affect well-being adversely. In fact, there is some evidence that – at low to moderate levels of involvement – combinations of caring and volunteering do have positive effects on well-being.

Two studies based on recent longitudinal UK data have shed light on this (Sacco et al., 2021; Van der Horst et al., 2017). Both focused on people aged 50 or over and investigated whether, as people transition out of paid work into retirement, role substitution or role extension were taking place. Role substitution means that people need to find something that substitutes for paid work; role extension means that participation in one role (e.g. paid work) expands the opportunities to participate in another (e.g. workplace networks give access to opportunities for volunteering). Using data from the BHPS and ELSA, the authors analyse the multiple pathways that individuals navigate between paid work, caring activities and formal and informal volunteering.

The sequences of activities are complex. These studies cross-classify the different frequencies (e.g. monthly, weekly, daily) of three types of activities (paid work, caring, volunteering) with different measures of commitments (e.g. full/part-time work, number of hours committed to caring activity) to produce several hundred potential trajectories which are followed over successive survey waves. The authors focused on the more prominent of the pathways through which people might move as they approached retirement. Sacco et al. (2021) identified three of these: 'full-time work to low activity' (over time, employment commitments remained high with a lower probability of engaging in unpaid activities of any kind); 'part-time and in-home work' (a lower likelihood of full-time work and a higher probability of working part time and providing informal care to kin); and a 'multiple activities' pathway (a substantially higher probability of volunteering and civic engagement than the other two classes).

As an example of an ideal-typical pathway, if role *substitution* were taking place, one would expect a gradual reduction of paid work commitments balanced by a gradual expansion of involvement in volunteering. As a challenge to this view, in neither study was there evidence of substantial growth in volunteering as individuals got older. But nor was there evidence of role *extension* – that is, the baseline level of volunteering remained broadly stable over time. The most consistent messages were that those whose life-courses had contained significant periods of no or limited employment were least likely to become engaged in volunteering, pointing to work as a source of social integration. In contrast, those in what was termed a 'multiple activities' pathway (i.e. combinations of caring and work that were mainly part time, along with volunteering) were more likely to demonstrate evidence of prior volunteer involvement.

The message is that it does not make much sense to analyse discretionary activities such as volunteering, which tend to absorb relatively small amounts of time, without reference to activities which occupy a much greater proportion of a person's waking hours, such as paid work or the provision of unpaid care. This is why theorists of household divisions of labour insist on conceptualising volunteering as part of the total social organisation of labour – that is, as one component of everything that individuals and households do to sustain themselves (Taylor, 2004; 2005; see also Chapter 1). The stylised volunteering trajectories shown earlier (Figure 6.1) may be largely explicable in terms of pressures from these other commitments. Second, focusing on individuals who are approaching the end of their working lives, there is relatively little evidence of extensive shifts taking place from paid to unpaid work (while van der Horst et al. (2017) suggested that there may be evidence of this for particular subgroups, such as higher-educated members of upper socioeconomic strata, sample size restrictions limited what could be said). Finally, and relatedly, there are strong socioeconomic gradients in volunteering trajectories – those most able to sustain consistent participation are those with the most resources.

Qualitative analyses of volunteering trajectories

Longitudinal surveys provide a somewhat stylised portrait of voluntary action; for more in-depth analyses of volunteering trajectories we turn to various qualitative accounts, which explore in more detail routes into voluntary engagement, pathways through it and circumstances surrounding cessation.

The first is a study of 38 writers for the MOP, whose demographic characteristics broadly reflect those of long-term volunteers in the wider British population (Lindsey and Mohan, 2018). The MOP recruits volunteer writers who receive 'directives' on topics of interest, to which they are free to respond as they see fit. Various directives have asked respondents to describe and comment on topics of relevance to voluntary activity – such as 'unpaid work' (1996), 'voluntary organisations' (1990) and the Big Society (2012). We traced numerous individuals who have responded to these directives consistently. We reconstructed volunteering trajectories for those people, for as much of their life-courses as the material allowed. This enabled a mapping of each writer's movement in and out of volunteering across time, situating changes and continuities in engagement alongside different life-course events. In a separate study, researchers drew on a study of social participation and identity (Brookfield et al., 2014), which used a structured interview guide to prompt individuals to recall lifetime histories of participation (see Chapter 4; Brookfield et al., 2014; 2018a; Parry et al., 2021). Other studies have also used retrospective interviews to establish histories of engagement (Hogg, 2016; Sherrott, 1983; Brodie et al., 2011).

Typologies have been applied to volunteering trajectories, such as Hogg's (2016) categories of constant, serial and trigger volunteers. This typology denotes the diverse ways in which individuals may remain with the same organisation for long periods, move between volunteering opportunities (including periods of non-engagement) or respond to ad hoc events or invitations to become engaged (possibly as direct consequences of changes in personal circumstances). Complete non-engagement – arguably a further trajectory – is considered in Chapter 4. Such typologies cannot capture every potential trajectory but they serve as useful heuristic devices. Taking advantage of the richness of the MOP data, my work with Rose Lindsey further broke down potential trajectories into a fourfold typology (Lindsey and Mohan, 2018).

First, we identified continuous committed volunteers, labelled *stickers*, who in their MOP writings showed *continuous* voluntary commitment to one or more organisations or individuals. This could involve a complex and evolving journey, in which the depth of engagement, and the relationships built up through it, changed over time. One respondent had initially volunteered as a library home-visitor delivering books to housebound beneficiaries, a role which she combined with bringing up her family. Over nearly a quarter-century, she developed close relationships with her clients, to the point where she was actively providing informal support (companionship, phone calls and shopping). She developed a deep personal commitment to this activity, insisting that it was something which she would always prioritise.

Second, there was a category of *natural switchers*: long-term volunteers who moved between organisations or causes. Longitudinal surveys cannot easily capture the detail of 'careers' in volunteering, in which people move from one volunteer opportunity to another (Musick and Wilson, 2008: 224). The biographical data in our study enabled the identification of people who committed several years to volunteering for an organisation or beneficiary, then moved on. As one respondent put it:

> As with most of my activities I have moved on after a time ... Not that I get bored; it just seems that something else might be more interesting and I dislike routine.

Writing in the tenth decade of his life, this respondent's voluntarism had included a mix of one-off actions (e.g. irregular street collections) and longer-term commitments to administrative roles. He had always volunteered but switched between roles as work and family commitments permitted. Others linked their volunteering trajectories to lifecourse events such as relocation or retirement; one married woman, who had relocated regularly as a result of her husband's careerrelated moves, described a parallel volunteering career in which she had started, stopped or continued a variety of other voluntary roles. Just over a quarter of our sample in this study described wanting or needing to vary and swap their volunteering activities throughout their life-course.

Other respondents appeared to have less scope for agency. We characterised them as *pragmatic switchers*: their routes into volunteering seem to have been determined by life-course events and family needs, such as establishing or supporting the provision of pre-school services. Such family-related examples also capture the sense that, in some circumstances, there can be an element of self-interest in engagement. Whether 'forced' or not, such activity could still trigger longer-term commitment, exemplified by one woman who helped establish a community centre in a new residential development and three decades later was still involved in its management. The behaviours of a further quarter of the study sample were interpreted as encompassing this kind of pragmatic switching. In some cases, volunteering journeys were largely determined by family circumstances, but for other 'switchers' the drivers seemed to be largely those of personality and motivation.

A fourth category in our work acknowledged that there are volunteering trajectories encompassing short-term and episodic activities. Without the biographical information derived from their writings for the MOP, they might have been classified as short-term formal or informal volunteers. Each had unique routes into their short-term voluntary engagement. One example was prompted by a search for an alternative career after a respondent left her teaching job due to stress-related depression. Over a period of years she balanced work and voluntary commitments, acquiring new skills which – she believed – helped open up a wider range of employment opportunities. This additional volunteering was of an interim and somewhat 'episodic' nature (Macduff, 2005). Another writer described a disparate range of apparently discrete and time-limited voluntary actions; it proved impossible to assess whether her engagement was continuous or not. She described herself as someone who did not volunteer, but her writing clearly identified several periods in which she was undertaking *formal* volunteering as well as actively providing *informal* support for friends and neighbours. We characterised this respondent as a *stop-starter* because she described these as a series of one-off activities.

There is no watertight schema for classifying volunteering trajectories. Taxonomies can be affected by the quality of the evidence provided, which will reflect the ability of respondents to recall (perhaps selectively) events over long time frames and the many other events that occur within an individual's life-course and the life context of the individual, which are possibly of greater significance to the individual than instances of volunteering. Nevertheless, a key message of the diverse and complex volunteering histories, as revealed by the studies discussed here, is that most people participate as and when they can; the question raised is how to understand the circumstances which enable or constrain that participation.

Accounts of moves between non-engagement and disengagement

What makes people move into or cease volunteering? Insights from the key qualitative studies discussed here make several points. First, for many people, caring responsibilities, and active informal volunteering, such as supporting immediate neighbours, formed a constant accompaniment to the accounts they gave of more formal instances of volunteering (Lindsey and Mohan, 2018: 96–102; Parry et al., 2021). As the quantitative evidence (see Chapter 2) indicates, most of those who are involved in formal volunteering are also engaged in informal activities. Second, volunteering trajectories begin at home:

important influences on them are therefore household resources and behaviours, including parental example.

We know from survey data that there are variations in volunteering related to age and household characteristics. For these reasons volunteering in early adulthood to middle age initially tails off then builds up again, as people start families and are drawn into child-related voluntary activities. Engagement at later life stages then depends not just on circumstances such as resources and capacities but also on other responsibilities that people have and on changes in jobs and places of residence. The ways in which these work out for individuals necessarily involves quite complex biographies.

Recollections of the commencement of volunteering do not often report a systematic search for opportunities but rather highlight the 'contingency of everyday life' in which engagement has more to do with 'accidental and arbitrary factors' than self-motivation or a predetermined plan (Roberts and Devine, 2004: 287–90). Having said that, the process is not completely random across the population.

Individual accounts emphasise a mix of circumstances (Brodie et al., 2011: 29). Parental influences feature strongly, whether these are the example set by parents (e.g. the importance of civic duty or trade union commitments) or the ways in which children joined in with the collective activities in which their parents were involved (church groups, the Scouting movement). As noted above, these influences are likely to be socially stratified.

Once family formation begins, direct connections made through children drew people in (Brodie et al., 2011: 29), whether they or not they had previously been nonparticipants. Parenthood opens up participation opportunities, though it also limits the time and energy individuals have available to participate, while also reorienting voluntarism towards child-related settings and activities. Engagement in volunteering for organisations and activities where their children or grandchildren were beneficiaries was extensive; over half of Lindsey and Mohan's sample of Mass Observers had taken active roles in nurseries, playgroups, PTAs, school activities, youth clubs and Scout or Guide groups (2018: 102–3). These met an immediate need for the families concerned – people became involved either because a particular service wasn't available or because they wanted to help improve the quality of what was on offer. Initial involvement was driven partly by self-interest (or at least family interest), but some individuals nevertheless continued in their volunteering roles for some time after their children had moved on. Thus, what began as a fairly informal and small-scale part of someone's life could develop into long-term involvement, entailing significant commitment and responsibilities (e.g. Lindsey and Mohan, 2018: 74).

Being asked is known to be crucial to volunteering, and qualitative studies shed light on how volunteer roles derive from personal connections established through business networks (often recruiting people with high levels of economic, social and cultural capital to positions in entities such as the Rotary Club), workplaces and trade unions, places of worship and (especially for men) engagement in leisure and cultural organisations (Brodie et al., 2011: 28, 46; Brookfield et al., 2014: 21, 24, 26; see also Bennett, 2013, for survey evidence). Over half of the regular participants in one study had become involved because of direct requests (Brookfield et al., 2014: 21). A veteran Mass Observer explained the volunteering activities in which he had become involved as a combination of invitations from individuals with whom he had either weak social ties (through church and workplace) or strong social ties (his extended family) (Granovetter, 1973). These points of entry were not accidental – his business connections and social and cultural capital made him an attractive recruit for governance roles – so this example somewhat contradicts Roberts and Devine's (2004) observations as to the chance nature of engagement. It wouldn't be surprising that such routes into volunteering – targeting individuals with desirable skills – are likely to mean that those recruited are not a random cross-section of society. The distinctively *local* character of voluntary action also emerges as a strong theme, where the initial connection was with a community-wide matter which united people around a shared issue or challenge, initially as supporters but which again drew them in to more sustained roles. Again, this illustrates Roberts and Devine's (2004) point about the 'accidental' nature of routes into participation, in the sense that engagement was precipitated by an unanticipated event.

We also gain insight into *disengagement* from voluntary action through these accounts. Changes in personal circumstances can lead to commencement for some but curtailment of involvement for others. The transition to retirement is sometimes seen as a trigger for volunteering. Some Mass Observers with no prior history of volunteering were enthusiastic about pursuing volunteering opportunities on retirement, but their ability to take advantage of them depended very much on contingent circumstances. One busy executive strongly insisted in 1996 that he would commence volunteering once he retired. We were able to trace his subsequent responses to Mass Observation directives. He followed through on this intention, but 13 active years in various roles eventually ceased in response to increased caring responsibilities. Another writer had pledged that she would take up volunteering opportunities upon retirement, but after a lifetime of difficult personal domestic circumstances and arduous work she focused her retirement on taking advantage of opportunities to relax and enjoy life without financial or domestic concerns (Lindsey and Mohan, 2018: chapter 7).

Other respondents positively relished the chance offered by retirement to cease volunteering, as part of a concerted relinquishment of established routines and constraints, and to seek opportunities for leisure and enjoyment. The experience of volunteering could also play a part in this. The studies reviewed here certainly found individuals who felt they had been more or less expected – if not coerced – to take on volunteering roles, and who expressed concerns that they would be unable to step aside from them. Others felt that they had contributed as much voluntary effort as could reasonably be expected and resented being asked to do more (Lindsey and Mohan, 2018; Lindsey and Bulloch, 2013). Thus, respondents actively welcomed changes in circumstances which freed them to move on, such as retirement. This is evidence of volunteer burnout – and if there are concerns about the availability of volunteers, this needs to be taken seriously. It was certainly a strong feature of some attitudinal work on volunteering – notably in response to the Big Society – while recent work suggests that those who volunteer are finding the experience less enjoyable than their counterparts did in an earlier study from the 1980s (see Chapter 11).

As regards the cessation of volunteering, the qualitative accounts strongly featured family commitments, work pressures, disadvantage and physical and mental health. Commitments to caring for close relatives were one reason why some Mass Observers' plans to engage in volunteering on retirement were not fulfilled. The intense nature of such commitments help explain why a small number of Mass Observers showed little or no evidence of voluntary action post-retirement. Gendered family expectations – for instance, the presumption that women would do the bulk of housework and take primary responsibility for unpaid care – also feature strongly (Brodie et al., 2011: 28, 40); the 'long arm of the household' (Parry et al., 2021) constrained involvement for many.

Experiences of health and disability were highly salient, restricting the time available for volunteering and impinging on people's ability to commit to it, especially for people who have taken on significant caring roles. One disabled respondent acknowledged the isolation of her position and had hoped that volunteering would provide social contacts, but being unemployed she was also concerned about the likelihood of benefit sanctions. She seemed to lack the education and social capital that might have provided a route into engagement, and as far as can be judged she remained a non-volunteer (Lindsey and Mohan, 2018: 174–5). The greatest and most persistent challenges to volunteering commitments seem to have been those relating to physical and mental health and to the onset of the challenges of ageing (Brodie et al., 2011: 40; Brookfield et al., 2014: 20). Even so, it was found that some individuals adjusted by changing the kinds of activities they did and/or by reducing the hours they committed to (see also Chapter 4).

One might also expect the changing character of the labour market to influence whether or not individuals could engage. The main studies covered here have rather fewer younger respondents, limiting the evidence they provide on recent labour market conditions, such as casualisation and precarity. Nonetheless, heavy, inflexible, unsociable and unpredictable work commitments are the most frequently cited reason for nonparticipants in the wider range of social participation activities in one study (Brookfield et al., 2014; 2018a). For those already engaged in volunteering, shift work, career ladder pressures and changing working patterns could render involvement difficult, though more frequently the impact was in terms of restricting how often and how intensively individuals were able to participate, rather than on whether or not they were able to participate at all. Flexible working patterns, in particular, limited the scope to engage in activities that required regular, consistent time investments. Conversely, self-employment appeared to offer flexibilities that made room for participation and/or volunteering (see also Chapter 3, in which self-employed and small business owners appear to have above average levels of involvement in volunteering).

Conclusions

Large-scale quantitative studies characterise the broad pattern of life-course changes which influence the volunteering pathways of individuals; in-depth qualitative work offers perspectives on how individuals contextualise and account for those pathways. Longitudinal studies show that, over people's lifetimes, the proportion of individuals who *never* engage at all in voluntary action is really very small (Chapter 4). Less positively, for most people volunteering is something in which they engage intermittently, depending on other individual and household priorities and on the effects of circumstances such as job loss, an expansion of caring responsibilities or separation.

For those interested in how volunteering rates might be increased, or gaps in the distribution of volunteers closed, research on moves into and out of volunteering is not completely encouraging. Certainly, longitudinal surveys indicate that once experience of volunteering forms part of individuals' lives, they are more likely to persist in it (Dawson et al., 2019). There is also positive news from longitudinal studies on the effects of retirement on volunteering (Eibich et al., 2022). However, longitudinal qualitative studies provide strong support for Roberts and Devine's (2004) emphasis on the accidental and contingent nature of commencement of volunteering. Social networks and shared mutual interests account for the ways in which people are first of all asked to engage and then commence their volunteering journeys. These processes aren't easily manageable or amenable to policy intervention. Such routes into engagement mean that participation is heavily influenced by pre-existing informal networks within communities and by perceptions of immediate need (often that of family, not more distant others). It follows that appeals to engagement that are based on abstract notions of a contribution to community well-being are likely to gain limited long-term traction.

If journeys into volunteering can be ad hoc and circumstantial, the broad patterns of routes out of it seem more systematic. Economic pressures, the burden of illness and competing family demands are more likely to adversely affect participation among those with fewest resources and social connections (see Chapter 3). This is reflected in qualitative research: when individuals give accounts of constraints on engagement they are focused on material needs such as making a living, caring for family members or finding a place for volunteering among the combined demands of work, family and leisure.

The barriers which inhibit people becoming involved are structural, though this isn't always acknowledged. Brodie et al.'s (2011) influential *Pathways through Participation* report, widely cited even a decade after its publication, summarises the factors that prevent people becoming involved in terms of an absence of practical resources, learnt resources and felt resources, only acknowledging to a limited degree that these are socioeconomically structured. Obviously, practical resources (time, money, security) will reflect an individual's economic capital; Brodie et al.'s 'learnt resources' (the skills, knowledge and experience that make them attractive recruits and support their engagement) will surely reflect the resources of the household in which they grew up and the opportunities to which they were exposed; while their dimension of 'felt resources' (confidence, sense of efficacy) could be better rephrased as one of cultural capital: the interpersonal skills necessary for successfully participating in a voluntary organisation.

Over and above these resources, many different circumstances – and changes in these circumstances – may affect an individual's ability to engage in social and collective activities; the patterns of some of these are more predictable than others (e.g. the effects of retirement or economic dislocation; see also Chapter 4). If we are to understand participation over the life-course, it is vital that the importance of transitions be built into this picture. There is a need to recognise the ebb and flow of demands on people's time and to appreciate how these demands can inform a person's willingness and ability to become and/or stay involved. Understanding the effects of these influences seems a more promising line of inquiry than seeking explanations in terms of who is, or is not, infused with character traits such as a 'habit of service' (Taylor-Collins et al., 2019).

Finally, circumstances surrounding current life transitions are not propitious and are likely to pose problems for proposals to increase volunteering. Retirement is often beneficial for volunteering, though many citizens who are at or near retirement age are increasingly caught between supporting very elderly parents on the one hand and children and grandchildren on the other. Moreover, the positive benefits of retirement for volunteering are likely to be attenuated as the state pension age rises. Communities where higher proportions of the population rely heavily on the state pension in retirement may also find that more of their residents have little choice but to continue in paid work. While volunteering rates among those above retirement age have remained relatively stable in comparison with those of younger generations, much will therefore depend on the circumstances in which individuals retire and their other commitments.

There is also – for more recent birth cohorts particularly – casualisation, precarity, rising housing costs and indebtedness. As shown in other longitudinal studies of behaviour (in this case crime), *when* we are matters in the same way as *who* we are: living through shared experiences such as war or a significant disruption to ordinary life is something which acts as a long-term shock to individual behaviours, including civic engagement (Sampson and Ash Smith, 2021: 60). Such recent disruptions and their impacts are considered in Chapters 11 and 13. Long-term trends in volunteering suggest that we are now witnessing a significant downturn in activity that is concentrated in particular age groups. This looks like a severe engagement penalty of the times through which we are currently living, and from the qualitative accounts we have from individuals, which mostly refer to less austere and challenging times than the present, the solutions to it are not likely to lie in exhortations to individuals to form good habits.

Part III

Impacts

Introduction to Part III

Volunteering is promoted by governments and its stakeholders because, aside from its direct impacts, it also offers a range of broader benefits to individuals, communities and society in general. The direct benefits are those intended by the individual or organisation promoting them and result from the contributions of volunteers such as running a group, delivering a service or providing advice. Individuals, voluntary organisations and communities all benefit directly from the actions of volunteers, and there have been considerable efforts to quantify the time that goes into volunteering, count the numbers of people involved in it and impute a monetary value to it (Chapter 2). In addition, there is now widespread recognition of the indirect impacts of volunteering, sometimes referred to as unintended or latent outcomes of actions, which were neither consciously intended nor recognised by participants in an action (Kamerāde et al., 2015). For instance, individual volunteers might benefit indirectly from their involvement – for example, by developing stronger relationships with fellow citizens, enhancing their skills or engaging in political deliberation. These, in turn, might enhance their well-being, increase their chances of finding work or promote social trust. The community will benefit indirectly too, through enhanced levels of local citizen engagement which strengthen social connections.

A rare public discussion of such public benefits occurred on the BBC's topical *Any Questions* programme during the 2015 British general election campaign. The only specific pledge made by the Conservative Party in relation to voluntary action was a proposal that employees in establishments with at least 250 staff would be guaranteed three days of unpaid leave to volunteer. This uncosted idea was celebrated by Grant Shapps MP (at that time, co-chair of the Conservative Party), with generalised claims about the societal benefits of volunteering such as increased productivity and better health – for example, the evidence that in companies with employer-supported volunteering schemes, sickness absences among employees were reduced.[1]

Other participants in the discussion focused on how the costs of the scheme would be covered. To estimate this, in 2015 some 10 million employees in the UK worked in establishments with 250 or more employees. Were they all to take three days' unpaid leave for volunteering, this would have equated to at least 30 million days of lost productivity. If it were all costed at the national minimum wage – around £7.50 per hour at that time – this would have amounted to around £1.7 billion. Suppose that the government believed this could be resourced, and employers compensated, by savings to the public purse arising from reduced pressures on the health service – for example, from fewer people being seen by general practitioners (family doctors or GPs). The annual cost of the GP service was in the order of £9 billion per annum at the time of the 2015 general election. Thus, in order to pay for the policy, GP consultations would need to have been reduced by around 20 per cent.

The programme chair remarked that, on the logic of this policy, the government ought to extend the promise to 100 days of volunteering, at which point the population would be so healthy that hospitals would not be necessary. Shapps retorted that his interlocutors were taking the discussion too far, too seriously and too literally, but deterministic claims are regularly made for the benefits of voluntary action. Sometimes these are rhetorical statements from stakeholders, think-tanks and politicians. But consider the definitive statement by Lawton and Watt (2018: 12) that 'volunteering is going to help you get on in life by helping you gain new skills, feel better about yourself and improve your health and happiness', and that the key message for under-represented groups in the volunteering population is: 'YOU CAN DO IT' (2018: 12). While there is certainly some evidence that points in these directions, I'm not sure we can be so confident that the spirit of service will have such dramatic effects for everyone, everywhere.

Evaluating claims about the beneficial impacts of volunteering raises some generic questions about the causal mechanisms involved, the measurement of those impacts and the formulation of an appropriate analytical strategy for determining whether claims for volunteering's benefits can be sustained. Consideration of those generic points is the subject of Chapter 7, which is then followed by chapters

---

[1] BBC, *Any Questions*, 10 April 2025 – recording available at www.bbc.co.uk/sounds/play/b05prq80 – at 2'30".

that review evidence on the impact of volunteering on employability, health and civic engagement. These are all entrenched policy challenges for the UK and other societies. Structural economic change since the 1970s has reshaped the labour market and demanded a broader range of skills and aptitudes from workers. In health inequalities, there is a recognition of both the material and social determinants of illness – health is in part a function of one's social environment, and so if isolated individuals can be connected up to constructive activities, there are potentially salutogenic impacts. Disengagement from political affairs is a further dimension of social exclusion, and the growing sense of political alienation prompts calls for the promotion of opportunities – especially at formative stages of people's lives – to engage in voluntary action, and thereby to promote active citizenship, political engagement and trust.

7

Do not expect miracles: the impacts of voluntary action

Introduction

The obvious and perhaps most influential place to start in assessing volunteering's impacts is by considering the work of Robert Putnam on social capital. Putnam argued that societies with high levels of social capital – networks, norms and trust, born out of regular interaction between citizens in non-hierarchical contexts – were also characterised by improved social outcomes on a number of fronts: health, economic performance, social cohesion and the strength of democratic institutions (Putnam et al., 1993; Putnam, 2000).

Putnam's claims were sometimes non-specific, as in his argument that volunteering was 'part of the syndrome of good citizenship and political involvement' (Putnam, 2000, 132), and at others deterministic. Commenting on the association between social participation and health, he suggested that, in terms of reducing mortality risk, 'if you smoke and belong to no groups, it's a toss-up statistically whether you should stop smoking or start joining' (Putnam, 2000: 331).

Voluntary action played a major part in Putnam's work, and his ideas were enthusiastically received in some quarters, such as governments seeking policy solutions that were costless, placing the responsibility squarely on citizens and communities to sort out their own problems. Academic authorities were more sceptical. Alejandro Portes cautioned that it was 'a sociological bias to see good things in sociability' (1998: 15), while Ben Fine (2010) considered that social capital was a route through which entrepreneurial academics were able to behave badly and opportunistically, making exaggerated claims for social capital and for the activities that produced it. These are important warnings, for volunteering is often presented as an unproblematic good, generating benefits for individuals, the communities in which they live and the societies of which they are a part. While some such benefits do accrue from voluntary action, we need to be aware of the challenges of identifying them and the risk of exaggeration.

In this part of the book we consider three principal types of beneficial impacts of volunteering: the effects on employability, health and political participation (Chapters 8–10) respectively. To frame the discussions in the next three chapters, this chapter discusses the generic issues that affect our ability to capture the distinctive impact of volunteering. First, there is a consideration of the mechanisms through which volunteering might affect these outcomes, paying due attention to the diversity of voluntary action and the range of activities and settings that it encompasses. Whether these heterogeneous activities can all have beneficial impacts is questionable. Then there is the question of the quasi-pharmacological approach that essentially regards volunteering as a solution that can be prescribed to resolve a problem. This is followed by the challenges associated with measuring the impact of volunteering, where there is a hierarchy of evidence: it is often believed that volunteering has positive outcomes for individuals but such claims are often based on self-reports by individuals at one point in time. Longitudinal surveys tracking individuals over time allow us to get some purchase on the effects of volunteering. Finally there are analytical issues. Individuals cannot – by definition – be prescribed (mandated) to undertake volunteering, generating problems such as selection bias (volunteers are not generally a cross-section of the population) and reverse causation (improved health leads to volunteering, rather than volunteering leading to improved health).

Mechanisms

Volunteering takes a range of forms and it happens in various settings so the content, meaning and impacts of voluntary activities will vary. Yet there are highly generalised claims about the effects of volunteering for third-sector organisations, as if those organisations and their activities were homogeneous. Furthermore, participation in volunteering is stratified and unequal (Chapter 3), so the impacts of involvement can vary between different groups in society.

Voluntary organisations differ in relation to basic organisational characteristics (size, sources of funding, balance of unpaid and paid personnel), orientation (the cause served and its beneficiaries) and the nature of their activities. Organisational types within the voluntary sector range from large professionalised organisations delivering substantial and often complex services and providing specialist expertise and advice, to small-scale, volunteer-run grassroots groups operating in an informal way to meet immediate personal needs. Then there are different 'paradigms' of voluntary action, denoting the orientation of different types of organisation: the 'dominant paradigm' is largely about large charities delivering services; the 'serious leisure' paradigm references many member-oriented organisations, from self-help groups for individuals with specific health needs to hobby clubs, Scout groups and sports clubs. Such groups are mainly oriented towards the needs of their members and are routinely listed as by far the most popular causes to which individuals provide unpaid help (Lindsey and Mohan, 2018: 92), though by being focused on the needs of a particular group they may be less likely to promote the interaction and debate with a cross-section of people that is said to generate latent benefits from volunteering. Finally, there is the 'civil society' paradigm, consisting of groups oriented towards campaigning and social change (Chapter 1), including political associations, environmental groups or entities helping disadvantaged members of society. These may provide direct benefits to recipients, but their main purpose is to bring about changes in society (Salamon and Sokolowski, 2003).

The nature of activity within voluntary organisations, and the ways in which their operations are structured, are also consequential for the indirect benefits to society of organisational life. For instance, do all organisations promote public deliberation on political issues across their membership? Do they engage a broad cross-section of society? (Not according to data on the diversity of volunteers: see Chapter 3.) Thus 'cheque book participation' is very unlikely to produce beneficial effects on individuals as compared to active and regular involvement in the activities and debates of an organisation. Wollebaek and Selle (2002) argue that passive memberships cannot generate civic skills, so that there is no necessary pay-off for democracy; they see some voluntary associations as an institutionalisation of engagement (attracting those who are already participating) not a generator of it.

In a similar vein, critics of the dominant paradigm in voluntary action, and with the colonisation of voluntary activity by the contract culture – in which voluntary organisations become bureaucratised and professionalised – might suggest that the benefits to the individual would be minimal and indistinguishable from those of paid work (Chapters 1 and 2; see also Overgaard, 2019; Aiken and Taylor, 2019).

Beyond organisational context, simply stating that an individual is a volunteer does not tell us anything about the content of the activity that they undertake, yet the nature of that activity may be pertinent to understanding its impact. For example, engagement in governance roles may produce consequences which are good for democracy if that engagement entails deliberation about policy choices, opportunities and constraints. Providing direct support to an individual through a mentoring programme might well produce the 'warm glow' effect that is associated with health benefits (Andreoni, 1989).

Tasks may equally be mundane, so the mere fact of involvement in voluntary action does not necessarily mean that indirect benefits will follow. Some of these benefits also depend on the nature of interactions between volunteers. For social capital to be produced, with its wider associated benefits, it is generally argued that individuals need to encounter people from a wider range of backgrounds than they otherwise would through connections made via work, church or family. This exposes volunteers to perspectives arising from interaction with diverse individuals; such experiences translate into wider awareness of social challenges and into increased levels of participation. Yet we cannot assume that this is the case for all voluntary organisations. Many voluntary organisations are stratified, drawing membership from a particular local community or ethnic or religious group, or recruiting people who have particular skills that often require a demonstration of ability.

The nature of volunteering and the interactions that take place through engagement in it are therefore important. Beyond this, if we accept that there are benefits to volunteering, how much of it and over what time period are required to produce the desired effect? Bekkers and Verkaik (2015) ask us to imagine that the spirit of service is distilled into a 'vitamin V', which can be taken in doses of varying sizes and frequencies. In a clinical context, when developing a new medicine, a researcher would investigate the dose that would be required to induce the relevant response. However, there is uncertainty about efficacy: we cannot say what frequency of dosage of vitamin V (yearly, monthly, weekly or more frequently) would be required to obtain the benefits of volunteering. Intuitively the reinforcement one receives from turning up regularly, not intermittently, might be expected to have a larger effect. However, it might not do so: the effects of a larger dosage of vitamin V are not always in one direction; indeed, some literature on links between volunteering and employability suggests that above a certain point *too much* volunteering is less beneficial as it interferes with job searching (Chapter 8).

Would a certain size of dose be important as well as frequency? For example, would a minimum time period of involvement matter? Even regular and committed individuals only volunteer a certain number of hours in the course of a week. In the UK the typical (median) volunteer of working age will commit some 2.5 hours per week to volunteering (though of course subsets of the population do considerably more; see Chapter 4). This is fewer than 3 per cent of the waking hours of a typical individual and is likely to be dwarfed by the amount of time devoted to unpaid care, household tasks and paid work. Volunteering is, however much we might like to pretend otherwise, something of secondary importance – measured only in terms of time spent on it – in the lives of most people. So we ought not to expect too much of it.

What about the level of concentration in the dose – in other words the intensity of the activity? Do small doses – 'micro-volunteering' in which volunteering is done as a secondary activity, or donating 'slivers of time' (Cabinet Office, 2011) – have beneficial effects? Would such a form of engagement be given equal weight to lengthy face-to-face connections in terms of its potential contribution to well-being? Is face-to-face involvement with other human beings essential for impacts to be realised? This might be highly relevant to debates about the benefits of online forms of volunteering. Online mentoring may well have valuable effects on the recipients of support and advice and be satisfying in its own way to the volunteer providing it, but if relationships are important, would it be as beneficial as activity that involved direct personal contact? As yet, and despite the enthusiasm for technology-enabled forms of support, knowledge is lacking as to whether they have these latent benefits.

Measurement and analysis

A challenge in this field is obtaining reliable measures of relevant outcome variables and then assessing causality through an appropriate analytical strategy. Many studies rely on self-reports of potential outcome variables. All the measures of volunteering's benefits reported in an early British publication, *Volunteering Works* (Ockenden, 2007), are self-reports from individuals; the same is true of the recent NCVO publication, *Time Well Spent* (Kanemura et al., 2023). Similar questions are asked in the main national social surveys. Naturally, these are questions asked solely of those who actually volunteer and they are potentially susceptible to social desirability biases. This problem is also found in evaluation studies – for instance of programmes designed to improve employability through volunteering, which typically rely on measures of whether participants *think* that volunteering has enhanced their skills or job prospects. Without an independent measure of the outcome (in this case whether someone has obtained work), this does not demonstrate that volunteering has indeed had the desired effect.

At a minimum, researchers need to measure change over time in the chosen indicator. An example would be someone's sense of well-being. At any one point in time, we might find a cross-sectional survey that suggests this is associated with volunteering (i.e. that well-being is higher for volunteers), but we need to obtain measures of that outcome variable for more than one point in time, for the same respondents, to judge whether volunteering has had an impact.

The UK's longitudinal surveys provide some useful evidence. The BHPS captures indicators at regular intervals of health and well-being, such as the General Health Questionnaire, a standard 12-item scale for producing an assessment of how healthy individuals believe themselves to be (see Chapter 9). For employability, the BHPS data do capture whether or not individuals were in employment at each wave of the survey. Longitudinal research into the relationship between volunteering and civic engagement has relied on questions about interest in politics but has rarely been able to determine associations with whether or not people actually voted. So while the BHPS is strong on individual self-reports at more than one point in time, it does not always have independent measures on relevant outcomes of interest.

Demonstrating volunteering's impacts is difficult unless participants in studies are tracked and information sought about whether they had, for instance, obtained jobs or actually voted. There is also a growing movement to capture biomarkers – measures of stress levels recorded through blood tests, for instance – from respondents to British social surveys which will potentially be beneficial, but as yet there is no published literature using these.

Even with good-quality longitudinal data, we then have problems of selection bias. Volunteers differ systematically and in statistically significant ways from non-volunteers, typically being more highly educated and well-off compared to non-volunteers (Chapter 3). Hence they are also likely to score more highly on potential outcome indicators of the benefits claimed for volunteering (such as well-being or physical or mental health). The problem is one of reverse causation: the better health of volunteers could be due not to volunteering but instead the cumulative result of life-course influences and experiences; vitamin V is operating on people who are, on average, relatively healthy to begin with and it's not necessarily the case that volunteering improves health. In the case of employability, for example, a limitation is that both volunteers and people who have higher chances of regaining employment share many similar individual characteristics; they are likely to have better educational qualifications, higher occupational status, better technical and social skills, be better socially connected and be physically and mentally healthier than people who are either not volunteering or who are likely to remain unemployed for longer periods of time (Wilson, 2000; 2012). Therefore it is plausible that those unemployed volunteers who were able to secure a paid job might have done so even without the help of volunteering (see also Chapter 8).

A related issue is that of ruling out confounders or alternative explanations. Any positive (or negative) association between volunteering and an outcome may be attributable to characteristics of the individual that are not observed and which can affect both their likelihood of engaging in volunteering and the outcome variable (e.g. well-being, civic engagement). For instance, there could be an unobserved personality trait which predisposes certain sorts of people to volunteer. A statistically significant association may therefore capture both the direct impact of engagement in volunteering and the effect of individuals' (unobserved) characteristics that led them to engage in the first place. This imposes demanding requirements on data collection, which are rarely met, because one would need to gather data on a range of personality traits in addition to all the socioeconomic and demographic data typically collected in a social survey.

These issues pose real problems for research that draws on observational data about individuals – whether those data are cross-sectional (at one point in time) or longitudinal. In an influential paper in demography, Ní Bhrolcháin and Dyson (2007) argue that causal interpretations from observational evidence can be justified in certain circumstances. The temporal sequencing of events needs to be securely identified, a clear mechanism needs to be at work and all potential confounders or alternative explanations need to be specified. Longitudinal studies do allow researchers to overcome the problem of temporal sequencing. If an individual is observed at intervals – for example, every year or two in the UK's Understanding Society panel survey of households – we can measure both changes in their life circumstances (e.g. moves into and out of work or changing health status) and changes in volunteering and see which of these is associated with changes in the variable of interest. Thus, if we know that unemployed individuals who engaged in volunteering at time t were then more likely to be in employment at time $t + 1$, adjusting for other characteristics and circumstances, this would be more informative than knowing about the relative employment status of volunteers and non-volunteers at a single point in time.

As to assessing the impact of volunteering, an ideal would be a randomised controlled trial in which individuals receiving a treatment were assigned to two groups, one of which would engage in volunteering (Kamerāde and Ellis Paine, 2014). However, this is almost impossible to achieve in this field. The problem is that volunteering – requiring a conscious choice by individuals to opt into an activity – is not something that can be treated in the manner of a clinical trial. However, even if controlled trials are not feasible, there are some approaches which allow the effects of volunteering to be analysed. A quasi-experimental longitudinal design, for instance, would capture prior and posterior measures of a particular state – for example, health status – among groups of participants exposed to a treatment that is non-random (in this case, volunteering) and would analyse differences in the health status of volunteers and non-volunteers over time. A less rigorous – and essentially observational – approach would be to take a cohort of volunteers and see how their lives changed as they continued to volunteer or, alternatively, as they quit. Detailed case studies of small numbers of individuals might also reveal something of the influence of volunteering on various outcomes.

In practice, there are very few studies which meet such exacting standards. Bekkers and Verkaik (2015) reviewed 452 studies which had appeared in a Google Scholar search for the phrase 'effect of volunteering'. However, fewer than 10 per cent of these (33) contained both a measure of volunteering activity (at least a dichotomous indicator) and an outcome indicator (i.e. a benefit to the volunteer). The majority of studies concerned either health outcomes or subjective well-being. Most involved either the analysis of cross-sectional data or quasi-experimental analyses of longitudinal data, in which the same individuals were observed and in which, therefore, measures could be taken of a change in their state (e.g. subjective well-being) over time. Almost no randomised controlled trials were undertaken. Other reviews have been conducted, mainly in relation to the impact of volunteering on health, but because of the challenges of study design, reviewers have found relatively small numbers of studies which are considered definitively to have demonstrated volunteering's impacts (see Chapter 9).

Conclusions

The aim of this chapter has been to provide a general overview of the challenges that face studies of the impact of volunteering. But the discussion of the effects of policies to promote volunteering does pose the question of how valid and reliable the claims being made actually are. There are significant generic challenges of measurement and study design. Individual voluntary organisations may well believe that volunteering makes a difference for their clients, in terms of social connectedness, mental health or employment prospects. Cross-sectional surveys certainly suggest that volunteers do better on a range of social outcomes than non-volunteers. But teasing out the causal connections requires complex datasets which are expensive and time-consuming to collect.

This means that, despite over 25 years of policies to promote volunteering in one form or another, the evidence base for those policies is still developing, though it is growing. In Chapters 8–10, we present a review of available UK evidence regarding the impacts of volunteering on employability, civic engagement, health and well-being, and community-level social capital. Echoing the conclusions of Bekkers and Verkaik (2015), the collective message is one of realism: even when causal connections are evident, the effects of volunteering on social outcomes are small. Thus, they argue, we should not expect miracles, and if there are policy proposals to invest in supporting voluntary action, it is arguable that they should rest on the benefits of volunteering for its own sake rather than on the basis of imprecise claims about latent impacts.

8

Volunteering, employability and policy

Introduction

In recent decades, high levels of unemployment, and the growing evidence of precarity and casualisation of existing employment opportunities, have stimulated interest in the contribution that volunteering might make to the pursuit of 'employability' (V. Smith, 2010: 279). This term denotes an individual's ability to move into and maintain employment, and to advance within the labour market.

Volunteering may contribute to employability if, through it, participants gain the chance to develop new skills, to build CVs, to try out potential new occupations and to gain references. Framed in this way, the focus is on the supply side of the labour market, and employability is an individual responsibility. Questions of the demand for labour remain unaddressed, including whether jobs are available and whether or not employers value the skills that individuals have gained from volunteering.

Volunteering might plausibly affect labour market outcomes for individuals through the acquisition of skills and work-related experience, the expansion of an individual's social networks and ability signalling (Bruno and Fiorillo, 2016; Baert and Vujić, 2016; Qvist and Munk, 2018). The first draws on human capital theory, which suggests that labour market outcomes reflect differences in cognitive abilities (e.g. educational qualifications) and job skills (e.g. work experience). Through volunteering, people develop 'hard' skills, which equip them to perform particular roles, and also 'soft' or relational skills that enable them to work better as part of a team (Kamerāde et al., 2015).

The second channel, social network expansion, draws on social capital theory, which suggests that the positioning of individuals in labour markets reflects the density and quality of their social connections, which may be acquired from volunteering. Volunteers tend to have more social capital than non-volunteers: they belong to more associations and have more diverse social networks and more extensive connections to people outside their immediate work setting (Musick and Wilson, 2008; Egerton and Mullan, 2008). Causality may therefore run in the opposite direction: people in strong positions in labour markets may be more likely to be *asked* to volunteer.

Finally, volunteering has a signalling function, providing potential employers with indications as to an individual's abilities and commitment. Carrying out volunteer roles in a workplace is informative about their suitability for particular roles or their ability to learn new skills. It may offer evidence of desirable qualities such as reliability and trustworthiness (Bruno and Fiorillo, 2016; Petrovski et al., 2017; Qvist and Munk, 2018).

The prospect that volunteering might contribute to improved labour market outcomes has informed policy interventions by successive British governments. Volunteering might be thought to have obvious instrumental benefits. Recalling earlier discussions of the blurred boundaries between paid and unpaid work (Chapter 1) (Taylor, 2004; 2005), volunteering – certainly in formal organisational settings – replicates some features of the workplace. Moreover, recent British governments have sought to develop policies to support people into paid employment. This is a general rationale for intervention: more specific programmes been have designed to offer volunteering opportunities to groups, or communities, considered to be at risk of exclusion and disconnection. The connection with unemployment and, therefore, with benefit receipt, provides policy levers that can be pulled which involve opportunities for compulsion and sanction, such as withdrawal of benefits for those who do not take up volunteering opportunities.

The chapter begins with an overview of efforts in Britain to develop programmes that encourage people to volunteer, with the aim of enhancing their employability and increasing their chances of securing paid work. Consideration is then given to the evidence base on the strength of the connections between volunteering and employability. The evidence base ranges in quality from many small-scale studies featuring self-reports by individuals, through narrowly defined programme evaluations, to quasi-experimental longitudinal analyses. Studies show that the benefits of volunteering for employability are limited, stratified and contextual. Given this, it may not be surprising to discover, from studies of how individuals and organisations engage with volunteering initiatives that are designed to promote their employability, that the outcomes of those initiatives are contingent and partial and may result in frustrated expectations. There is a particular focus on evidence regarding young people, since these (especially young school leavers with few or no qualifications) are a core target group for volunteering initiatives. Finally, in the light of the limited positive evidence in relation to the instrumental benefits of volunteering for employability, the chapter considers a recent argument that a justification for the use of volunteering to address unemployment may be found in its contribution to self-respect.

Volunteering and employability: policy and programmes

Official policy pronouncements, the mission statements of prominent organisations and communications from voluntary sector trade bodies have promulgated a broadly consistent message that volunteering contributes positively to employability and provides a route to employment. Other justifications have been provided for policies to support volunteering, but the discussion here is of those policies and programmes where increased employability was as at least one of the stated objectives.

The return of mass unemployment in the early 1980s directly stimulated significant programmes to promote volunteering as part of policies to get people back into work (Sheard, 1995: 118). Penny and Finnegan (2019: 152) use the term 'unemployment-related support for volunteering' (URSV) to distinguish policies which are components of policy responses to unemployment from policies designed to promote volunteering in general. The following is a summary of some key policy developments; for more detailed accounts see Kamerāde and Ellis Paine (2014: 260–4) and Hardill and Baines (2011).

Numerous volunteering programmes were created by the Conservative governments from the early 1980s, and were designed to facilitate entry into work in specific sectors (health and social care) or to create opportunities for particular groups, such as the long-term unemployed. Volunteering was also part of the labour market programmes introduced by the subsequent Labour governments. While the Conservative initiatives were seen as instrumental in character, with an emphasis on the management of mass unemployment, under Labour such goals were subsumed under a philosophy that emphasised the broader goals of increasing engagement in volunteering. Such programmes did not always have an explicitly stated aim or objective relating to employability/employment but they did make references to the potential utility of volunteering experience in job applications. For example, a major initiative promoted by Labour, the youth charity *v*, had the primary goal of raising youth engagement substantially. However, *v* also pointed (in their recruitment strategies) to the potential utility of skills development through volunteering and the potential value of a history of volunteering in job applications.

Even Labour's flagship New Deal for Young People did not explicitly employ anything that might be recognised as URSV, although it did offer an option to socially excluded young people to gain work experience through a placement in the voluntary sector (Penny and Finnegan, 2019: 153). But the 2008–9 financial crisis and subsequent recession prompted significant efforts to engage the unemployed in unpaid voluntary work, and the policy rationales for these were explicitly couched in terms of skills enhancement, boosting CVs and raising self-esteem (see Kamerāde and Ellis Paine, 2014). Various initiatives provided additional advisory support and opportunities for Jobseeker's Allowance claimants, such as targeted help in finding them volunteering opportunities.

These programmes had funding at levels which compared unfavourably with flagship initiatives such as *v*. But after the 2010 election, and despite the apparent prominence of voluntary action in government rhetoric, the only Coalition government initiative in this area was Work Together, largely a combination of JobCentre Plus staff signposting the unemployed towards relevant opportunities and engaging with local voluntary organisations to develop opportunities for the unemployed to volunteer. No specific funding was attached to this initiative.

The subsequent administrations have eschewed large-scale central government volunteering programmes, though an exception is the flagship NCS for young people, the recipient of over £1 billion of public funding to date. Participants engage in social action projects in their own communities as well as residential courses that involve team development activities. NCS is packaged and sold to young people in terms of social mixing, independent living and acquisition of a sense of social responsibility.[1] But it also emphasises the inculcation of self-discipline, as well as the value of gaining experience of social action in order to strengthen one's CV.

In summary, while some funding streams associated with government policies towards volunteering were initially motivated by concerns about employability, in general these are less prominent, and

---

[1] https://wearencs.com/.

funded at a lower level, than 'flagship' initiatives such as *v* or NCS. The initiatives that had as their principal objective the improvement of employability through volunteering all emerged during periods of economic downturn. Where such programmes have been implemented, they have focused firmly on the supply side, that is, on the personal characteristics and behaviours of the unemployed.

Moreover, compared to the scale of central government expenditure on wider employment and training initiatives, the amounts concerned with volunteering are small. At the end of the period of office of the Blair and Brown governments, Finnegan (2012) estimated these as, at most, in the region of £100 million over a number of years, which is a fraction of the sums subsequently provided for NCS.

Other non-governmental policy actors believe in the value of initiatives in this area, such as campaigns to raise the level of engagement by young people in 'social action'. In addition to stressing the direct benefits to communities of voluntary action undertaken by young people, publicity emphasises instrumental benefits to young people in terms of the skills and networks that can support their future employment (#iwill, n.d.; see also Chapter 12). The value of volunteering, in terms of enhancing employability and providing a route into paid work, is commonly asserted by individual voluntary organisations, producing positive individual illustrations from the court of experience that may not easily support wider generalisations as to volunteering's impacts (see, e.g., Hogg and Smith, 2021). In order to clarify what can and cannot definitively be said about these claims, in the next section I present a summary of the academic literature in the UK. I also draw on wider international studies where they are comparable and appropriate.

Volunteering and employability: what does the evidence tell us?

The literature in this field covers several potential outcomes of volunteering: employability, including the effect of volunteering on people's skills and self-confidence; progression into employment; and incomes. I begin with a summary of studies based largely on self-reports by individuals – evidence which Bekkers and Verkaik (2015) would regard as least reliable in terms of demonstrating outcomes. The bulk of this section then summarises analyses of longitudinal datasets, from the UK and elsewhere, on various labour market outcomes.

Self-reports of effects on employability

Much British evidence initially drew on reports from individuals contacted through organisations operating at the interface between the voluntary sector and the management of unemployment. Studies typically found a belief among volunteers that aspects of their employability had been enhanced (Gay, 1998; Nichols and Ralston, 2011; Kelemen et al., 2017). Studies of some specific volunteering programmes (e.g. in conservation or in overseas volunteering programmes) claim that high proportions of volunteers subsequently became employed and/or employed in fields directly related to their volunteering. However, these are fields which often attract people with prior commitments to a particular cause, so it is not possible to rule out selection bias. Generally, findings which have solicited opinion from participants in a volunteering programme about whether they believe that volunteering has helped them gain employment have produced ambiguous findings (summarised by Kameräde and Ellis Paine, 2014). Usually, studies have found positive endorsements of volunteering experiences, combined with beliefs held by participants that they would probably have found employment without volunteering. Those who felt that their volunteering experience had helped them gain employment were in a minority. Some evaluations, however, suggested that volunteering initiatives had not provided claimants with a direct 'stepping stone' into paid employment or links to real labour market opportunities, while others suggest a belief among clients that even if volunteering had helped them gain employment, they were no better off, financially, than they had been when claiming Jobseeker's Allowance. Slightly more optimistic data are available from the formative evaluation of *v*, which reported that 15 per cent of the participants moved into paid work after volunteering (Natcen et al., 2011). Perhaps unsurprisingly for an initiative making grants to organisations involved in the provision of youth-volunteering opportunities, it was found that 90 per cent of grant recipients – the organisations managing programmes – believed that receiving funding had improved their clients' chances of getting a job, though as recipients of grants these organisations arguably had an interest in providing a positive perspective on the scheme. In another study, although a high proportion of respondents believed that volunteering had helped or would help them to gain employment, there was no evidence that volunteers and non-volunteers differed in terms of labour market outcomes.

Expectations for the impact of volunteering on employability and employment would be anticipated to be highest for programmes which had employability as their principal objective. However, the intended beneficiaries of such programmes were also more likely to be generally the most disadvantaged in the labour market (e.g. the long-term unemployed). Those groups are also most vulnerable to variations in the demand for labour as a result of economic cycles. Combined, these pose particular challenges for achieving employment outcomes.

Like volunteering itself, outcomes are stratified. Within one initiative, targeted at young people from low-income backgrounds, an evaluation reported that levels of progression into employment after volunteering varied greatly according to the prior qualification levels of participants. Those without qualifications were about half as likely to obtain employment as a result of the programme than better-qualified groups. It is not clear what proportion of those moving into work attributed the change in their status to volunteering in these programmes.

The limitations of these studies include reliance on self-reported outcomes, the absence of comparable control groups of people not taking part in the respective programmes and the lack of longitudinal tracking of programmes. While individuals may therefore report beliefs that they have derived benefits from these initiatives, which is desirable in itself, this does not justify some of the more enthusiastic public claims made for the benefits of volunteering.

Longitudinal analyses

A key challenge in evaluating the impacts of volunteering is the availability of appropriate longitudinal datasets, but the BHPS provides such high-quality data and it has been used in several studies of volunteering and employability. The BHPS (now absorbed into the larger UKHLS) was a long-running panel study with data available for an 18-year period from 1991 through to 2008–9. The survey included questions on a range of standard human capital and demographic variables, including education, occupation, age, gender, earnings and hours worked.

From 1996 onwards, respondents were asked a relatively narrow question about volunteering (see Chapter 2), namely whether they carried out 'unpaid voluntary work' in their leisure time and the frequency with which they did so. Typically, around a fifth of the adult population reported that they did 'unpaid voluntary work' in any one wave of the survey, but many moved into and out of volunteering from one wave of the survey to the next (see Chapter 6).

Ellis Paine et al. (2013) deployed longitudinal data from the BHPS to test the effect of volunteering on employability – specifically access into employment, employment retention and progression in terms of remuneration. They drew data from the seven BHPS waves in which the volunteering question had been asked (between 1996 and 2008), containing over 92,000 observations (25,000 different individuals observed for an average of close to four of the relevant waves of the survey). Comparing the current employment situation of the respondents with their situation from one year previously, the analysis assessed how the association between the two was mediated by reports of whether unpaid voluntary work had been carried out.

The study used three outcome measures: moving into work, remaining in work and earnings levels. Each model controlled for education and other socioeconomic characteristics which were thought likely to be associated with elements of human capital and therefore likely to influence moves into paid work (Ellis Paine et al., 2013: 360–9). The analysis considered changes in employment status and wage levels as a function of a range of individual characteristics, including histories of volunteering at different points in the survey. The findings gave some limited support for a positive effect of volunteering on the likelihood of obtaining paid work, but the positive effects were by no means consistent across all groups.

First, the frequency of engagement appeared to matter but not in a consistent way. The effect was not necessarily larger as the 'dose' (effort committed to volunteering) increased. Monthly volunteering was positively associated with the chances of people not in work one year ago moving into paid employment. However, those volunteering on a weekly or yearly basis had *lower* than average chances of moving into paid work. This might be explicable in terms of time committed: *too much* volunteering might obstruct job searches while infrequent doses of vitamin V were inadequate to gain any benefit. Importantly, given the policy concerns about youth unemployment, there was no evidence of a positive effect of volunteering on the employment chances of young people (16–25-year-olds). It was only among people aged 45–60 years old that volunteering had a positive effect, and then only if undertaken on a monthly or slightly less frequent basis.

The effects of volunteering on moving into work also varied according to the reason why people were not employed – for example, whether respondents reported disabilities, caring responsibilities or being full-time students. For the unemployed, weekly volunteering had a negative effect on the chances of moving into employment, though volunteering several times a year had a positive effect; a similar pattern was observed for those out of work with family caring responsibilities. For students, the effect of volunteering appeared to be negative or insignificant; among people with disabilities, volunteering several times a year was found to have a positive effect on the move into employment, while doing more or less than this had little effect either way.

Overall, this analysis suggests that some volunteering *could* have a positive effect on the likelihood of movement into employment, but the impact depends on who you are, why you are out of work and how much volunteering you do. Doing 'too much' volunteering (i.e. on a weekly or more frequent basis) had a universally negative effect, particularly among young people and/or students. There are no consistent or unequivocal findings here.

If volunteering provides those who undertake it with enhanced levels of human and social capital, one might expect a positive impact on job retention, but Ellis Paine et al. (2013) found no particularly strong evidence for this, with the exception of those aged 16–24 who volunteered at least once a month (though findings for other frequencies of volunteering were inconsistent).

Does volunteering facilitate progression within the labour market, indexed by remuneration? The findings here are also inconsistent. Some positive assessments are based on cross-sectional data for one point in time and are unable to track individual respondents. Ellis Paine et al. (2013) assessed the effect of a change in the frequency of voluntary work and found that frequent (weekly) volunteering and infrequent (several times or once a year) volunteering had a negative effect on wage rates, while the effect of monthly volunteering was not significant. According to this analysis, volunteering doesn't appear to help people get on in their career (in terms of earning more), and if anything it has the opposite effect. This is consistent with equivocal results from other European studies of the impact of volunteering on remuneration. Qvist and Munk (2018) argue that studies demonstrating positive effects are usually based on cross-sectional data and therefore cannot demonstrate economic returns on voluntary work over the course of the working lives of respondents (see also Petrovski et al., 2017; Bruno and Fiorillo, 2016).

Is there evidence that volunteering specifically benefits *young* people in their transition to employment? Hoskins et al. (2020) analysed the Citizenship Education Longitudinal Study (CELS) – a nationally representative cohort of young people in England over 11 years, recruited in 2003 when they had just entered secondary school and tracked until the ages 19–20 (2011) and 22–23 (2014). Their first finding was that the social background of respondents, measured by numbers of books in the households and parental occupation, influenced their access to forms of work experience: the higher the level of social and cultural capital in the household, the more likely young people were to have done unpaid voluntary work (as with other studies of the beneficial impacts of volunteering, this shows how family circumstances influence the likelihood of engagement, and thus access to potential benefits of volunteering; see also Chapter 10). Second, they actually found a significant negative relationship between 'participating in unpaid work in charities and voluntary organisations' and employment in the final wave of the study.

The latter finding was the result of a cross-sectional analysis, so causality cannot be determined from it. The authors suggested several potential interpretations of this result. First, it was possible that volunteering experiences were having negative effects on individuals' employment prospects. Alternatively, not being in work might be what is driving individuals to engage in volunteering, in order to do something useful with their time. Conceivably, young people were so busy in volunteering that they were not actually available to work. More negatively, it could be that respondents were less likely to get a job anyway, and so were keeping busy by volunteering. With the available quantitative data it was not possible to determine which of these explanations was the more likely, though the results of qualitative research (see below) point in interesting directions. Finally, in a longitudinal analysis, Hoskins et al. (2020) found no relationship between volunteering in 2011 and the likelihood of being in paid work in 2014.

Summarising this research, in common with other claimed impacts of volunteering, it appears that its beneficial effects on employability are limited. There may be plausible reasons for hypothesising that volunteering may benefit individuals but there is little hard evidence that it does. Some of the challenges reflect data limitations. Binary indicators of whether or not someone participates in volunteering are not very informative about the extent of involvement or, to use the terminology of vitamin V, the extent of the dose. The nature and frequency of volunteering, the character of the voluntary roles carried out, how volunteering is structured and managed, and the nature and extent of unemployment might all be consequential for employability, but no longitudinal survey gathers such detailed data on volunteering. Similarly, surveys do not have strong data on the labour market histories of individuals. British data only provide information about respondent employment status at intervals and not on what happened between waves of the survey.

As a consequence, there is a disjuncture between the positive responses of individuals to the benefits of volunteering and the negative or inconclusive evidence from large-scale quantitative analyses. In the concluding section of this chapter, I consider the wider issues raised by this challenge. Prior to that, I consider how those engaged in the volunteering field manage programmes that are concerned with employability, and how their clients respond to those programmes, as this may shed further light on why the expectations of volunteering are somewhat dashed in practice.

How do people and organisations engage with employability initiatives?

Employability ranks some way down the list of reasons given by individuals for becoming involved in volunteering. In social surveys conducted in the UK over the last three decades, respondents have been given menus of up to a dozen possible reasons for engagement. In rankings of these reasons in order of popularity, employment-related options such as 'learning new skills' or 'giving the chance to use existing skills' are typically preceded by numerous others such as a desire to improve things, meet needs in the community or act in a manner consistent with the respondent's philosophy of life (Lindsey and Mohan, 2018: table 6.1). Asked to describe the various types of satisfaction that they obtained from volunteering, fewer than 5 per cent of volunteers reported that 'it gives me the chance to improve my employment prospects', and responses seemed to be consistent regardless of employment status.

Despite this, the provision of volunteering opportunities and experiences to those on the margins of the labour market has been the subject of considerable policy interest. It therefore seems reasonable to explore studies which have examined how volunteering is managed at the points in the life-course in which individual behaviours can be influenced. This points to educational settings (both schools and universities) and transitions into the labour market as key sites of policy.

On some accounts, volunteering can now be regarded as obligatory in young people's lives (Hustinx and Meijs, 2011: 17; Dean, 2014a: 233). Schools are the first point at which children are exposed to that view, but by the time pupils and students are presented with volunteering opportunities, they have already acquired resources which influence their ability to take advantage of them. These include shared family histories of volunteering, economic resources, social capital from friends and social networks, and perhaps direct connections to the voluntary sector organisations themselves (Dean, 2016: 97S; Hoskins et al., 2020: 9–12).

Dean (2014b) argues that schools in effect serve to socially stratify the availability of volunteering opportunities, which then has effects on the social mix of volunteers. In an education authority which had retained selective education at age 11, he found that grammar schools engaged in concerted efforts to cultivate prosocial attitudes among their students through structured programmes of voluntary work. However, non-selective, comprehensive schools seemed to attach less priority to such efforts, probably because of the requirement to deal with a broader cross-section of pupils. Dean shows how schools strongly emphasised the ways in which experience of volunteering could be sold as giving pupils a competitive advantage over other pupils who had no such experience, to the point where volunteering was difficult to distinguish from work experience (Dean, 2014a: 238; see also Taylor-Collins, 2022). Even so, he questioned a policy that prioritises the quantity of voluntary participation as opposed to the quality of its outcomes (Dean, 2014b: 654).

The formats in which students were introduced to volunteering also mattered. A growing number of UK schools now promote the International Baccalaureate (IB), which has a compulsory community service element. Dean found concerns from providers of volunteering opportunities about the lack of commitment of IB students. The incorporation of experiences of volunteering and social action in school curricula might seem to be a route through which pupils would receive broadly equal exposure to opportunities, but there are variations between schools in the extent to which volunteering is promoted. Taylor-Collins's (2022) qualitative study of three schools indicates the variations. In one, there were numerous opportunities to volunteer but little scope for wider reflection by the students on the volunteering experience; in another, the school put relatively little into supporting social action because they did not believe it was valued by Ofsted (the school inspectorate); in a third, social action was said to be integral to the ethos of the school. If these cases are typical, the opportunities available to pupils would vary in terms of extent and quality. Nor are those opportunities equally available to all even within schools – for example, access to these opportunities was sometimes tied very closely to standards of behaviour and achievement (Taylor-Collins, 2022).

The way in which volunteering is marketed to students may also limit the benefits which it confers. It would hardly be surprising if, having been encouraged to volunteer largely for instrumental reasons, students then explained their motivation as an instrumental one and did not develop a wider sense of social citizenship or civic responsibility. In an economic environment dominated by risk and uncertainty, such dispositions are not seen as priorities by young people (J. Dean, 2013: 59). Indeed, one manager of youth-volunteering programmes interviewed by Dean declined to spend time with participants talking about 'nebulous' concepts such as responsibility and instead focused on the 'get the certificate, get out' culture engendered for her clients by short-term projects (J. Dean, 2013: 58).

Turning to young adults seeking to use volunteering as part of a strategy to gain employment, Hoskins et al. (2020) complemented their quantitative work by interviewing selected individuals from the CELS about their experiences. Interviewees identified with the potential instrumental goals of volunteering experiences, such as keeping busy, becoming more motivated and helping with self-confidence. But they felt that positive outcomes in terms of employment were very limited or non-existent. For individuals lacking family resources or personal connections, and often in possession of few qualifications, the experience of volunteering was confined to the public sector or to poorly resourced charities. Few of these were able to provide employment opportunities, while provision of training and opportunities for career development were very limited. Finally, the study also considered the experiences of a small number of people compelled to work unpaid either as a condition of benefit receipt or as a result of community punishment orders (CPOs). These respondents felt that the work contributed little to employability, since it was largely menial in character and the requirement for uniforms marking out those who had received CPOs did nothing to motivate the individuals concerned. The experiences revealed by these studies show that the labour market outcomes of volunteering were highly stratified according to socioeconomic status and to the context in which volunteering was undertaken.

The findings also carry warnings for those who anticipate major contributions by the voluntary sector to the goal of giving opportunities that will facilitate employability. The exigencies facing many small, local agencies also meant that their ability to engage with employability programmes was limited (Leonard and Wilde, 2019: 134). Some were able to generate opportunities but had little concern beyond that for how those options were filled or by whom. Thus the experience of volunteers could be of low quality, carrying out work with limited scope for personal development. Providers could also engage in 'gaming' in order to demonstrate results and guarantee payment: one of Dean's interviewees referred to how they focus attention on the 'less complicated' volunteers (Dean, 2016: 106S). Thus those engaged in volunteer 'brokerage' were 'unadventurous in their recruitment practices' (Dean, 2016: 109S)

Project workers in voluntary organisations were sceptical about targets which emphasised volunteering – that is, as a placement opportunity for young people – but nevertheless they, and their organisations, benefited from engaging in such programmes (Dean, 2014a: 242). And organisations did actively contest narrow notions of employability. Leonard and Wilde found clear recognition that for many young people seeking to gain volunteering experience, especially those at a greater distance from the formal labour market, it was more realistic to emphasise the sense of self-worth that volunteering might offer (2019: 137).

Finally, do employers in fact value the experiences gained by volunteers? There is little hard evidence about how their recruitment practices are influenced, if at all. The predominant focus of policy and research appears to have been on what voluntary organisations and volunteers *believe* might influence employability of those looking for work (the supply side) and not what employers are *actually* looking for when hiring staff (Kamerāde, 2013). One interesting study suggested that volunteering can enhance the prospects of those who have engaged in it, at least in terms of positive feedback from employers; the implication is that employers do recognise the value of volunteering. Baert and Vujić (2016) conducted a randomised field experiment in which they submitted pairs of fictitious job applications in response to real vacancies. For each vacancy, one of the two applications was randomly assigned to a 'treatment' of volunteering – that application described volunteer work carried out by the fictional applicant while the other did not. The applications therefore only differed in one respect, namely whether volunteering experience was reported, and therefore the unequal treatment of applications from volunteers and non-volunteers could reasonably be attributed to the evidence of volunteering submitted by the fictitious applicants. Applications were sent to vacancies for a range of commercial and administrative white-collar occupational positions. Candidates with volunteering experience were 7.3 percentage points (significant at the 1 per cent level) more likely to receive one of a range of positive reactions from an employer (including, but not confined to, a job interview) and 2.8 percentage points more likely to obtain an interview (only statistically significant at the 10 per cent level). There was a higher premium for women but no suggestion that an increase in the numbers of types of voluntary engagement had any positive effect. Though this clearly implies that employers valued volunteering, there are some limitations. By definition, it was not possible to assess the final outcome of the applications, and the range of vacancies was limited to white-collar positions. Also, it was not possible to determine what exactly about volunteering it is that is valued by employers: did they welcome volunteers for reasons of their possession of enhanced levels of human or social capital, or because their volunteering experience was held to be informative about their motivations?

Conclusions

There are several reasons why the employability gains from volunteering might be limited. Returning to the conceptual frameworks that suggest why volunteering could have beneficial labour market outcomes, the skills that might be gained from volunteering in most cases tend to be basic organisational attributes (turning up on time, carrying out assigned tasks, working with people), the use of informal social ties to obtain jobs declines with age and labour market experience, and the signalling value of volunteering depends on how far employers actually value the experience of voluntary work. These suggest that the employability returns from volunteering are likely to be strongest for those at or near the point of entering the labour market for the first time and for people at an early stage of their career. The effects are not homogenous, with positive effects for young people being cancelled out by small or negative economic returns to volunteer experience for people who are in the middle or later stages of their working life (Qvist and Munk, 2018: 188–207). Self-reports from individuals do suggest that they feel they benefit from participation, but we do not have conclusive evidence that this translates into enhanced employability, whether that is defined in terms of access to paid work, job retention or remuneration.

Moreover, programmes to support volunteering all have an emphasis on the supply side; the responsibility is placed firmly on individuals to render themselves employable. But positive gains to 'individual employability' factors cannot be expected to overcome the structural inequalities which limit the chances of certain people moving into paid work, such as the demand for labour in a particular locality or occupation, or the prejudices of employers. Furthermore, volunteering is stratified, so its use as a route into the workplace will reproduce that stratification. Young people from well-connected middle-class backgrounds are likely to have had access to volunteering opportunities through family connections, and the school system reproduces this. As Dean (2014b: 657) puts it: 'the structures and practices that enable and deliver youth-volunteering programmes have helped to reinforce barriers to voluntary action among socially-disadvantaged students and those not at selective schools'. This reproduces the social advantages of those who attend selective schools and also excludes those furthest from the labour market through the opportunities they make available and the ways they manage programmes. Interestingly, though, while the qualitative studies reviewed here cannot trace whether or not school-level encouragement of volunteering has an effect on employability, there is quantitative evidence that former pupils of private schools in the UK are no more likely to volunteer in early adulthood than their state school counterparts (Green et al., 2020).

In short, there are clear limits to what we can expect from promoting volunteering on the grounds that it facilitates employability. Furthermore, it may be unreasonable to expect it to do so, given that many individual volunteers have no expectation or aspiration for volunteering to enhance their employability and many are engaged in activities which are not connected to employability-related opportunities or programmes. There is also an obvious dilemma in encouraging volunteering on the basis that it will help get people into jobs. There is a widely shared view that young people should undertake some service to their community and that volunteering will become a normal part of growing up in Britain. But surely it is the case that the more that volunteering becomes a social norm, the less it becomes a point of distinction that an individual has engaged in it. This would erode any employability benefits to be gained.

Given the limited evidence that volunteering has beneficial labour market effects, should policymakers and funders cease to fund programmes that claim to have such effects? More modesty in claims-making might be beneficial, certainly. It is surely overegging the pudding to claim that there is 'compelling evidence' for volunteering's effect on social mobility as a result of the contribution it makes to employability (Hogg and Smith, 2021). When compared to other well-attested influences on social mobility – household circumstances, early years education, access to education and access to employment opportunities – the influence of volunteering on social mobility is likely to be small.

An alternative justification for policies aimed at supporting those not in paid work to volunteer is proposed by Penny and Finnegan (2019). They contend that volunteering is used by many individuals not as a route into paid work but as a substitute for it, especially in contexts where little paid work is available. Paid work not only provides a person with an income but also with time structure, social contacts, collective purpose, social status and activity opportunities which are important for psychological well-being. Evidence suggests that there is a replacement effect of volunteering among those who have limited or no engagement with the formal labour market, perhaps because of illness, caring responsibilities or disability (Baines and Hardill, 2008; Hardill and Baines, 2011). Thus, volunteers engage not because they anticipate a transition into paid employment but because of the benefits volunteering offers them: structure, relationships with others, a sense of contributing to their community and recognition of that contribution.

On this view, a defence of policies to provide URSV might be better founded on the ability of volunteering to provide self-respect for citizens who are affected by unemployment or labour market inactivity. In contrast to evidence about the employability benefits of volunteering, there are much firmer grounds for believing that it has positive effects on self-esteem and well-being (Chapter 9). Therefore, Penny and Finnegan (2019) make an argument, drawing on normative political theory, that states have a duty to ensure that citizens have access to self-respect in their everyday lives. Therefore, they suggest that states should avoid enabling or permitting social conditions to emerge and persist if those conditions are harmful to self-respect. One of those conditions is structural unemployment. Arguments for policies to support volunteering based on self-respect would seem to carry weight. They would arguably be a more ethical foundation for policies to provide support for the unemployed to become engaged in volunteering than neoliberal discourses around the 'fantasy of employability' (Shachar et al., 2019: 252) that are currently hegemonic in policy discussions.

9

Volunteering, health and well-being

Introduction

Health inequalities in the UK are long-established and persistent. While many factors are implicated, substantial public funding to address the root causes seems unlikely for the foreseeable future. Understandably therefore there has been growing attention to features of society that might deliver health benefits for relatively modest cost. While the improvement of one's health status is not something regularly offered to individuals as an option in survey questions about their reasons for taking up volunteering, there is a widely held view that a latent benefit of this activity can be improvements in health and well-being (Jenkinson et al., 2013: 773). Consequently, there is growing interest in the opportunities that volunteering might contribute to the reduction of health inequalities.

According to the *Daily Telegraph*, the 'hot new zeitgeist you need to get involved in … is volunteering'; as well as its direct benefits to those helped, 'volunteering will do you the world of good too'. An endorsement by the NCVO claims that volunteering 'improves well-being, reduces loneliness and increases opportunities for all who get involved' (Garlick, 2021). NCVO's evidence for this is largely what people who volunteer tell them about their well-being, rather than any independent measures or analyses of changes over time (see Chapter 7 for why this matters for the strength of claims that can be made about causality). More expansively, Robert Putnam has claimed that nowhere is the 'importance of social connectedness so well-established as in the case of health and well-being' (Putnam, 2000: 326). His work was on all forms of civic participation, but a growing body of work assesses claims about the direct health benefits of volunteering.

What might cause volunteering to improve the health of those who participate in it? Can we be confident that someone volunteering for the first time would become more healthy as a result? And how widespread might the benefits be? First, are the benefits of volunteering due to the activity itself as opposed to its specifically *voluntary* character? For instance, volunteering for environmental charities might involve serious outdoor exertion, so if a volunteer increased their level of physical activity by participating, then (especially if they weren't previously doing any exercise) they could improve their physical strength, stamina and cardiovascular fitness. But those benefits could be obtained from other forms of exercise. As to acceptance of the invitation to volunteer, that would depend on the time and resources available to the individual; unsurprisingly, therefore, we find that not only are volunteers drawn largely from middle-class, prosperous and educated groups, they are healthier than average to begin with, since they have the resources to maintain healthy lifestyles. Thus, if volunteering were to be treated in clinical terms, as a kind of intervention, you cannot easily randomise the allocation of groups to it. Furthermore, if those who are receiving the benefits of the activity differ substantively from the population as a whole, it is not defensible to conclude unambiguously that volunteering is responsible for improvements in health.

Before considering the evidence for volunteering's health benefits, then, the first question is what is distinctive about the mechanisms through which volunteering could affect health. There are also analytical challenges (see Chapter 7) – especially problems of selection bias and reverse causality – which limit our ability to show conclusively that volunteering has health benefits. Following discussion of these points, the chapter considers the existing evidence in relation to three issues: psychological well-being and life satisfaction; mental health; and physical health and mortality. These are illustrated with specific examples of studies from the UK. The chapter concludes with consideration of the growing policy focus on 'social prescribing' and whether this might be a route through which the benefits of voluntary participation are developed, with a view to improving population health.

Mechanisms and analytical challenges

A range of health benefits of volunteering have been identified by reviews of the relevant literature, including claims as to greater longevity, improvements in ability to carry out routine tasks, adoption of healthy lifestyles, improvements in quality of life, social support and self-esteem, and reductions in psychological and physiological symptoms (Casiday et al., 2008). However, what plausible routes are there through which volunteering might have health benefits? Three broad categories of mechanism have been suggested.

First, there are physical and cognitive mechanisms: volunteering involves combinations of physical, social or cognitive activities, which may enhance physical fitness and offer some protection against cognitive decline. Second, there are social ties: participation enables individuals to forge new connections, thereby expanding their social networks. This could enhance social trust in general while, in relation to health specifically, it could provide more information on health issues and possibly access to informal support. Third, there are psychological advantages: by contributing to collective activities and contributing to the collective achievement of organisational goals, volunteering can provide individuals with a structure, interaction with others, self-esteem and a sense of purpose. Indeed Fujiwara et al. (2018: 25) argue that 'first and foremost volunteering is important for our well-being because it brings a sense of purpose to our lives'. Engagement in prosocial behaviour may also provide the 'warm glow' effects attributed to volunteering and charitable giving (de Wit et al., 2022: 1190; Steptoe and Fancourt, 2019: 1207). Given this multiplicity of mechanisms, we could expect volunteering to have impacts on a range of outcomes – for example on life satisfaction and quality of life, meaning or purpose, reduced depression or levels of anxiety. These pathways make intuitive sense to volunteers, as shown by numerous qualitative studies in which volunteers have given their own accounts of the benefits of engagement (see Stuart et al., 2020, for an overview of these studies). However, the nature of those studies (often of small groups operating in a particular niche in the voluntary sector) limits the extent to which it is reasonable to infer causality from them.

We may hypothesise that some benefits may be greater for specific groups of the population – for older age groups, volunteering enables people to maintain activity and social connections. It also offers role substitution: members of older age groups typically have a diminished number of familial or social roles and volunteering may therefore compensate for the loss of these – perhaps especially the absence of the routine and goal orientation of paid work. This is in contrast to younger adults who are likely to be combining volunteering with a range of other roles. Benefits for health and sense of well-being may also be greater for those who are less healthy to begin with, for the marginal impact of frequent volunteering for someone who is already happy is likely to be rather less than for someone who is not (Binder and Freytag, 2013: 110).

Many studies have detected an association between volunteering and measures of health status using cross-sectional surveys or qualitative interviews, but they are no substitute for longitudinal surveys. These offer an improvement, because they follow the same individuals over time and can therefore analyse changes in outcome variables following a change in a volunteering 'state' such as a movement from non-volunteering to volunteering. However, there is still the possibility that even very large-scale studies are unable to control for a sufficiently large range of factors that could affect either volunteering or health. Thus, selection bias is still possible: healthier or richer people volunteer who also have higher levels of well-being or better health to begin with (Lawton et al., 2021: 606); and both the volunteering and the higher well-being could be jointly caused – for example, by higher levels of income. There is also the risk of reverse causation – a relationship between volunteering and well-being is observed because volunteering is the result of higher well-being and not the cause of it (see Chapter 7).

For these reasons, De Wit et al. (2022) argue that researchers are likely to overstate the impacts of volunteering on health and well-being. Even when analysing a range of high-quality longitudinal studies comprising large panels tracking the same individuals, they found that associations between volunteering and subjective well-being were principally due to selection processes. People with higher levels of subjective well-being were more likely to commence volunteering and less likely to cease doing so subsequently (de Wit et al., 2022: 1194). While longitudinal work can control for a wide range of factors that have an impact on well-being, it does not provide definite proof of causation. Rather, it shows the extent to which differences between volunteers and non-volunteers in well-being result from selection (approximately 70 per cent of these differences could be accounted for in this way).

Finally, there are a small number of studies which approximated to an experimental design, broadly mimicking a random assignment between volunteering (treatment) or non-volunteering (control) groups, to enable the comparison of experiences before and after volunteering. Such studies can support the contention that differences between groups are solely due to the 'intervention' – in this case, the experience of volunteering. Two such examples are discussed below.

As a result of these challenges, literature reviews of the health effects of well-being therefore characteristically find only a small number of studies worth detailed consideration. The great majority of studies do not involve trials of any kind; a number use longitudinal data, so it is possible to make some claims about associations between change over time in volunteering and changes in outcome variables, but inference of causality is inherently limited.

Subjective well-being and life satisfaction

Volunteering is widely held to be associated with positive feelings about one's life and well-being. A common approach to assessment of well-being and life satisfaction is to ask the respondent to state how, on a scale (e.g. 1 to 5), they would rate their 'health in general' or their degree of satisfaction with their lives. In some more extensive sets of questions – for example the General Health Questionnaire (GHQ) 12-point scale (known as the GHQ-12) on mental health – such responses are combined to give a more multidimensional picture. Some surveys provide cross-sectional data which are of limited value for inferring causality, but a number of major longitudinal surveys track the same individuals and enable assessment of whether *changes* in the former between waves of the survey are associated with changes in the latter.

In a substantial analysis covering pooled data from six large longitudinal studies in Europe, De Wit et al. (2022) found that, without adjusting for individual characteristics, volunteers have better wellbeing, better mental and physical health, and live longer than nonvolunteers. However, most of the differences in well-being in such studies were accounted for by individual characteristics. The remaining differences in well-being tend to be small in magnitude.

A very well-known study in this area, which arguably approximated to an experiment in which one group of people were subject to an exogenous shock and a comparator group were not, is the longitudinal panel study of adults living in Germany around the time of the country's reunification (Meier and Stuzter, 2008). The economic collapse of East Germany meant the closure of most of the organisational infrastructure through which volunteering was managed. This created an exogenous shock: people in East Germany lost the opportunity to engage in volunteering, whereas those in West Germany did not. The analysis compared the life satisfaction of those in East Germany with their counterparts elsewhere in the reunified country. The authors argued that reunification approximated to a 'random manipulation of the extent of volunteering' (2008: 43), in which people were forced to cease volunteering regardless of underlying factors or personality traits which could jointly affect both volunteering and life satisfaction (Lawton et al., 2021). Residents of the former East Germany, deprived of the chance to volunteer, experienced a statistically significant drop in life satisfaction. That is an unusual case, though an opportunity for a similar analysis in the UK was provided by the disruption caused by the COVID-19 pandemic (Dolan et al., 2021; see below).

Numerous studies have deployed longitudinal datasets to explore whether changes in volunteering status have discernible effects on aspects of health. Thus, Binder and Freytag (2013) used UK survey data and found that volunteering at least weekly was associated with increased life satisfaction even after allowing for personality traits, trust and social networks. This positive impact was found among those with lower rather than higher levels of well-being, suggesting the effects of volunteering were 'driven by reducing the unhappiness of the less happy' (2013: 97), and that benefits of volunteering were likely to be greater for those whose initial health or well-being was worse. In a follow-up study, Binder (2015) again found a relationship between volunteering and life satisfaction, but he also concluded that volunteering's beneficial effect was also felt by those who were happier to begin with – though the effect was substantively small.

Positive associations between volunteering and life satisfaction were also found by Lawton et al.'s (2021) analysis of British longitudinal data. They controlled for a wide range of individual socioeconomic and demographic characteristics, as well as analysing the influence of prior levels of well-being and the incidence and frequency of volunteering over time. They investigated the effects of volunteering on well-being by considering the effect of changes from previous time points (or waves in the surveys) at which those items were measured; for example, is a change in volunteering status – from non-volunteering to volunteering – associated with a change in well-being? They showed that while it wasn't possible to eliminate completely the possibility that changes in life circumstances were happening which simultaneously caused respondents to take up volunteering *and* also made them happier, they could conclude that their results gave plausible evidence for a beneficial effect of volunteering on well-being. The magnitude of the effect was small but not negligible, and they sought to quantify this by estimating a financial equivalent value for the well-being impact of volunteering. They term this the 'compensating surplus' – the amount that someone on the median UK income would have to sacrifice to compensate them for the increased well-being experienced while volunteering and bring them to the same expected level of well-being as someone who doesn't volunteer. They estimate this equivalent well-being value to be £911 per year. This is substantially lower than several earlier estimates (Lawton et al., 2021: table 9), which they argue was because previous studies had not accounted as fully as they did for the factors that influence the relationship between volunteering and well-being.

The effects of volunteering on changes in an individuals' sense of purpose in life, and their feeling that things in life are worthwhile, have also been examined. Steptoe and Fancourt (2019) analysed the English Longitudinal Study of Ageing, concluding that regular volunteering at least once a month predicted higher levels of feeling that life was worthwhile two years on. The study also found that changes in the feeling that life was worthwhile did not predict changes in volunteering two years later, indicating a possibility that the causality might be from volunteering to well-being, not the other way around.

Finally, a recent analysis of volunteering under COVID-19 conditions suggests support for the positive impact of volunteering on well-being. Not unlike the study of German reunification described previously, it exploited differences in the opportunity to volunteer to identify the well-being impact. Dolan et al. (2021) surveyed several thousand individuals at the point at which they registered for the NHS Responders scheme during 2020. Large numbers of people had signed up for that scheme – which sought to recruit volunteers to carry out tasks to support vulnerable individuals in their own homes and to reduce social isolation – but not many were called upon, and therefore whether or not an individual was assigned to a volunteering opportunity could be regarded as a largely random process. The study therefore analysed differences in levels of reported well-being between those who had signed up for the scheme and *were not* allocated a task, and those who had signed up but *were* allocated a task. The authors argued that (controlling for demographic characteristics) any identifiable differences in well-being between the two groups over time were down to whether or not they had experienced volunteering as a result of the NHS Responder initiative. Even small acts of volunteering, including talking to at-risk individuals on the phone or helping to deliver groceries to vulnerable people, boosted participants' sense of well-being and increased feelings of belonging within the local community. The positive impacts on well-being lasted up to three months after the last task had been completed. Volunteers who had carried out a task rated their life satisfaction as 0.17 points (on a scale of 0–10) higher than the comparison group. This effect was broadly comparable with the findings from other studies of the relationship between volunteering and well-being.

Volunteering and mental health

Several mechanisms may explain the beneficial links between mental well-being and volunteering. Benefits might result from an expansion of an individual's social networks, from the personal sense of accomplishment that someone gains from volunteering activities or from gaining a sense of purpose, particularly for those people who have lost roles (in the workplace or the home) that previously provided it. These mechanisms do not, however, necessarily mean that everyone's mental health will benefit from volunteering to the same extent. We know from earlier chapters that there are considerable variations over individual lifetimes in the amount of volunteering people carry out, and that participation is something they accommodate alongside their other activities in the public and private spheres. So we might reasonably surmise that not only will volunteering commitments vary but so too will their impacts on individuals; the implication is that volunteering cannot be thought of as something which can benefit everyone, at any stage of life. Many studies of the relationship between health and volunteering have focused on older individuals, but in our work (Tabassum et al., 2016) we used the BHPS, analysing information on volunteering and self-reported mental health for survey data gathered in alternate years from 1996 to 2008. The final sample comprised 66,343 observations (person-years) with no missing data. The outcome of interest (the GHQ-12 score) was a proxy for mental well-being measured at each wave of the BHPS. It is derived by combining self-completion responses to the GHQ, comprising 12 questions. Each question has four categories (scored 0 to 3, giving a potential maximum score of 36) that assess happiness, mental distress (such as existence of depression or anguish) and well-being. Our main explanatory variable was the frequency with which individuals carried out 'unpaid voluntary work', in four categories, depending on the frequency of the volunteering (at least weekly; at least several times a year; once a year or less; and never). Other independent variables thought likely to influence mental well-being were included (gender, age, gross household income, occupational class (manual and non-manual), respondent's highest educational qualification, marital status and number of children in the household). We also included organisational membership (in line with literature, which argues for the health benefits of social participation even at lower levels of intensity) and a measure of general health status.

We investigated the main effects of age and volunteering status on GHQ scores, holding all other covariates constant. The full analysis is reported in Tabassum et al. (2016); Figure 9.1 represents the results graphically. It plots the predicted GHQ score, by age, for different levels of volunteering, after adjusting for all other covariates in the model. An increase in GHQ indicates, generally, that mental health is getting worse. The GHQ scores were lowest at the youngest ages among those who never volunteered but then increased sharply with age, peaking at 11.6 when participants were aged 45–50. At younger

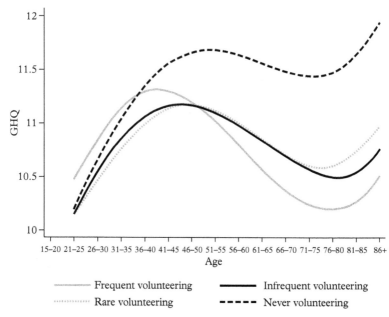

Figure 9.1 Trajectories in GHQ scores by volunteering status and age, BHPS, 1996–2008. Source: Tabassum et al. (2016).

ages, GHQ scores are indistinguishable across different levels of volunteering. The effect of volunteering frequency on GHQ scores emerges in early middle age: as can be clearly seen, for those who never volunteer, GHQ scores rise and then remain at broadly similar levels before increasing once again much later in life. By contrast, for those who volunteer, GHQ scores decline with age until later in life (from the mid-seventies onwards) when they turn upwards again, and the reduction in GHQ score is more evident for frequent volunteers.

What explains this pattern of associations? At early adulthood, volunteering is competing with many other daily activities (careers, starting families and so forth), all of which influence our mental well-being; put simply, other things are going on in people's lives that influence health to a greater extent than does volunteering. As people become older, it is conceivable that volunteering fulfils a number of functions – perhaps it offers a sense of accomplishment and purpose or helps to maintain or expand social networks. The findings appear to hold regardless of frequency of engagement, suggesting that even a relatively small dose of 'vitamin V' may have a protective effect on health. This echoes earlier findings in this field (van Willigen, 2000).

The findings suggest that the association between volunteering and mental well-being varies at different points in the life-course. This is an important counterbalance to an undifferentiated message about the benefits of volunteering. Even though it is well-known that middle-aged people (from the mid-forties upwards) do engage in volunteering at a relatively high level, this work suggests that, for those in these age groups who are not engaged in it, there may be benefits to be obtained from volunteering.

Volunteering, physical health and mortality

Based on what we know about the effects of volunteering in general, we can see that it has some effects on various dimensions of self-reported health, such as mental health or subjective well-being. But could volunteering be related to your chances of dying – or of dying sooner than you might have expected? This might not be entirely implausible – indeed, some authors contend that the health advantage gained from volunteering is approximately equivalent to being a year younger (de Wit et al., 2022: 1198). If the advantage cumulates, could it hold off the Grim Reaper? Some British evidence suggests that this might be so, at least on a modest scale.

International reviews have suggested that volunteering is associated with reduced risk of mortality, albeit with qualifications depending on age group, intensity of volunteering and location (most mortality-related studies took place in the USA, a society characterised by strong traditions of volunteering and wide disparities in health). However, the studies in question were all observational, so they could not determine whether lower mortality attributed to volunteering was a result of volunteering or a consequence of the characteristics of the volunteer population (O'Reilly et al., 2017b: 1296; Jenkinson et al., 2013: 5; Filges et al., 2020). Observing drily that the ideal study design (a randomised controlled trial) is 'impractical where mortality is the outcome', O'Reilly et al. (2017b: 1296) took a novel approach to the subject. Survey data can never cover the whole gamut of unobserved characteristics that might influence a social outcome, but one response to this challenge is to undertake comparisons within families. Married and cohabiting couples have in common the same environment, albeit with some differences (e.g. couples may not work together), and there is ample evidence that members of such households are similar in relation to health-related and other behaviours. So if there is a lower mortality risk associated with volunteering, it could be caused by many unobservable factors, and if these influences are not fully accounted for in statistical analyses, that lower risk will be visible among the non-volunteering partners of the volunteers. However, if there is a real protective effect of volunteering, it should be visible in the differential mortality experience of those in households where one person volunteers and the other does not. 'The mortality advantage should not necessarily be evident' for the non-volunteering partner of a volunteer (O'Reilly et al., 2017: 1297).

Northern Ireland presents researchers with a unique opportunity to test these ideas because its individual-level decennial census data for the entire population (c. 1.5 million people) are linked over time, and they are also linked to administrative data such as mortality records. In 2011 the Northern Ireland census also asked respondents whether, in the previous year, they had 'helped with or carried out any voluntary work without pay'. By the standards of some UK surveys (Chapters 1 and 2) this is a general question, and the proportion assenting is low (around 16 per cent of the adult population), albeit comparable with the results of survey questions framed in similar general terms (Chapter 2). However, the answers to it – when cross-referenced to data on age, gender and educational qualifications – indicate that the social profile of volunteers is highly consistent with expectations from other surveys in the UK (O'Reilly et al., 2017b: table 1b). Volunteers in the Northern Ireland census were generally more affluent, better educated and more religious than their non-volunteer counterparts. The census also asks about self-reported health status and the presence or absence of specific chronic conditions. The linkage to mortality enabled an analysis of the risk of mortality during a follow-up period (the 33 months from the census to December 2013).

The authors identified 308,733 couples (617,466 individuals) living in the same household with complete data on a large range of individual characteristics; of these, 15.7 per cent of males and 16.9 per cent of females reported volunteering at the census. There were 12,260 deaths in these households during the follow-up period, equivalent to roughly 2 per cent of the study population, but just under 1 per cent of volunteers died. This sounds like a very large mortality advantage of volunteering, but after adjusting for socioeconomic characteristics and baseline health status, volunteers had approximately 25 per cent lower mortality risk than their non-volunteering peers. A crucial feature of the study was the comparison of volunteers and non-volunteers within the same households. For the non-volunteers, having a partner who was a volunteer was not associated with a mortality advantage. Therefore the authors could rule out the possibility that the apparent connection between volunteering and health was the result of the influence of unmeasured characteristics of households that affected the mortality risk of both volunteers and non-volunteers. This work consequently increases the plausibility of a causal influence of volunteering on mortality risk.

Volunteering and health policy: what about social prescribing?

What might be the practical implications of the finding that there are some benefits to health and well-being from volunteering? One obvious problem is that one cannot compel people to volunteer: vitamin V can be prescribed, perhaps, but there is no guarantee that the medicine will be taken, nor that it will be equally efficacious for everyone. Based on the evidence discussed here, if policy interventions (Chapter 12; see also Rochester et al., 2010: chapter 7) succeeded in raising the level of volunteering then we might expect some positive impacts on health. But how can volunteering be "prescribed"? Here there is a narrower focus on a recent field of policy innovation: social prescribing.

Social prescribing is an approach to health inequalities which connects people to activities, groups and services that will meet practical, social and emotional needs that affect their health and well-being. These activities may or may not involve volunteering – some opportunities to volunteer may be offered, but mostly individuals will simply be presented with suggested connections to groups that engage people in educational, cultural or recreational activities. Patients will be directed towards services in the community, which are mostly offered by voluntary and community organisations. Social prescribing now forms part of long-term NHS planning (NHS England, 2019). It is primarily intended to support people who have chronic conditions, are lonely or isolated, need support with mental health and/or have complex health needs affecting their well-being. People in such circumstances do not necessarily volunteer in large numbers, and consideration needs to be given as to how they might best be supported to do so. Research on volunteer recruitment, management and retention has always emphasised the importance of a positive and engaging experience. If volunteering is to work for the purposes of social prescribing, it needs to be properly planned and resourced, with volunteers being integrated into organisational activities and not just carrying out mundane tasks. Especially with regard to groups who have chronic conditions or mental health issues, volunteers need to feel that they are supported and valued and that expectations are realistic (Turk et al., 2022).

There are broader questions to ask about social prescribing. In the context of a *universal* health service, how can a service that relies on the local distribution of voluntary organisations and their activities be available to all who need it? There is widespread acknowledgement of geographical variations not just in volunteering (Chapter 5) but also in the distribution of voluntary organisations (Clifford, 2012; McDonnell et al., 2020). This suggests that if social prescribing initiatives are being rolled out, they are more likely to be available in communities with a more substantial organisational base. But if it is to be part of the NHS's approach to health inequalities, shouldn't social prescribing be available everywhere? Or is it to be left to local initiative and perhaps charitable resources?

Furthermore, to what extent is social prescribing an approach which attempts to deal with issues – health inequalities – that are deep-rooted and structural in character and which are therefore not capable of resolution through individual initiative? Mackenzie et al. (2020) suggest that social prescribing initiatives are developed with the best of intentions since they are offered to individuals to support them in dealing with social determinants of health status. However, in isolation from wider redistributive efforts, social prescribing risks highlighting individual lifestyle choices rather than structural features, such as the contexts of entrenched deprivation in which the study by McKenzie et al. was set.

Conclusions and policy implications

To summarise, as with other dimensions of the impacts of volunteering on social outcomes, its effects on health are discernible but relatively small scale and variable. In addition to the general points made here there is some evidence of a dose–response effect, with benefits being related to the frequency of engagement, and a suggestion that sustained and moderate involvement in volunteering may be better than intense engagement (Binder, 2015; Lawton et al., 2021). Though volunteering is differentiated in terms of the field of activity and the roles taken by volunteers, evidence on which organisational settings and activities are beneficial is an area for further development (Stuart et al., 2020). As far as the distribution of benefits is concerned, again there are heterogeneous findings. Volunteering can be beneficial at some points in people's lives but not at others (e.g. Tabassum et al.,

2016; van Willigen, 2000), and there are particular groups (e.g. the unemployed or those whose well-being is lowest to begin with) who appear to benefit more than others. Generally, though systematic reviews (Jenkinson et al., 2013; Filges et al., 2020) acknowledge that there are some benefits to health from volunteering, they concur that currently there is not enough robust research to underpin volunteering as a public health intervention.

If volunteering is to form part of a strategy for the reduction of health inequalities, the first point to note here is that gaps and gradients in health status show no sign of diminishing; the reverse is the case, according to authoritative reviews of evidence on health inequalities (Marmot et al., 2020). Even prior to COVID-19, the consequences of austerity were evident in worsening health standards and life expectancy. As in the case of the impacts of volunteering on civic engagement (Chapter 10) and employability (Chapter 8), there needs to be realism about what volunteering might be expected to achieve. The marginal effects of volunteering on well-being, self-reported health status, mental health and mortality are relatively small, compared to the effects of austerity on, say, the height of children, where Britain now has the shortest five-year-olds in Europe.

Given that some of the demonstrable benefits of volunteering seem to be larger for those in poorer health to begin with, it could be argued that if only citizens are made aware of the instrumental benefits of volunteering the scales will fall from their eyes and they will rush forwards to volunteer. Chapters 3–6 of this book provide evidence as to the extensive and enduring nature of inequalities in participation in volunteering, and also the unequal distribution of the obstacles which get in the way of engagement. These are unlikely to change anytime soon, given the adverse circumstances affecting British society; the ongoing steady decline of volunteering rates provides ample testimony to that. Interventions such as social prescribing may make some difference in the opportunities that become available for individuals, but since there is uncertainty about the precise mechanisms through which volunteering has effects on health status, actually targeting and implementing such interventions is not a guarantee of success. Moreover, such efforts are not costless: they require funding. While there is considerable enthusiasm for health-related initiatives that involve volunteering, such initiatives are swimming against a very strong tide.

10

Volunteering and civic engagement

Introduction

Concerns are regularly expressed in the UK about inequalities in and the decline of political participation, as manifested by low levels of turnout at elections. Most recently, the issue has been raised in policy proposals by the Onward think-tank for a national service scheme in the UK which specifically draws attention to the association between low levels of volunteering and voting among young adults (Valentin and Hawksbee, 2023: 16). Volunteering has featured in policy proposals to promote social mixing, raise the level of civic engagement and reduce socioeconomic inequalities in participation. Faith is placed in the ability of volunteering to promote generalised social trust (itself strongly associated with engagement in political affairs) by facilitating face-to-face contact and the discussion of social issues with various dissimilar others. If these arguments are valid, then successful efforts to raise engagement in volunteering ought to promote enhanced trust as well as greater engagement in politics.

Public policy in the UK has promoted volunteering for both its direct benefits and its latent, or indirect, benefits. One of the latter is the enhancement of political engagement. The assumption is that voluntary action provides a grounding in citizenship and that this will have positive spillover effects into the wider civic sphere. This is not a new concern. William Beveridge's *Voluntary Action* saw voluntary initiative by citizens as an essential civil defence against totalitarianism, which would contribute to ensuring that 'the night's insane dream of power' would fade (Beveridge, 1948: 324). The MOP researchers engaged by Beveridge in the 1940s expended considerable efforts, during their investigation of a working-class community in Birmingham, in seeking to show that *not* belonging to a voluntary organisation meant that citizens were less likely to vote (and therefore were 'apathetic'). In fact, a greater percentage of the *non-voting* sample were actually members of associations, though the differences were not statistically significant (Child, 2020).

More recently, politicians have also espoused the view that volunteering enhances political participation. David Blunkett, when Secretary of State for Education and Employment, argued that voluntary action embodied 'principles of commitments and engagement that are the foundations of democracy' (Blunkett, 2001), while Tony Blair encouraged volunteering as an expression of 'civic patriotism' (BBC, 2000). The Coalition government's *Giving White Paper* (2011) spoke of the ways in which volunteering could strengthen society through its effect on relationships and trust (Cabinet Office, 2011: 4). The subsequent NCS scheme had, as one of its objects, equipping young people with the skills they needed to be 'active citizens' (Gov.uk, 2010; Weinberg, 2021), and proposals for some form of genuinely national service share similar objectives (Valentin and Hawksbee, 2023; Hague, 2021).

The baton has been picked up by high-profile initiatives to promote youth volunteering and social action, such as the #iwill campaign, which stress the wider societal and civic pay-offs of volunteering (Alma Economics, 2021). Some quite definitive claims have been made as to the benefits of volunteering, including the arresting statement that participation in youth social action was a 'powerful generator' of political efficacy (i.e. encouraging individuals and communities to exercise power and seek to effect change), since 'participation in youth social action *makes a person much more likely* to be an active citizen in later life, developing individual and community political efficacy' (Birdwell et al., 2020: 46).

As supporting evidence, Birdwell et al. (2020) cited a study in which participants in the City Year initiative in the USA were followed up at intervals subsequent to their participation. City Year volunteers in Boston, the original base for the initiative, are full time for 11 months of community service, leadership development and engagement; they receive a stipend of $20,000. We may ask where a remunerated experience which is practically full time fits into a discussion of voluntary activity. The study compared 107 City Year participants with 85 who had been accepted for the programme but did not take up the offer. Thus, the two groups being compared were broadly similar; while not a randomised controlled study, the groups who differed only in whether or not they had actually participated in City Year or not. One outcome cited as evidence of beneficial impacts was that voting rates among participants (41 per cent) were higher than the comparison group (33 per cent), although with these sample sizes the differences are at best marginally significant. Positive outcomes were cited for some years but not for others, perhaps suggesting that effects were not evident consistently over time. Moreover, picking up Bekkers and Verkaik's (2015) discussion of the doses of 'vitamin V' required to produce an effect (Chapter 7), City Year is a very well-resourced and full-time service programme, with a support infrastructure for its participants that has been built up over a 30-year period. If the only demonstrable benefit of City Year were to be an increase in civic engagement, that would be an expensive way to promote it.

What does the wider literature – which, for the UK, is a small one – say about whether participation in voluntary action enhances the likelihood of engagement in politics and formal acts of participation such as voting? And what are the challenges associated with measuring relevant constructs and developing appropriate analyses (see the next section on 'Previous literature')? Academic analyses of longitudinal surveys in the UK cover the relationship between volunteering in early adulthood and political and civic behaviours some decades later, including the influence of volunteering on outcomes such as political interest, political action and support for political parties (see section on 'Impact of volunteering on political engagement and interest'). In addition, there are emerging evaluations of initiatives such as NCS for young people (see section on 'National Citizen Service and its effect on political interest and engagement'). The findings of this work do not show strong evidence that volunteering promotes engagement in politics and the chapter concludes with reflections on why this is so.

Previous literature

Engagement in voluntary action is said to promote political engagement through the fostering of civic values and skills and the facilitation of public deliberation. Civic virtues inculcated through participation in voluntary associations are said to include deliberation, tolerance, self-confidence, efficacy and respect for diverse others and the rule of law (Fung, 2003: 520). The argument is that these skills are carried over into the political sphere. This argument can be dated to de Tocqueville's famous study of the role of voluntary organisations in promoting democracy in the USA (de Tocqueville, 2000 [1835]). In this line of reasoning, voluntary organisations are 'schools of democracy'. However, the evidential base for this argument is not especially robust, sometimes resting on apparently strong associations at the level of countries between the levels of voluntary action and political participation, which are not then also found at the level of individuals. It is also possible that the relationship at the individual level could be due to a selection effect (Dekker, 2014: 45; Van Der Meer and Van Ingen, 2009: 303; see also Van Ingen and Van der Meer, 2016).

Alternatively, the connections between political engagement and voluntary action could also be largely explicable in terms of a resource model: individuals in possession of higher levels of social, economic and cultural capital (see also Chapter 3), as well as of free time, are more likely to engage in both types of activity (Brady et al., 1995). From this perspective, voluntary organisations are 'pools' of democracy, attracting those who are already highly engaged and actively interested in politics, and who have the resources required to engage (Bolton, 2016; Kamerāde et al., 2015; Binder, 2021).

Volunteering is also said to influence political engagement via its effects on trust, generalised reciprocity or, more generally, social capital. Direct, face-to-face interaction means that volunteers learn to cooperate with others, thereby building up their levels of generalised trust. If that proves to be the case, we might anticipate an impact on political engagement, since those who possess high levels of trust are also more likely to vote, be interested in politics and be engaged in civic and community organisations (Putnam, 2000: 132). Participation in volunteering may also enable individuals to enhance their knowledge of political affairs through interactions with others in the community. Voluntary organisations may facilitate this because participants will exchange information in ordinary social interactions, while meetings may promote active discussion of political issues and challenging of political views (Hooghe, 2011; Sobieraj and White, 2004).

Although these mechanisms have some theoretical plausibility, there are important issues to resolve. Volunteering is a small part of most people's lives – for all but the most committed, it amounts to a few hours a week – and political socialisation may take place in various other contexts, such as family, school or the workplace, in which individuals spend much more of their time. So we need to understand more about those contexts and how they might influence individual political engagement as well as volunteering. The apparent correlation between volunteering and political engagement may be artefactual if both are related in similar ways to upbringing, education or socialisation, or if they derive from a common influence (such as the workplace) – for example, union activism might heighten political awareness but also bring someone into contact with networks through which they then get asked to volunteer.

It is also easy to overgeneralise about the benefits of volunteering; it is not – how could it be? – a uniform, undifferentiated activity. As with other outcomes of volunteering (see Chapters 8 and 9), impacts may differ depending on the size and type of organisation in which a volunteer is engaged (Maloney et al., 2008). The type of voluntary activity undertaken will also influence whether political engagement is promoted through organisational structures and activities (Lee, 2022). Civic outcomes might be expected to vary depending on whether an individual carries out governance roles in an organisation or simply a routine task such as transporting clients (see also Chapter 3). Importantly, there is concern that 'chequebook participation' in associations, though by no means a novel phenomenon now, may be less likely to promote the development of civic skills (Wollebaek and Selle, 2002). That might also be said of distanced, largely online forms of volunteering, which must reduce the intensity of interaction associated with volunteering, though that does not imply that such engagement is entirely passive. The connections between volunteering, associational membership and subsequent civic engagement may also vary according to the outcome variable – for instance whether the concern is with political interest, political understanding or political engagement. Compion and Janoski's (2020: 681) provocative review takes this line of argument further, suggesting that it is easy to exaggerate the benefits of volunteering for political interest and engagement. They divide voluntary activity into 'the good, the bland and the ugly': they acknowledge that some forms of participation (the 'good') and some types of organisations certainly promote active deliberation about political affairs and in that sense may stimulate political engagement on the part of volunteers. However, and without being disrespectful to large numbers of organisations, they class many as 'the bland': entities in which there is little evidence of political discussion. Indeed, some studies (Eliasoph, 1998) suggest that many organisations regard themselves as non-political, preferring to concentrate on the immediate issues they are tackling, while many people may well engage in volunteering precisely because they distrust formal political structures. For those reasons we might expect the impacts of volunteering on political engagement to be attenuated (Eliasoph, 1998: 277). Finally, there is the 'ugly' side of associational life: groups that do not cultivate virtues of democracy and tolerance, breeding parochialism and distrust (Compion and Janoski, 2020: 690).

Given such criticisms of the underlying processes, it is not surprising that Dekker (2014) summarises the evidence base indicating a connection between volunteering and political engagement as 'fragile', with evidence of association rather than causality. This conclusion is largely endorsed by Binder (2021; see also Quintelier, 2008; Musick and Wilson, 2008: chapter 20; Bolton, 2016).

As with our other discussions of the impacts of volunteering (Chapters 8 and 9), there are selection biases: those who volunteer are also those who are likely to engage in political debate or join political parties. There are also issues about assessing the outcome of interest: if evaluating the impact of volunteering on political engagement, the gold standard measure would be whether or not individuals have voted subsequent to gaining experience of volunteering. Longitudinal studies do not always collect that information and studies may have to resort to questions about political interest or party support. Likewise, measures of volunteering are limited, often lacking in detail beyond an indication of whether or not a respondent participates and the frequency with which they do so. Information about the type of organisation in which an individual participates is rarely present, so we cannot answer questions about whether variations in the nature of volunteering influence associations with political engagement.

Finally, in order to assess causality, we need to know the temporal sequencing of events and actions. In the UK, volunteering will, by definition, precede voting for anyone who engages in voluntary activity before their eighteenth birthday, but it does not follow that volunteering causes a young person to exercise their democratic right to vote once aged 18. Moreover, even when we possess complex and detailed data on individual characteristics and are able to follow individuals over time, we may not be able to capture an underlying unobserved individual characteristic which precedes *both* volunteering and political engagement. Put simply, it may be the case that both political activity and volunteering are jointly caused by aspects of individual characteristics or of the household in which they grew up (Theiss-Morse and Hibbing, 2005).

Evidence of the impact of volunteering on political engagement and interest

The UK's high-quality longitudinal surveys have formed the basis for a small number of studies of the effects of volunteering experiences on subsequent political behaviours and attitudes. The investigations discussed below are the only British studies known to the author which have explicitly considered the relationship between volunteering (however it is measured) and subsequent forms of action which may be regarded as political (Bolton, 2016; Binder, 2021).

The impact of volunteering in early adulthood on subsequent civic engagement

The UK's NCDS tracks people born in one week in April 1958, at intervals of roughly seven years (with some gaps). Data on civic and social participation have been collected regularly. Vicki Bolton (2016) used data on volunteering and voting collected at ages 23 and 50 (in 1981 and 2008 respectively) to investigate whether experiences in early adulthood influenced outcomes in middle age. Information on volunteering was sought through a question on 'unpaid voluntary work'; respondents were advised that the work ought to be 'of service to others apart from [the respondent's] immediate family', but no other information was available to prompt recollection. Those who reported volunteering more than once a year in the year before the survey were counted as volunteers.

As a measure of political engagement, cohort members were asked about their turnout at the previous general election (in 1979 and 2005 respectively) for the two waves of survey data used (1981 and 2008). Bolton controlled for individual- and household-level factors such as gender and social class at birth; controls from subsequent waves of the study included characteristics of the cohort members (e.g. educational qualifications and test scores), class, religion and aspects of their social participation. The control variables were clearly related to social class: more participation and higher educational test scores were found in those from social classes I and II (professional (I), managerial and technical (II) occupations). Conversely, a propensity to be married and start a family in young adulthood was associated with social classes IV (partly skilled occupations) and V (unskilled occupations).

Those who reported volunteering at age 23 were more likely to vote and volunteer when aged 50. Volunteering at age 23 was associated with a substantially increased likelihood of doing so later in life: those volunteering at 23 were twice as likely to volunteer at age 50, compared to those who were not volunteers at age 23; they were also more likely to go on to vote at age 50. This suggests a relationship between experience of volunteering early in adult life and later involvement, but in addition there was clearly a strong relationship between volunteering, voting and social class at birth. Individuals born who grew up in households from social class I were much more likely than others to engage in either volunteering or voting, while those from social class V were the least likely to do so. Therefore, the direct relationship between volunteering at age 23 and later political and civic behaviour is likely to be in part a function of the social class background of the cohort members (Bolton, 2016: table 2.1).

The study does indicate an effect of early adult volunteering on political engagement. Bolton found a strong relationship between volunteering at age 23 and voting at age 50, although it was less strong than the relationship between volunteering at 23 and volunteering at age 50. As with the volunteering outcome at age 50, there was both a class effect and an effect of the interaction between social class and volunteering. Thus Bolton's conclusion was that the effect of volunteering on civic engagement is different for different socioeconomic groups; the 'civic pay-off' from volunteering increases towards the upper tiers of the socioeconomic structure.

Bolton demonstrates the effect of the interaction between social class and volunteering at age 23 by calculating the predicted probability of being a voter at age 50 (Figure 10.1, vertical axis), having accounted for the effects of social class and volunteering at age 23. The likelihood of voting at 50 was lower for volunteers in social class V than for non-volunteers; volunteers in more skilled or professional social classes, on the other hand, see a positive effect on voting that is attributable to volunteering, the gap in the likelihood of voting between volunteers and non-volunteers is maintained across social

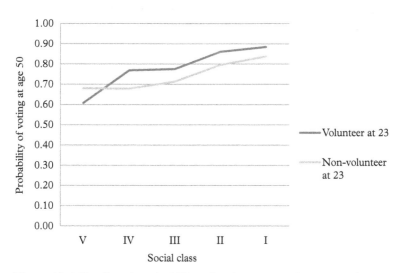

Figure 10.1 Predicted probability of voting at age 50, accounting for social class and volunteering at age 23. Source: Bolton (2016).

classes I to IV, and the probability of volunteering increases the further up the social hierarchy one goes.

Bolton concludes that the effect of volunteering in early adulthood on voting and volunteering in middle age is inextricably linked to social class, the effect of which is reinforced by experience of involvement in civic affairs at an early stage of one's life. People from households in upper socioeconomic strata were more likely to volunteer and to hold pro-civic values. Cohort members born into the professional and managerial classes were more likely to volunteer as young adults, and in turn their educational, social and workplace networks (through association with other individuals like themselves) were likely to be those that presented opportunities for further engagement in civic affairs and voluntary organisations.

These processes were cumulative; if volunteering in early adulthood, cohort members were more likely to become politically engaged subsequently if they had been born into professional or managerial homes. Volunteers born into social class V (supported by unskilled, manual workers) received no civic dividend at all: in fact, 23-year-old volunteers from class V were *less* likely to vote at age 50 than non-volunteers. This unequal volunteering effect was just one part of a greater inequality between social classes; elsewhere, Bolton's (2016) work shows that the volunteering experiences of the different social classes were different too. Volunteers from professional and managerial social classes were more likely to be in positions of responsibility, perhaps serving in governance roles, than volunteers from lower social classes (see also Table 3.2 above on stratification in volunteering roles).

Second, Bolton found a relationship between volunteering at age 23 and voting and volunteering at age 50, even having accounted for potential confounders. In other words, uneven civic participation was reinforced rather than reduced by volunteering in early adulthood. Early volunteering experience among groups of higher socioeconomic status was translated into higher levels of civic engagement in middle age. Thus, as Bolton put it, volunteering and voting are connected in a virtuous circle, but it is a privileged one.

Volunteering, political interest and political party support

Important recent studies by Bolton (2016) and Binder (2021) reach broadly similar conclusions on the question of whether individuals who volunteer are more likely to become politically engaged. The previous section of this chapter concentrated on volunteering as a formative experience. To extend this work, what are the effects of trajectories (Chapter 6) of volunteering in adulthood on other acts of civic or political engagement, or on interest in politics? Volunteering is not just something that people do just once; for many people, it becomes a habitual behaviour, which people engage in repeatedly over their lives (Bellah et al., 1985). Of course, persistence in volunteering could be a function of the resources that people possess, and there could be a selection bias in any study of the effect of volunteering on political engagement: people with the resources to engage in volunteering consistently also have the resources to engage politically. The aim of the work by Bolton and Binder is to explore links between volunteering and political engagement over a period of several years, with strong controls for selection. Both authors used the BHPS.

They examined political engagement using questions about political interest and political party support. Cohort members were asked whether they were not at all interested in politics or whether they had varying degrees of interest. The studies divided responses into those who were 'not at all' interested, contrasted with any who expressed at least some degree of interest in politics. Likewise, a variable for political party support differentiated those who could not say that they were closer to one political party than another from those who had expressed support, in varying degrees, for a political party.

Volunteering is measured in the BHPS as one of 12 possible responses to a question about 'the things people do in their leisure time'. Respondents are asked if they do 'unpaid voluntary work' and also about how frequently they do so. Because respondents are not presented with a definition or any examples of this activity (e.g. by comparison with the Citizenship or Community Life Surveys; see Chapter 2) reported rates are low, though they are still within the normal range of responses in British social surveys (Staetsky and Mohan, 2011).

BHPS panel members were asked how often they did voluntary work (at two-year intervals from 1996 to 2008). Bolton (2016) defined a volunteer as someone who volunteered 'several times a year' or more; Binder (2021) used the available categories of volunteering frequency (never, at least annually, at least monthly, weekly). Rates of volunteering in the BHPS were fairly stable over the seven waves in which panel members were asked about it, and there was little movement in and out of volunteering (see also Chapter 6). The relatively stable nature of volunteering meant that it was reasonable to suppose that changes in behaviour by individuals would have measurable effects on other outcome variables.

Both authors include a range of controls for individual characteristics (age, gender, marital status, educational attainment, self-report health, income); measures of class, employment status and the numbers of children in the household were used by one, but not both, studies. These analyses of panel data have a binary outcome (politically engaged/not engaged) and were conducted as logistic regressions, estimating the log-odds of engagement (Bolton, 2016: 41–60; Binder, 2021: table 4).

The findings are summarised in Table 10.1. Firstly, there was evidence from Binder's (2021) work that membership of, and activity in, voluntary organisations had small positive effects on political engagement and interest, though with the caveat that the beneficial impacts were largely associated with involvement in certain types of organisation. This is in line with literature which suggests that the type of organisation in which someone participates (or volunteers) is consequential for the outcomes of volunteering (see pp. 137–9 and 180, this volume). Secondly, there was a positive effect of volunteering on political interest. Bolton found that the odds of being politically interested were 1.2 times greater for volunteers than for non-volunteers. Her approach used took account of many characteristics of individuals which might have confounded the results, so we can be confident there is an effect of volunteering on political interest, albeit a small one. In Bolton's work, volunteers were more likely to be interested in politics than non-volunteers, but the relationship was not a straightforwardly linear one: somewhat counterintuitively, monthly volunteering appeared more strongly linked to political interest than volunteering at least weekly, though the relationship did not attain statistical significance (Bolton, 2016: figure 3.1; Binder, 2021: table 4). Binder echoed these conclusions, finding that political interest was more strongly associated with volunteering at least monthly and also with volunteering weekly (for which Bolton had found no significant effect).

Models were also fitted for political party support by both authors. Without controls, there was a positive and significant effect of volunteering on the outcome, in this case whether or not a respondent supported any political party. However, once appropriately adjusted for individual characteristics, no consistent effect remained. Nor was any consistent effect observed when volunteering was broken down into four frequencies, suggesting no detectable 'dosage' effect (e.g. whether a more frequent experience of volunteering had a larger impact; see Chapter 7).

In an attempt to disentangle further the effects of volunteering, Binder restricted analysis to a subset of respondents who, when first observed in the study, reported neither any prior experience of

Table 10.1 Relationship between volunteering and membership of groups and aspects of political engagement and interest

Author	Independent variable of interest	Outcome of interest		
		Political party support ('do you think of yourself as a supporter of one political party?')	Strength of political party support ('would you count yourself a very strong/strong/not very strong supporter?')	Interest in politics ('not at all vs. expressing some degree of interest')
Binder				
	Member of one or more types of organisation	Some types of group membership (environmental and sports) significant		Some types of group membership significant (e.g. tenants, religious, trade union)
	Active in at least one type of organisation	Yes (significant at 1% level)		
	Frequency of unpaid voluntary work	Inconsistent effects (positive effect for yearly and monthly volunteering, but not for weekly volunteering)	Not pronounced (significant only for those least engaged in volunteering)	Odds of being interested in politics greater for those who volunteer monthly/weekly
Bolton				
	Does unpaid voluntary work	No effect	No effect	Odds of being interested in politics greater for volunteers than non-volunteers
	Frequency of unpaid voluntary work	No effect	No effect	No effect of frequency of volunteering

Source: Binder (2021): tables 4, 5; Bolton (2016).

volunteering nor any interest in or engagement in politics, but who began to engage in volunteering at some point during the study. He did not find evidence of an association between these initial experiences of volunteering and the likelihood of engagement or interest in politics.

In summary, the important analytical challenge for this topic is that volunteers are more likely to be engaged with politics than non-volunteers; at the same time, however, volunteers are also more likely to be well-educated people with professional jobs who come from middle-class homes with parents who socialised them to engage in this way. The approach taken by these authors accounts for these effects. These longitudinal studies analyse the influence of volunteering on political engagement for a period of over a decade in the lives of survey respondents, investigating whether volunteers are more likely to become politically engaged. Volunteering is linked to political engagement in several ways (through skills, knowledge, socialisation and trust), and the academic literature suggests that early life experiences will influence both volunteering and political engagement (Stolle and Hooghe, 2005). However, the effects are not strong.

If we are considering the potential to use volunteering as an instrument of policy, on the basis of its potential to raise civic engagement, then the first stage in the 'civic journey' is the development of political interest, which is clearly a prerequisite for further engagement in politics. The evidence in the findings considered here, that volunteering experiences are associated with political interest, reinforces previous literature (Maloney et al., 2008; Wollebaek and Selle, 2002). Volunteering was not, however, a driver of political party support. Volunteers were no more likely than non-volunteers to become a supporter of a political party, and nor did volunteering affect the strength of their support for one. The effect of volunteering on political engagement is therefore not consistent over different types of political engagement. The type of outcome variable matters. Volunteering does not influence all types of civic behaviour, and if there is a sickness in the body politic, indexed by declining engagement and interest, volunteering cannot therefore be reliably prescribed as a remedy.

National Citizen Service and its effect on political interest and engagement

Given the claims made for the value of the UK's NCS programme, one rationale for which was to increase civic and political engagement among young people, is there any evidence that the cohorts of young people who have participated in NCS's activities, with their emphasis on social action, have been more likely to engage in politics after having experienced NCS? Evaluations of the scheme have not followed up participants to enquire about post-NCS political interest or engagement, but participants are asked about the likelihood of them voting 'at the next General Election or referendum'. At first sight there was evidence that participation in NCS was associated with a significant increase in intention to vote. It is relatively marginal – a 0.6 point increase on a scale from 1 to 10, where a response of 1 means being absolutely certain of not voting and a score of 10 implies absolute certainty about voting. Note, however, that authoritative studies of electoral behaviour conclude that young people consistently overstate their likelihood of voting (Kantar and London Economics, 2020: 54 and table 6.11).

NCS also had different impacts on different social, economic and demographic groups of young people (Jump Projects and Mime Consulting, 2020). There were two key messages in support of the contention that experiences such as NCS would increase the likelihood of voting. First, there was a stronger positive impact on likelihood to vote among those from areas of greater deprivation (measured by higher scores on the IMD). This is a welcome finding if an aim of policy is to close gaps and reduce gradients in volunteering. Second, analysis suggested that, compared to a control group, there was a larger positive impact of NCS on the likelihood of voting for those people who joined with a *lower* intention of voting to begin with (Jump Projects and Mime Consulting, 2020: 36).

These studies demonstrate limited *general* effects of engagement in social action on the entire population; but might exposure to volunteering experiences be valuable in terms of closing gaps between groups in the likelihood of civic engagement? This was explored by Stuart Fox in a study of the relationship between youth volunteering and individual attitudes to politics, including likelihood of voting (Fox, 2023). He concentrated on young people who were about to reach voting age in the mid-2000s and used individual- and household-level data from the UKHLS. He concluded that there were weak, though statistically significant, effects of volunteering on political interest and on whether individuals saw voting as a duty. However, these were evident only in a relatively small subset of individuals – those raised in households which were disengaged from politics. Thus, he argued, volunteering could be expected to make only a marginal contribution to reducing inequalities in engagement that originate in early socialisation and socioeconomic circumstances. If the goal was to increase voter turnout, volunteering would therefore be less effective than encouraging higher levels of participation or addressing the inequalities that underlie civic disengagement more generally.

Conclusions

There are some impacts of volunteering on political engagement. Studies using UK data have demonstrated such effects: for a cohort of individuals born in 1958; for the population enrolled in the BHPS and its successor, the UKHLS; for a subset of young people whose households were part of those surveys; and for young people who took part in the evaluations of NCS. Generally, those who volunteered as young adults were more likely to vote than their non-volunteering counterparts when aged 50; volunteering has some small effects on interest in politics, and on intention to vote, but not on party identification or party support; and some young people from households characterised as 'disengaged' from politics showed an effect of volunteering on the likelihood of voting and on interest in politics. These are robust findings from well-designed studies which use longitudinal data. This enables people to be tracked over time (in some cases for five decades) and to use modelling strategies which control for individuals' birth circumstances, their upbringing, personality and education, and all their life experiences prior to the point of data collection. A corollary of these extensive controls is that the statistical effect of our variable of interest – volunteering – on our chosen outcome variables (political interest and engagement) is likely to be reduced, and this is what these studies have found (as was the case in studies of health outcomes: see Chapter 9). The effects of volunteering on political engagement are small and not consistent across different dimensions of political interest and engagement. They are also constrained by social class.

Volunteering may have beneficial effects on political engagement and interest for some groups of people, but exposure to it is not – in itself – going to have much effect on increasing civic engagement or closing gaps in engagement. The effects of volunteering on civic and political engagement are strongest for those who are already most likely to be engaged. Bolton's work, in particular, shows that raising rates of volunteering in early adulthood would produce a civic and political benefit mostly among the middle classes, whose rates of engagement are already higher. Results from the evaluation of the NCS scheme are a partial exception (there appears to be some civic dividend for people from disadvantaged communities) as is Fox's (2023) finding of a weak but statistically significant positive effect of volunteering for young people from civically disengaged households. As Fox observes, however, this is only a small subset of households in the UK so it would have limited effects on the overall level of political engagement.

The practical implications of this work are that it is not obvious what policy levers might be available to promote political engagement through volunteering. So many measures of political interest and engagement are likely to be jointly caused. The same household and individual influences that drive voluntary association membership and participation are also those associated with interest and engagement in politics. The result is that those groups with least power and most limited resources are unlikely to be the most active participants in volunteering and civic affairs, so raising volunteering levels without doing something about those inequalities will have only marginal impacts on political participation. This is a further illustration of why a socially stratified phenomenon such as volunteering can be expected to do little to reduce social inequalities.

There may be other ways to encourage civic engagement than investing in support for volunteering opportunities for young people with the prospect of relatively limited returns. Higher returns might be generated if society communicated to individuals that their civic participation is valued, by making it easy for them to vote, rather than limiting the number and types of forms of identification through which they secure their citizenship rights, as is currently the case with the recent introduction of a requirement for voter identification at polling stations (the list of acceptable forms of ID is more restrictive for young people than for the elderly). Rather than approaching the raising of democratic participation indirectly, through volunteering, it may be more productive to address education and resource inequalities, as well as the question of access to the ballot box.

Part IV

Changing contexts

Introduction to Part IV

This final section explores scenarios for voluntary action in the future. As we have seen earlier in this book, there is a long history of calls for people to come forward to engage in their communities as volunteers, but responses have been limited and not sustained. Why is this so, and what might be done about it?

First, the key determinants of levels of voluntary action relate to demographic change and economic circumstances (Chapter 3), but levels of precarity and insecurity are rising, posing questions about whether citizens have the resources necessary to sustain participation. The belief that a strong welfare state would provide people with the resources that enabled them to contribute to voluntary action now looks optimistic: economic security (whether in retirement or not) is feasible for many people but not for all. Similar points can be made about the argument that increased health and longevity would provide an enlarged pool of the baby boom generation, with the resources and energy to engage actively in their communities. Many people are certainly in that position, but some other evidence points in a more negative direction. The combination of welfare state shrinkage and changing economic circumstances mean that volunteering becomes one of many potential claims on the time of individuals, as they juggle extended careers (due to the effects of economic disruption on their careers) and unanticipated caring responsibilities. Consequently, when we look at people's retirement intentions there are also some grounds for scepticism about whether we can rely on an increase in volunteering from those generations who are coming up to retirement, since voluntary action comes some way down the list of options considered in their accounts of how they envision post-retirement lives. Therefore, we might ask questions about which individuals, families and communities would be best placed to respond to demands for greater voluntary effort.

The nature of working life has also changed irrevocably and again this will have consequences for voluntary action. The importance of stable and secure employment as a basis for civic participation and community engagement has been recognised by social scientists for generations – going back at least as famous interwar studies of the social consequences of the loss of major employers in communities. Recent evidence, using both survey data and qualitative material, provides clear warnings of the impact of adverse economic circumstances on individual behaviours. This suggests that we cannot take for granted the ability of individuals to volunteer. What about public attitudes to doing so? There is often scepticism about responding to calls from government for more engagement. In Chapter 11, therefore, I consider evidence which bears on the question of how confident we can be about the sustainability of volunteering, drawing on studies of attitudes to volunteering, people's visions of their retirement priorities, the impact of economic dislocation on engagement and responses to the Coalition government's Big Society proposals.

This discussion is followed by Chapter 12, on policy responses. I begin with a discussion of the general approaches taken by governments, including political rhetoric around the topic. Different approaches to policy are then considered, including the question of the setting of targets for participation, the focus of policy on particular groups (especially young people) in the belief that strong formative experiences will lead to persistence in volunteering, the use of volunteering as an instrument of specific policies in the field of labour market policy and the potential for 'nudging' techniques to stimulate behavioural change. The chapter concludes by discussing what a broader framework for cultivating and conserving the 'spirit of service' might entail.

I follow this with a reflection on voluntary action in the time of COVID-19 in Chapter 13. This was a period in which voluntary action had a very high profile, but in hindsight it is arguable that it was another temporary blip in engagement, which was not sustained. I consider the volunteering response to the pandemic, using both quantitative data on involvement and qualitative investigations of the mobilisation of volunteers. The volunteering response to the pandemic was not as large as originally hoped, nor was it sustained. Perhaps surprisingly, the evidence from large numbers of charities is that their volunteer numbers did not collapse – a finding which seems at odds with survey reports for the COVID-19 period. Moreover, to a large degree, it appears that relatively few new volunteers came forward and, where we have reliable data, the socioeconomic patterning of volunteers was not that dissimilar to that revealed by two decades of prior surveys. These points run counter to optimistic claims that the COVID-19 mobilisation reached groups not previously noted for their high level of involvement in volunteering.

Finally I return, in the Conclusion, to various views of what the 'spirit of service' might mean. Early 2024 saw the latest evocation of this idea from the Labour leader, Keir Starmer. Recent decades in the UK have seen much evidence of Gramsci's 'cult of the volunteer' but it is not a time for uncritical paeans to the benefits of volunteering (Bolton, 2014; Hawksley and Georgeou, 2019). I consider the relationship between volunteering and national identity, whether the spirit is manifested in volunteering 'habits' and how best to promote them, the clinical properties of the spirit, the circumstances in which the spirit can be sustained and divergent views about potential future policy responses.

11

Demographic change, economic circumstances and attitudes to volunteering

Introduction

What would enable the spirit of service to be activated? One argument is that put forward by William Beveridge (see chapter 1): there was an underlying willingness to engage in voluntary action which could be activated once people's immediate material needs were met through the framework of a supportive welfare state. The idea that post-war prosperity and the ageing, and retirement, of a well-off cohort of baby boomers would boost volunteering rates can certainly be traced to discussions in the 1960s. It featured in Thatcher's public statements on volunteering and still had traction 20 years later, when the Conservative MP Oliver Letwin argued that increased longevity meant that a 'huge new well' of potential volunteers would become available, comprising active, healthy, energetic, experienced and intelligent people who were retired or approaching retirement; what was needed was a way of tapping that resource (Letwin, 2003).

Letwin didn't develop ideas on how that well might have been tapped. Unlike a natural resource such as oil, which can be extracted, gushing forth as the drill breaks into the subterranean reservoir, volunteers do not automatically come when they are summoned. In recent decades optimistic commentators have nevertheless anticipated a sustained increase in volunteering not just because of favourable demographics but also because people wanted to be part of something bigger than themselves. Attempts to mobilise that spirit have accompanied major sporting events or national celebrations (the Commonwealth and Olympic Games, King Charles' Coronation). Others pointed to the compassionate response to support neighbours and front-line workers in the COVID-19 emergency as something on which to build. Approaching from a different direction, proponents of the Big Society asserted the need for a different way forward, a society in which communities would welcome the opportunities provided by the Coalition government's shrinkage of the state. Those short-term responses have certainly raised the profile, though not the level, of volunteering; rates of engagement have stubbornly flatlined. Why might this be so?

The demographics appear favourable, so to help understand the public's apparent unwillingness to engage, we need to consider social attitudes and economic circumstances. We know relatively little about attitudes to volunteering. A small number of robust national surveys are now somewhat dated but are revealing about individuals' perceptions as to the necessity and desirability of voluntary action. Nor do we know very much about future intentions regarding voluntary action. However, we do have studies of retirement intentions from longitudinal surveys, which offer interesting insights, though the somewhat negative message is that volunteering is largely absent from the imagined futures of most respondents (see section on 'Social attitudes to volunteering').

Economic circumstances have fluctuated in the UK in recent decades and social divisions have widened. The insight that economic precarity reduces the likelihood of social and civic engagement is not novel (Clark and Heath, 2014: 1), but there is strong evidence from both quantitative and qualitative research as to its adverse effects on engagement (see section on 'economic circumstances, social change and volunteering'). The chapter considers two studies of the constraints imposed by economic circumstances on voluntary action: one from a longitudinal study, which tracked people for over half a century and which detected civic 'penalties' from earlier periods of economic hardship; the other a cross-sectional analysis of the effects on volunteering of the 2008–9 Great Recession. Combined with other biographical evidence from individuals (see Chapter 6; Lindsey and Mohan, 2018: 153–82), this paints a clear and strong picture of the negative effects of economic adversity on volunteering.

Finally, responses to requests to engage, and the views that people have about their experience of volunteering, feature in the section on 'Responses to the Big Society'. Volunteering research has always emphasised the importance of *being asked* to volunteer as a key influence on participation. The nature of 'the ask' is also relevant to the ways governments convey messages about volunteering. We can see this from responses to the post-2010 Coalition government's Big Society policies. Though individuals were not always opposed to the ideas, key themes were cynicism about the motivations for the policy but also narratives conveying a sense of exhaustion from people who were already very active. There may be a reserve of willingness, but whether that reserve is mobilised depends very much on the context of the appeal and the circumstances of individuals, not whether they have somehow internalised a 'spirit' or 'habit' of service. Finally, and as if to emphasise the points made by those respondents, volunteering is simply something that we do not enjoy as much as we used to, as shown by a comparison of time use diaries from the mid-1980s and 2015.

Social attitudes to volunteering

Occasional studies of volunteering intentions are claimed to indicate a pent-up desire for engagement in voluntary action. A recent Pro Bono Economics study (December 2022) made such a claim, projecting an increase of several million volunteers on the back of a survey which stated that a quarter of adults *intended* to volunteer during 2023 (Jemal et al., 2022). If shown to be true, this would have been a completely unprecedented increase, but the survey didn't appear to distinguish those who *intended to continue volunteering* from those who were contemplating *doing so for the first time* (a proportion actually likely to be quite low, for reasons discussed in Chapter 6).

Can we rely on what people say about whether or not they intend to become engaged in voluntary action? Evidence of short-term change has been taken for a fundamental shift in the public mood, as in Philip Blond's argument, around the time of the 2010 election campaign, that volunteering rates among the professional classes and the young had 'doubled' in a short time period (Blond, 2010b; Jackson, 2009). It was never clear what evidence there was for this claim, other than contemporaneous newspaper reports of an increase in the demand for volunteering opportunities, but there was no evidence of a spike in volunteering, sustained or otherwise, around the time at which Blond was writing (Hill, 2011).

The problem is the reliability of evidence of intentions. Volunteering is a socially desirable activity, and if asked about it we're naturally predisposed to respond in a way that we think will elicit approbation. But such responses are not a sure guide to how people will actually behave. A study claimed to have identified those who had acquired a 'habit of social action' as those who had volunteered and who had *expressed interest in doing so* in the future (Taylor-Collins et al., 2019). But simply flagging the intention to repeat an action at some point is hardly evidence that someone has internalised a prosocial disposition (see Chapter 6); the researchers were not able to follow up with their respondents to determine whether they had continued to volunteer.

Attitudes and behaviours are also framed by the economic and social context which influences the resources that people possess and the social networks they have. However, appeals to volunteer are framed very much against particular circumstances. Thatcher's positive rhetoric about volunteering in the early 1980s was set against the background of economic policies that deprived people of the resources that formed the basis for participation and provoked scepticism about the underlying motivation lying behind calls to volunteer (see section on 'Economic circumstances, social change and volunteering').

Attitudes to volunteering

While the UK possesses an exceptional time series of data on social attitudes, only rarely have questions been posed about attitudes to volunteering. In the NSVs conducted in 1981 and 1991, perhaps the most interesting feature was the response to the statement that 'if government fulfilled all its responsibilities there should be no need for voluntary workers'. The proportion agreeing with this rose from 23 per cent to 49 per cent in the decade between these surveys (Lynn and Davis Smith, 1991). Changes over time in these responses suggest increased awareness of the rolling back of the state during the Thatcher and Major years.

The authoritative and long-running British Social Attitudes Survey (BSAS) only explored attitudes to volunteering in the mid-1990s, a time when the Major government was seeking, through its 'Active Citizenship' policy rhetoric, to promote volunteering (see Chapter 13). There wasn't an unequivocal endorsement of volunteering – three-fifths of respondents felt that 'as a society, we rely too much on volunteers', and barely one-third agreed, and a slightly larger proportion disagreed, with the proposition that 'everybody has a duty to do voluntary work' (these surveys are summarised in Lindsey and Mohan, 2018: 184–6).

The BSAS data demonstrate a cyclical pattern of attitudes either for or against greater government intervention, self-reliance and higher welfare payments. Support for government intervention has waxed and waned depending on the state of the economy, and this has been particularly true of attitudes to statements about the need for people to be self-reliant and not depend on the state. Those trends bear no relationship to levels of voluntary action; if at times attitudes have shifted away from support for state intervention, behaviour was not switching in favour of greater voluntarism by individuals. Though the absence of long-term trend data on attitudes to volunteering limits what can be said on the topic, the national surveys that exist (especially the surveys on volunteering from 1981 and 1991) indicate that people are aware of whether or not government is delivering on its promises when they answer questions on the need for volunteers – a point to which we return later, in a discussion of public responses to the 2010 Coalition government's Big Society policies.

Intentions: can we count on the boomers?

Two pieces of evidence illustrate different aspects of the challenges that society faces in terms of recruiting more volunteers. The first comes from a module of questions issued to a subset of participants in the BHPS/UKHLS longitudinal surveys, namely people aged over 45 who were not retired and those of pensionable age, aged under 71, who did *not* consider themselves to be retired. They were offered 'a list of things that some people say are good about retirement' – being one's own boss and having time to take things easy, the opportunity to travel, time for family and friends, time for leisure and time for voluntary work – and asked to say whether these were very important, moderately important, somewhat important or not important.

Having time for voluntary work was the least popular option – around 12 per cent regarded it as 'very' important and 28 per cent rated it of 'moderate' importance. In contrast, between two-thirds and over four-fifths of respondents rated the options of relaxation, travel, time for friends and family and leisure pursuits as either very or moderately important, with over 55 per cent indicating that family and friends were very important to them. In these surveys, voluntary work always attracts the least positive endorsement. As an indication of the consistency of responses to this question over time, when these questions were first posed in 2001, 11 per cent and 27 per cent indicated that time for voluntary work was very and moderately important, respectively.

The second source is the NCDS, which follows a cohort of children born in one week in 1958 and surveys them at, approximately, seven-to-eight-year intervals. When cohort members were aged 50, in 2008, they were also asked to write a free-form response to an open-ended prompt inviting them to envisage what their life would be at the age of 60:

> Imagine that you are now 60 years old. Please write a few lines about the life you are leading (your interests, your home life, your health and well-being, and any work you may be doing). (Elliott et al., 2010)

Recall that this is a group born in what were very propitious economic circumstances – the first 25 years of their lives were generally characterised by steady economic growth, increased prosperity and widening opportunity.

In total, 7,378 cohort members responded, although in many cases only a few words or sentences were written. Frequency counts of common terms such as 'voluntary work', 'volunteering' or 'charity work' showed relatively few direct references to anything that was recognisable as voluntary action. There were 450 responses including the phrase 'voluntary work', 55 featured the word 'volunteer' and 141 mentioned 'helping'. References to 'helping' are not an unambiguous indicator of voluntary action outside the family, as a number referred to helping relatives. Differences in phraseology are fascinating: some report 'helping' in the charity shop while others characterise their activity as 'working' in it; another stated that in their future existence they would 'volunteer for a couple of charities and help at the hospice' – raising the question of whether there is a difference between volunteering and helping. Another describes *'taking part* in charity activities, [and] helping other people in my community' – perhaps echoing the lack of clarity about what counts as formal and informal volunteering (Chapter 1).

These basic frequency counts show that 11 per cent made some reference to activities of this kind. That proportion was around half the proportion (typically around 23 per cent) which reported involvement in 'unpaid voluntary work' in the same wave of this survey. Strikingly, women were nearly three times as likely as men to make some reference to prospective future community involvement, a disparity far greater than that revealed in responses to the simultaneous survey question on unpaid voluntary work. As expected from the wider literature there was a similar gradient for education. For those with degrees or higher qualifications, at least 17 per cent made some reference to future prosocial behaviour, compared to 7 per cent for those who had left school with very few educational qualifications. We would anticipate this, since higher-education qualifications are associated with stronger awareness of and empathy with the needs of others.

We also find a clear gradient in the responses between those who were already volunteering and those who weren't. Of those cohort members who were volunteering at least once a week in 2008, at least 15 per cent said that they would be engaged in volunteering at age 60, compared to fewer than half of that for those volunteering once a year or less. Perhaps surprisingly, as many as 4 per cent of those volunteering 'never or almost never' at the age of 50 indicated that they might be volunteering when they reached 60. Ongoing work, analysing this corpus of text in more detail, shows that, as with the survey data on retirement intentions, volunteering comes some way down the rankings in terms of its place in the imagined futures of respondents (Doodeman et al., 2023).

These pieces of work shed light on the willingness of citizens to become engaged and the place of volunteering in their priorities. Reassuringly, given the different ways in which data are collected across the two studies, the findings are similar – just over one-tenth of the population spontaneously indicate the possibility that they might get engaged in volunteering in later life (NCDS) or regard 'time for voluntary work' as a 'very important' aspect of the opportunities offered by retirement (UKHLS).[1] But the findings do not provide optimism about the scope for a potential upsurge in the spirit of service.

Finally, and perhaps pointing in the direction of broader social changes, we aren't enjoying volunteering as much as we used to, relative to other activities. This might appear surprising when we recall that national surveys on volunteering elicit highly positive responses to questions about the enjoyment and personal satisfaction it provides (Lindsey and Mohan, 2018: table 6.2). However, the framing of the questions does not allow for comparisons with other ways in which people might spend their available free time.

We can turn to the UK's Time Use Surveys for data that compare the level of enjoyment people experience across various categories of activity. Such surveys ask people to complete detailed daily diaries indicating what they were doing in defined (often as little as 10 minutes) intervals of time throughout a day. The diary responses are coded by research team members (Fisher, 2010). Some time use studies have also asked respondents to record *how much* they were enjoying themselves at a point in time, regardless of the activity being undertaken. Thus, once the activities that comprise people's daily diaries are classified, researchers can explore the levels of enjoyment associated with particular ways of passing the time. When the data are arranged by levels of happiness, activities such as job searching and routine domestic tasks are usually ranked lowest; activities such as outdoor leisure, playing with one's children and going to sports events or cultural performances are at or near the top. In the 2014–15 Time Use Survey (TUS), volunteering ranked 46th out of 63 separate categories of activity; the categories of activity ranked below it were associated with formal education, paid work and domestic chores. The level of enjoyment recorded while engaging in 'voluntary work' was

---

[1] Author's calculations based on UKHLS data.

directly comparable with that derived from various aspects of work, shopping and adult care.

For comparisons from a previous time period, Gershuny and colleagues drew on a survey of adults aged 16–65 conducted in 1986, in which 33 categories of activity were comparable with the 2014–15 TUS (Gershuny and Sullivan, 2019). The difference was striking (Figure 11.1). In the 1986 surveys, volunteering was ranked near the top of 33 categories of activity recorded. All the activities that were given scores clearly greater than that for voluntary work were to do with leisure in some form (sport, going out, music, pubs and restaurants). Volunteering ranked equally with sleep (which by 2014–15 was the most highly scored category of all), visits, hobbies and reading.

What might explain the differences between the two studies? The underlying approach was identical – time use surveys request a representative sample of individuals to complete time use diaries, text from which is then coded by research team members. Gershuny and Sullivan argued that the reduction in the enjoyment of voluntary activity could reflect reductions in state welfare provision and the consequent 'extra burden on people providing care for others on an unpaid, informal or voluntary basis' (2019: 314). This is certainly a possibility. Further support for Gershuny and Sullivan's argument might be drawn from research on attitudes to the Big Society (see section on 'Responses to the Big Society'), which convey a sense of weariness and cynicism about demands for engagement, suggesting that those respondents were at best not enjoying their voluntary activities but felt they had no choice but to continue in them. Even if the condition of the welfare state could not be held responsible, Gershuny and Sullivan have clearly shown how, over a period of some three decades, other priorities and necessities have come to be seen as more pleasurable than volunteering.

Economic circumstances, social change and volunteering

If it is agreed that volunteering is a behaviour that societies have an interest in sustaining, we might want to consider what causes people to cease doing it. One answer can be provided by economic circumstances: individual participation can be adversely affected by unfavourable economic events, which may produce traceable lifelong consequences for engagement.

Prominent explanatory accounts of the pattern of volunteering are heavily resource-based, placing an emphasis not just on economic

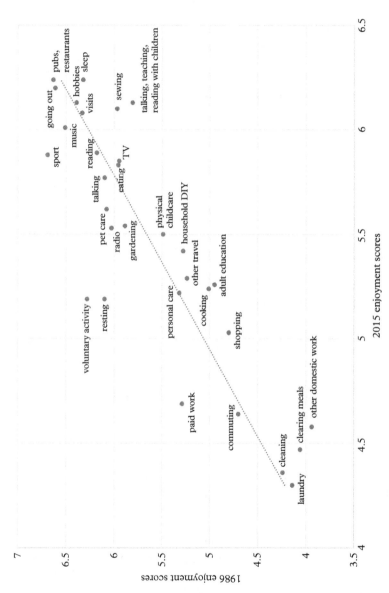

Figure 11.1 Comparisons of the enjoyment of activities in the UK, 1986 and 2014–15, for men and women aged 16–65. Source: Gershuny and Sullivan (2019).

capital but also on social and cultural capital. Based on such frameworks, increased prosperity, incomes and the availability of leisure time, along with rising levels of education, might have been expected to increase levels of volunteering but, as shown in Chapter 2, this has not happened. How can this be explained? One reason may be that the relationship between individual and household circumstances on the one hand, and the likelihood and level of participation on the other, may vary between birth cohorts (McCulloch, 2014). Specifically, the changing economic and social circumstances over post-war decades have weakened the economic foundations for participation in voluntary action and have affected cohorts differentially.

Labour markets have become increasingly insecure and casualised, the social safety net provided by the welfare state has become considerably less generous and the social structures conducive to voluntary engagement, such as trades unions, which often provided routes into active engagement in prosocial behaviours, are diminished in extent and influence. The free time available to individuals for participation has been squeezed by lengthy commutes, flexible but therefore less predictable working patterns, and the challenges for households in combining two or more jobs with their caring activities (see Chapter 6).

It would therefore hardly be surprising if there had not been significant changes in associational life in recent decades. McCulloch's study of cohort variations in voluntary association membership in Britain (McCulloch, 2014; see also Li et al., 2003) finds that there are statistically significant differences in associational membership between successive birth cohorts, with the earlier (1935–44; 1945–54) birth cohorts being more likely to have been engaged in associations than subsequent cohorts after adjusting for a range of individual characteristics. He attributed this to changes in the 'macro social and economic conditions experienced by different cohorts', which cumulatively reduced the resources and opportunities for organisational membership, and individuals' willingness to take part in collective action of all kinds (2014: 181). These changed circumstances particularly affected people born from the mid-1950s onwards who came to adulthood from the early 1970s, a period characterised by economic stagnation and some severe recessions, notably in the early 1980s.

Do we find similar changes in relation to volunteering? Clifford's (2020) study of charity trustees points in that direction – he finds a decline in the proportion of successive birth cohorts who have trustee roles in English and Welsh charities. He forms five-year birth cohorts for analysis – the 1945 birth cohort includes all those born in 1943–7.

As an example of the broad pattern of his findings, the proportion of trustees in the 1945 cohort at age 55 is 39/10,000 people, which compares favourably with the figure for trustees at age 55 in the 1950 cohort (37/10,000), the 1955 cohort (33/10,000) and the 1960 cohort (27/10,000). In other words, those born in the early post-war years have higher rates of trusteeship when observed at the same ages as later cohorts. This is broadly comparable with McCulloch's (2014) findings and suggests that one reason for the slow decline of volunteering is that the more recent birth cohorts are not engaging in it as much as their predecessors.

Research suggests that economic change casts a long shadow and may be partly responsible for this decline in engagement. A long tradition of social scientific enquiry has drawn connections between challenging economic circumstances and the withdrawal of individuals from social and civic engagement (Clark and Heath, 2014). Lim and Laurence (2015) provide a convincing demonstration of the negative effects of recession on engagement. Using the Citizenship Survey for 2009–10 they showed that levels of volunteering had declined in the most disadvantaged parts of England and Wales during the Great Recession of 2008–9. This raises the question of whether that reduction might be associated with economic circumstances.

For the period 2007–11 the Citizenship Survey provides data for each quarter of the calendar year. Lim and Laurence showed a reduction in the rate of volunteering when comparing 2008–9 with 2009–10, and also a detectable decline in the average number of hours committed by citizens to voluntary activity from 2008 onwards. The quarterly survey data for four years straddling the Great Recession enabled Lim and Laurence (2015) to examine what happened to individual reports of volunteering. They found a reduction in the proportions of the population involved in voluntary activity during the recession. The reduction was greatest for informal volunteering (down by 10 percentage points) and the decline was particularly evident in disadvantaged areas.

They also found a reduction in the *level* of engagement – that is, the estimated hours committed to voluntary activities. For both formal and informal volunteering there were substantial reductions in the hours committed, the timing of which coincided with the economic recession almost exactly. For formal volunteering through organisations, the average time commitment fell by nearly one-third between the third quarter of 2008, when the average time volunteered in the previous four weeks was 190 minutes, and the second quarter of 2010, when the figure was 130 minutes. Similar reductions were found for informal volunteering: help and support given directly to other members of one's own community. This was more surprising since such help does not depend so much on economic resources (see Chapter 3). Informal volunteering also fell by an average of approximately an hour. Lim and Lawrence (2015) explored year-on-year changes between 2007 and 2011 and found a combined reduction in formal and informal volunteering of just under one hour a month. Their estimate was that in total this meant that overall there was roughly a 25 per cent reduction in community engagement. On this measure the social recession was considerably bigger than the financial one (Clark and Heath, 2014: 125–6). The implication was that adverse economic circumstances had detectable and relatively immediate effects on individual engagement, weakening the capacities of communities to cope.

These scars may also be long-lasting. Laurence and Lim (2014) also show how labour market circumstances from the 1980s had traceable effects on engagement even decades later. They use data from the NCDS which, in addition to its questions on participation, has also gathered data on the lifetime labour market histories of respondents. Their key point is that, after controlling for numerous individual characteristics, adverse labour market experiences, particularly from the 1980s, were reflected in reduced levels of civic engagement even decades later. They emphasised in particular the effects of job *displacement* – involuntary job loss through mechanisms such as redundancy or workplace closures; individuals who lost jobs through such routes in early adulthood were significantly less likely to do unpaid voluntary work at the age of 50. The largest adverse effect was reserved for those men who experienced the loss of a job, followed by a period of not being employed for a least one month. Similar analyses for women found no significant effect. They postulated that this process might work in three potential ways. First, displacement might lead to downward socioeconomic mobility; second, that damage to individual psychological well-being led to a reduction in participation; and third, that displacement led to family breakdown, with a consequent negative effect on social networks. However, the effect of job displacement on participation persisted even after controlling for these.

They attributed these effects to the ways in which sudden job loss severed people's networks (workplace, unions) through which they found opportunities to develop and maintain social participation. The early and sudden interruption to workforce participation for these young adults removed those opportunities and placed them on a more truncated participation career. Groups who had not experienced job displacement continued to increase engagement as they aged;

in contrast, the rates of participation among the 'displaced' group initially remained stable, but subsequently those involved became increasingly likely to cease participation. Job displacement therefore gradually resulted in widening disparities in rates of participation.

These findings were reminiscent of sociological work from the 1950s in which – prior to the large-scale disruptions to labour markets of subsequent decades – scholars had discerned differences in the propensity to join associations between those at the core of the labour market (on stable and secure employment trajectories) and those in what they termed the 'chaotic' sections of it (Wilensky, 1961) – rhetoric which seems highly pertinent today given the growing evidence of precarity. The circumstances against which this book is written seem likely to run the risk of creating a generation of 'civically handicapped individuals' (Laurence and Lim, 2014: 25).

In short, people make their volunteering histories, but they do so not under conditions of their own choosing, and economic circumstances which expel people from the labour market may also disconnect them from the social networks which lead to civic engagement.

Responses to the Big Society: why should people do more?

The post-2010 Coalition government's Big Society policies envisaged a shrinkage in the role of the state, the creation of opportunities for citizens to run local services and an encouragement of voluntary action and charitable giving (Chapter 13; see also Defty, 2011; Lindsey and Bulloch, 2013; Ware, 2012; Alcock, 2010; Macmillan, 2013). We know that volunteering rates have not increased (see Chapter 2), but what do we know about the public's response to being called upon to do more volunteering?

I draw here on material generated by Mass Observation, the social research charity. Mass Observation recruits volunteer writers, who are asked to respond to 'directives', which solicit opinions about open-ended statements on topics of current interest or descriptions of aspects of the daily lives of respondents. There are issues with the representativeness of these respondents, who are not a cross-section of the UK population (Lindsey and Mohan, 2018: chapter 3), but by the same token they are reporting the perceptions of active citizens.

In 1996, Mass Observation issued a directive on unpaid work, while in 2012 a directive was commissioned on the Big Society, thus permitting comparisons between the Cameron and Major governments, both of which professed support for voluntary action. In both directives individuals were asked to comment on the voluntary activities they were undertaking in their communities, the meanings those activities held for them, and their attitudes, for example whether they would be willing to do more. The 2012 directive also explored views on responsibility for public service provision. Here, I summarise key findings from work done in collaboration with Mass Observation. The two studies respectively sampled 100 respondents to the 2012 directive on the Big Society (Lindsey and Bulloch, 2013) and 38 individuals whose responses to Mass Observation directives on voluntary action and civic engagement had been tracked continuously from the mid-1980s onwards, giving a unique longitudinal qualitative perspective on individual engagement (Lindsey and Mohan, 2018; Lindsey and Bulloch, 2013).

At both points in time respondents clearly articulated the view that socially necessary work ought to be properly remunerated, and they objected to *job substitution* – the use of volunteers to take over the running of public services, which they saw as central to austerity policies. Numerous respondents had histories of deep and continuous volunteering, but they emphasised that they were certainly not going to take on more commitments in response to negative messages. Scepticism about the underlying motivations of the Big Society was widespread. Clearly, a policy to expand levels of volunteering must emphasise to potential volunteers the intrinsic benefits, impacts and rewards of engagement, and not just the economic necessity of substituting for state withdrawal.

Despite Cameron's presentation of the Big Society as a novel and significant departure, it never gained traction. Even among the minority who were aware of it, barely a third felt they had some comprehension of what it meant; public interest was patchy and limited (Ferragina and Arrigoni, 2016: 362). Our findings suggested that a higher proportion of Mass Observers were aware of the Big Society than was the case for the population as a whole, but they also felt taken for granted by policies which were failing to acknowledge the enormous extent of existing voluntary effort.

Some three-quarters of these engaged individuals expressed negative views, with barely one-tenth welcoming the Big Society initiative. Some Mass Observation writers reported a total lack of understanding, dismissing the idea as vacuous, superficial and irrelevant to the social and economic challenges facing the country. The underlying political motivations were strongly criticised; the Big Society was characterised as a stunt to get people working for nothing, hypocritical propaganda at a time when the welfare state was under attack and part of a strategy to weaken organised labour by the substitution of unpaid labour for that of paid personnel.

The people expressing the foregoing views were, by and large, actively engaged in volunteering, but they did not wish to engage in an enterprise which they believed to be poorly thought-out and confused, neither novel nor distinctive, and driven by an ideological agenda. Such responses suggest that citizens required an explanation of the underlying policy framework, what was envisaged and to what ends. But what of the capacities of individuals and communities to take on more responsibilities?

The Mass Observation writers are highly engaged, active citizens, but when our Big Society directive asked individuals whether they felt they could do *more* voluntary work, it evoked strongly negative responses. Where respondents commented directly, a clear majority (over four-fifths) indicated that they lacked the capacity to do more, for various reasons: they were fully committed to existing activities, too stretched by their informal caring commitments and/or were seeking to cut back because of the effects of age and infirmity. A small proportion of respondents categorically attributed their motivations for not engaging in formal volunteering (or taking on any more commitments) to exhaustion, either because of paid work or looking after homes, children or family members, or otherwise attributed their unwillingness to volunteer to age, disability or sickness. A retired senior teacher recounted his lengthy experience of volunteering for what was in effect unpaid overtime on top of his educational roles, stating that his 'days of volunteering for anything were over'. This sentiment of having already contributed to society through and beyond paid employment was echoed in a small number of other scripts, where writers mentioned having to give unpaid overtime (whether in the public or private sectors) and feeling unable or willing to volunteer in their so-called spare time.

In summary, this study shows that there was little capacity or desire to take on more unpaid work; fewer than one-tenth felt that they could do more. Reliable national surveys of volunteering have found that up to one-third of respondents would like to spend more time helping groups, clubs or organisations. The Mass Observation research is not directly comparable to those surveys but the source material (written responses, some of considerable length) means that it is the outcome of a more extensive process of reflection than completing a questionnaire. Thus we would suggest that it casts some doubt on whether a *willingness* to do more can, in practice, be taken to signal that there is the *capacity* to do more.

What of the capacities of communities? Writers were asked whether the places in which they live have the capacity to meet the communities' needs. Respondents were certainly aware of the contrasting socioeconomic circumstances of communities. One highlighted the concentration in his area of retired people, generally in good health and with high disposable incomes, optimistically arguing that such people could reasonably be expected to contribute significantly to community life. Some nostalgically evoked a vision of a former country in which, for example, 'attributes once seen as "Englishness" still survive in districts such as ours [including] ... independence and respectability', with others seeing the Big Society as a reasonable characterisation of how small communities operated before the welfare state.

Others argued that returning to such a bygone era was obviously not realistic and pointed to challenges in places where 'community wealth' (Keohane et al., 2011; see also Chapter 5) was lacking, as in a disadvantaged ex-mining town beset by what the writer perceived as fatigue and fatalism. These comments echo Lindsey's (2013) research into voluntary action in two contrasting communities: the skills, energy, confidence and connections needed to take up the Big Society's opportunities were well in evidence in an area of affluence but singularly lacking in a very disadvantaged neighbourhood a few miles away (see Chapter 6).

A strong critique of the Big Society (Ware, 2012) – and by extension other policy initiatives relying on an expansion of voluntarism – was that the policy placed its faith in community-based solutions at a time when communities were declining as a base for social organisation (Sampson et al., 2005). Few Mass Observation writers positively eulogised their communities. Several longstanding respondents lamented the decline of the strong social networks they had built up over many years, and there was also an awareness of wider social changes consequent upon changes in the organisation of production. Respondents therefore regretted the passing of social institutions, including clubs and societies, built upon large-scale manufacturing operations; those networks had provided support to ex-employees in retirement and acted as an ongoing base for voluntary effort. Combined with lengthier commutes and more flexible working patterns, the consequence had been that residents were left with less time and energy for community-focused efforts.

Some expressed forthright views on the need for continued infrastructural support from local government – for example the view that voluntarism went hand in hand with a supportive state, which was needed to provide a basic level of support to communities if they were to manage their own needs. There was also the view that the scale and pace of austerity had negative consequences as local authorities had little alternative but to sell off open space, play areas and community facilities – spaces for interaction and voluntarism that were part of the infrastructure of communities (Klinenberg, 2018).

Conclusions

There have been repeated calls for the UK's citizens to become more involved in voluntary action, but none of them have resulted in a sustained increase in the proportion of the population who are engaged. Why might that be the case? This chapter has pointed to evidence regarding the attitudes and priorities of individuals, their material circumstances and their responses to a specific call for engagement – the Big Society policies of the post-2010 Coalition government.

Where we possess robust national surveys of social attitudes to volunteering, there are some very positive statements about volunteering and its place in society but more qualified verdicts about the reliance of society on volunteers and about whether citizens have a duty to volunteer. For evidence of the likely future behaviours of citizens, some survey data show that volunteering is relatively low on the ranking of priorities for those from early middle age onwards, lagging well behind family, leisure and travel. And when individuals at age 50 were asked to envision their life 10 years on, few referenced volunteering spontaneously.

This ambivalence about volunteering, and the apparently low priority attached to it, doesn't mean that it is not possible to engage people in volunteering, but doing so requires a positive vision of why they are being asked. What is much harder to change is the economic context. There is strong evidence as to the negative impacts of economic downturns on engagement and of their long-lasting effects. Sociologists over half a century ago identified the importance of 'orderly careers' as bases for sustained participation trajectories (Wilensky, 1961). UK studies from the 1980s and the early 2000s show clearly the engagement penalties paid over several decades by those forcibly ejected from the job market in the early 1980s and the shorter-term impact of the economic recession of 2008–9 on voluntary effort. It is fairly clear from aggregate data that it is the younger generations who are most affected by the current economic turbulence (see evidence as to rapid decline in volunteering in Chapter 2). Given the precarious prospects facing these groups, they seem unlikely to move into stable engagement pathways in the manner of previous generations.

There needs to be a conversation about this. Drawing a parallel from other studies of social behaviour – criminology – Neil and Sampson suggest that social scientists 'should really be looking at not what was wrong or virtuous with individuals of a particular cohort, but rather looking at *what was right or wrong with the larger social environment* during the historical period in which they happen to come of age' (2021: 1170, emphasis added). Living through substantial disruption, whether occasioned by war, economic decline or pandemics, has had substantial effects on the routine patterns of social life. In those circumstances the recent drop in volunteering among young adults would hardly be a surprise, since those groups are facing the greatest pressures from precarity. This shifts the emphasis in explaining behaviours firmly away from individual dispositions, but awareness of the effects of economic change on voluntary action is relatively lacking in many recent policy pronouncements and prominent inquiries in the field.

Sustaining voluntary action will therefore throw a considerable burden on groups who are most insulated from precarity, but whether those groups will answer the call for action will also depend on the nature of the request for their assistance. The most prominent effort to shift the frontier between statutory and voluntary effort – the Big Society – was little understood and, to the extent that the message percolated, came to be interpreted as an ill-conceived cover for austerity. The majority of the active citizens who were writing for Mass Observation were roundly critical and also quick to identify the unpromising context for demanding further voluntary effort. Their comments were of course directed at what they saw as a government request that they should pick up responsibilities jettisoned by the state; perhaps they felt that this was a particularly narrow vision of voluntary action, defined as a contribution to the delivery of public services and little else. In that sense, the views of people from organisations concerned less with delivering services and more with the pursuit of 'serious leisure' (Chapter 1) might have been less pessimistic. Even so, if governments in the future are to summon their citizens to commit more of their time to community initiatives, this suggests that they will, at the very least, need to communicate positive reasons for doing so. With this in mind, we turn in Chapter 12 to a consideration of policies designed to support volunteering.

12

Cultivating and conserving the spirit of service

Introduction

Voluntary action results from choices made by individuals in a private capacity, without compulsion. Can governments influence those choices? Since at least 1979, all UK governments, including the devolved administrations, have professed support for voluntary action per se, for initiatives designed to enhance the scope for voluntary action and for the non-state provision of public services. But the means through which governments have pursued those objectives has varied.

What then can governments do in order to influence volunteering? First, there are ways of framing policy such that economic security is maximised through strong welfare systems and the promotion of full employment. This is an intervention at the macro level and is considered further in the Conclusion. There is also the rhetoric used by government in their endorsement of volunteering, and the positions taken by governments over time, with a focus on the underlying philosophies (next section). Then there are a range of possible policy interventions. Governments might simply want to stimulate volunteering without regard for the resultant patterns (e.g. of inequalities in engagement); they might therefore wish to widen the availability of opportunities to engage, with a view to establishing a norm of participation. Or they could prioritise particular sections of the population, for instance encouraging young people to volunteer through educational programmes or bespoke volunteering opportunities. Steps may be taken to draw on hitherto untapped reserves of volunteers (Koolen-Maas et al., 2023; see also the Conclusion), by ensuring that access to volunteering opportunities is improved, including policies targeted at specific groups who are deemed to be under-represented. Volunteering programmes may also be developed to deal with particular issues, such as the management of mass unemployment. The broad repertoire of policy measures implemented is considered in the third section, 'Specific policy initiatives' (fuller descriptions of policies in previous periods are given in Rochester et al., 2010: 84–102; Lindsey and Mohan, 2018: 19–38). Note that quantifying government commitments in terms of expenditures is a challenging task and one not attempted here, because in principle initiatives in various government departments might or might not be regarded as related to volunteering. Consequently, where figures are quoted, they relate to some specific individual programmes.

Rhetoric

The first and most visible way governments promote volunteering is the language they use about it. Nostalgia for a golden age of voluntarism has various elements – its significance to national identity, the contribution it can make to the formation of character and resilience, its place in a strategy for emulating the social successes of other nations and as a driver of prosperity and generator of social capital – all of which feature at different times and with different emphases. The spirit of service is invoked and is a presence here, but it is malleable: voluntarism takes on the meanings that those invoking it want it to possess.

We see this from 1979, following the election of the Conservative government. Thatcher's policies (1979–90) were heavily driven by a sense of the need to reverse national economic decline, and this was mirrored in the social sphere with speeches about citizens developing a sense of personal responsibility towards family, neighbourhood and community. She felt that there was no substitute for intensive personal support for those in need from their families, friends and neighbours, support which was often sustained for a period of time. Though operating with a fairly narrow vision of voluntary action, the strong emphasis on the distinctive and personal contribution made by volunteers was intellectually coherent in a way that the subsequent Big Society policies were not (Slocock, 2019: 222–4). Thatcher (1981) eulogised the 'volunteer movement', with a particular emphasis on individual volunteers and small community-based groups, often local and spontaneous, which could be given continuity and support by the bigger voluntary organisations. On the other hand, the hopes invested in volunteering by her government were largely lacking in evidence (Brenton, 1985).

Given Thatcher's emphasis on the importance of reversing Britain's decline and the need to revive a tradition of voluntary action, it might therefore appear surprising that positive policy steps to support voluntary action by individuals were less evident during her time in office than during Major's term (1990–7). The Conservatives enjoined the beneficiaries of government economic policies to commit, as 'active citizens', to engagement in their communities. An emerging policy framework for the voluntary sector, developed under Major, was acknowledged by commentators as ambitious, innovative and volunteer-centred, in contrast to the Thatcher era (Rochester et al., 2010: 89–90). However, little was achieved before the Conservatives lost office.

The years of Labour government saw a different approach. The Labour leader, Tony Blair, took transatlantic inspiration from the social capital literature in suggesting that all 'successful societies' displayed high levels of voluntary initiative (Blair, 1999). The post-1997 Labour governments therefore embarked upon what Kendall (2009: 67) characterised as the 'hyperactive mainstreaming' of the third sector into public policy. Their policies in relation to volunteering embraced national targets for levels of volunteering, support for citizenship education in schools and a wide range of efforts targeted at under-represented groups. Investments were also made in the infrastructure for voluntary action, through local councils for voluntary service, one function of which is to facilitate the matching up of individuals with volunteering opportunities. Broader policy objectives espoused by Labour included increasing the contribution of the 'third sector' to public service delivery, including efforts to take account of the 'social value' provided by volunteers (Kendall, 2009; Lindsey and Mohan, 2018: 26–30). While welcoming Labour's engagement, critics drew attention to the implicit enlistment of volunteers in the service of political priorities, its instrumentalist conception of volunteering, with a focus on service delivery and the renewal of civil order (Rochester et al., 2010: 95–7), and its selective emphasis on formal and measurable acts of engagement in organisational settings, to the neglect of wider dimensions of voluntarism such as informal volunteering and support from neighbours, or campaigning and activism (Aiken and Taylor, 2019; Rochester, 2013).

The Conservative Party's pitch in the 2010 election envisaged a substantial expansion in the contribution of voluntary effort to the welfare mix, encapsulated in David Cameron's Big Society proposals. In this view, top-down state intervention had produced limited results and societal breakdown; to repair the damage, the government sought to take power away from politicians and give it to people, with a particular emphasis on local initiative. This Burkean vision of 'little platoons' combined elements of public sector reform, community empowerment and philanthropic action (Blond, 2010a; Norman, 2010). In sharp contrast to the predecessor Labour governments, the post-2010 period was characterised by general rhetorical exhortation and greater terminological vagueness about volunteering (e.g. a broader concept of social action rather than just volunteering; see Chapter 1), and no normative aspirations or targets other than a generalised desire to increase levels of engagement.

The heterogeneous origins of the Big Society concept provoked criticisms that it was a vague rhetorical device for distancing the Conservatives from their Thatcherite predecessors (Ware, 2012). The concept produced "grand theories, moral outrage, a Scotch mist of statistics, a litter of spoofs, ... and elevated paeans on human dignity' (Stewart, 2023, 99). Launched against a background of severe austerity, the Big Society struggled to gain traction and generated cynical responses (see Chapter 11). The encouragement of greater public involvement in their communities, and the transfer of public services and facilities to community control, were strong elements of the underlying ideas. In terms of specific initiatives that might bear on volunteering levels, the most substantial innovation was the launching of NCS (see the section on 'Specific policy initiatives'); though structured as being primarily about personal development, it includes elements of social action.

The short-lived premiership of Theresa May (2017–19), resulted in a civil society strategy statement (Cabinet Office, 2018). Despite its inclusive title ('a future that works for everyone'), references to volunteering were almost wholly directed to youth engagement; the rest of the adult population received little attention. Perhaps unwittingly it exemplified the challenges for government policy, hinting that in effect governments could do little for volunteering, other than by acting as a convener and facilitator (Bennett et al., 2019).

The term of office of Boris Johnson, and the efforts of his government to respond to the COVID-19 pandemic, prompted the Kruger (2020) report, which was an effort to build on the momentum generated by the enthusiasm for volunteering in the early stages of the pandemic. It asserted the importance of the 'ties that bind people and community together' in rebuilding the social fabric, calling with a grand rhetorical flourish for a 'new social covenant'. Precise recommendations and any prospective scale of investment were difficult to discern. The thrust of the argument was that there was 'an enormous capacity for action: every neighbourhood has latent reserves of manpower, expertise, compassion and wisdom that can be deployed to improve local life for everyone'. The assumption, plainly, was that everyone could step up and do more – a view which makes rather large assumptions about the public's willingness and capacity to engage, and about the provision of opportunities for them to do so. Kruger did acknowledge that the role of voluntary action was to complement the public provision of services with a 'more spontaneous, adaptive resource' (2020: 26); not a particularly contentious statement in itself but again one which makes assumptions about from whom, and where, this 'resource' might be found. (The government's response to Kruger's report did in fact acknowledge some of the barriers – caring commitments, working hours – that constrained volunteering; DCMS, 2022).

Recent policy initiatives from government in relation to volunteering include ongoing funding for NCS and other initiatives for young people. The policy conversation about voluntary action has instead been picked up by private initiatives, sometimes with government endorsement, which are nevertheless formally independent of it. One illustration here is the Vision for Volunteering (n.d.) campaign, which (with a grant from the Department for Culture, Media and Sport) brought together many key volunteer sector stakeholders in networks designed to reimagine what volunteering would look like over the next decade; others include the youth-volunteering campaigns Step up to Serve and #iwill, as well as the Helpforce initiative to support the NHS and the Big Help Out which took place on the weekend of the 2023 Coronation.

Shachar et al. (2019) draw attention to the growing role of external stakeholders on government policies in the sphere of volunteering, notably corporate actors who are not external to discussions about volunteering policy but integral to it. This is visible in corporate funding of pro-voluntarist think-tanks and high-profile national volunteering initiatives, such as some of those mentioned, encouraging public volunteering through funding and creating coalitions with non-governmental organisations. The hybrid settings in which volunteering takes place are shaped by the confluence of state, voluntary sector and market actors (Shachar et al., 2019: 251–2).

Outside government, therefore, we have a range of elite actors instructing citizens in their responsibilities. The eulogies to volunteering keep coming, even if the cavalry – the volunteers – are not arriving in the desired numbers. A recent example is former Conservative leader William Hague's (2021) argument that for the UK to survive it needs a new identity. What would this look like? According to Hague, several core issues form natural building blocks of national identity – one being 'active citizenship: a National Volunteer Reserve, a biosecurity citizens' army, an NHS reserve, a civilian conservation corps, based on mixing all communities' (see also Valentin and Hawksbee,

2023). But the aspiration so far is well short of the achievement and no political party is yet proposing an expansion of programmes of active citizenship on this scale. In similar vein, during 2023 the Coronation speech by Charles III referenced the idea of 'service', and the nationwide Big Help Out took place on the weekend of the Coronation, which aimed at bringing people together for – initially – a one-off voluntary effort which would then, it was hoped, lead to more sustained involvement. Early survey results for late 2023 do not suggest that this initiative has yet had a discernible impact (see Chapter 2).

Specific policy initiatives

In this section I draw together some key themes of volunteering-related policy initiatives, from which more general lessons can be drawn. These relate to the setting of targets, the changing focus of policies to provide volunteering opportunities for young people, efforts to encourage and extend generalised norms of prosocial behaviour and efforts to mobilise volunteers in support of wider policy initiatives.

Normative aspirations and targets

To what extent have governments set specific goals and targets for volunteering? Since an increase in volunteering requires more individuals to engage in it – a decision dependent on individual circumstances, resources and life stages – it might be imagined that governments would be wary of making specific commitments. On the other hand, since volunteering has become politicised, governments are tempted to claim credit for positive change.

Targets were not a feature of government policy on volunteering prior to 1997 but became a distinctive element of policy during Labour's period of office. The government soon spoke of attracting one million more volunteers and began to set up programmes on a large scale. Performance regimes for both central and local government included public service agreements around volunteering; for local authorities, the rate of volunteering formed part of a wide-ranging basket of performance measures. Given that so much of community-level voluntary activity is explicable in terms of the characteristics of people who live in different places (see Chapter 5), there seems to be little that local government agencies can do that would guarantee an increase in participation. Labour's targetry was criticised: the rationale for the targets was not obvious; there was (initially anyway) no concern about historically under-represented groups, though that omission was subsequently rectified; and an emphasis on 'dragnet' initiatives to achieve numerical targets was arguably at the expense of the quality of the volunteering experience (Nash, 2002: vi, 1–16).

Though elected on a pro-voluntarist manifesto, the Coalition government was somewhat agnostic about what volunteering meant, and its early decision to cancel the Citizenship Survey (on cost grounds) suggested indifference to measurement. Policy also came to be framed in relation to a broader concept of *social action* rather than just volunteering (see the Introduction and Chapter 1). A 2011 White Paper on giving and volunteering contained no normative or aspirational targets. It simply welcomed any kind of prosocial behaviour ('it doesn't matter how people give ... or what they give'). Such developments raised the question of how the government would know whether their policies had had any effect; within two years a revised survey was launched to enable measurement, and shortly thereafter the government was celebrating an apparent upturn in volunteering (see the Introduction).

Targets – or target groups of people and targeted types of activities – were not entirely absent from post-2010 discussions, however. To support the promotion of social action by young people, the government provided initial pump-priming support to the #iwill campaign, which had the ambition of doubling the numbers of people involved in what they termed 'meaningful' social action by 2020, so that the 'majority of young people' would be engaged. By 2015 a less ambitious target of a 50 per cent increase was indicated, and its more recent statements simply indicate a desire to make youth social action a norm (#iwill, 2019: 5). However, these ambitious targets have not been achieved, nor has the goal of closing gaps between disadvantaged young people and their peers (Simpson, 2020). If not spelling out targets for aggregate levels of participation, the Coalition government did emphasise the normative desirability of raising it – or at least of prioritising certain kinds of action. Examples would be Prime Minister Cameron's belief that everyone should be part of a neighbourhood group and support for the expansion of opportunities to engage in uniformed youth groups, particularly in disadvantaged areas (though the latter is not a narrowly Conservative policy). Perhaps a more important point to make about normative goals is the emphasis given to particular types of voluntary activity, and here the menu of opportunities presented to young people is particularly worth examining.

Cultivating and conserving the spirit of service 223

Round up the usual suspects?

There is broad agreement across party lines about a desire to engage young people in voluntary action at an early stage of their lives. Policy in this field has been motivated by a desire to respond to signs of social or economic dislocation, such as disorder among teenagers in the 1960s or concerns for youth unemployment in the 1980s. Aside from the immediate issue of offering opportunities for constructive engagement, the belief is that providing positive experiences at formative stages of young people's lives can inculcate practices which are then sustained. Policies have often been implemented in a negative way which has the potential to alienate young people through combinations of social discipline, compulsory service and supplementary instruction in their civic duties (Deakin, 1999; see the Introduction).

A more inclusive approach would arguably be to ensure that school curricula include some form of citizenship education for all; recommendations from the Crick Commission on Citizenship (Crick, 1998) were implemented in the national curriculum from 2001. Consistent with an emphasis on civil renewal in Labour's policies, the intention was to restore a sense of common citizenship and create common ground between groups from different religious and ethnic backgrounds. Crick's vision was a move away from *individualised* citizens to *justice-oriented* citizens; in relation to the concerns of this book, the former group would step in to volunteer in times of crisis whereas the latter would go well beyond this to challenge and change established systems and structures. Some 20 years on, commentators suggest that citizenship education has been insufficiently embedded into the core curriculum, that schools have honoured it more in the breach than the observance, and that a key challenge with school-based voluntary activity is the extent to which it depends on the status (public or private), resources and priorities of individual schools (Chapter 8). More seriously and fundamentally, recent assessments suggest a decline in and a narrowing of the focus of citizenship education. Weinberg and Flinders (2018) and Dean (2016) criticise pedagogy which, through the medium of character education, sidesteps collective and active citizenship focused on social change, offering instead a narrower focus on individual characteristics such as 'grit' and resilience.

Labour had also established the volunteering charity *v* (later vInspired, which folded in 2018) with significant government funding to deliver 'a step change in the diversity of young people who volunteer, in the quality and impact of their voluntary work, and in their numbers'

(Russell, 2005: 107). To do this, *v* sought to reach out to relatively under-represented groups, to engage young people actively in the design of initiatives and to deliver volunteering opportunities in new ways (including online activity such as e-mentoring).

Significant funding was subsequently provided by the Coalition government for the NCS scheme. This is a summer programme of activities aimed at the personal and social development of young people; it isn't solely about volunteering but an element of it has a focus on social action. The intention is to encourage young people to increase involvement in such action and enable them to mix with people from different backgrounds. NCS has been criticised for its high cost (Committee of Public Accounts, 2017), with some £1.5 billion being committed up to 2021. This largesse has been contrasted, unfavourably, with the effects on youth services of very considerable reductions in local government funding since 2010 (De St Croix, 2017; Davies, 2017). Evaluations have, however, emphasised the social returns on this investment of public money; such returns can, it seems, justify expenditures of hundreds of millions of pounds on youth volunteering (in sharp contrast to earlier periods of Conservative policy making which took no account of the social costs of economic policies, such as downsizing the coal and steel industries in the 1980s). Among the returns evidenced in favour of the scheme are its potential to foster intergroup cohesion among adolescents and a suggestion that participation increases the likelihood of voting. Evaluations suggest that the benefits have been greater for young people from more disadvantaged and more segregated communities, with some small impact on engagement with politics (Chapter 10; Laurence, 2020; Jump Projects and Mime Consulting, 2020).

The content of NCS has been compared, unfavourably, with the ideals of the Crick Commission on Citizenship. Here, it has been suggested that whereas the policy community views citizenship education as a school-based and collective endeavour that requires significant investment, the government sees citizenship education as an individualist project, focusing on the development of individual character and on instructing future citizens in their responsibilities (Weinberg, 2021). Similar points have been made about policies to support uniformed groups (Brown, 2018) and the provision of start-up funds to the Step up to Serve and #iwill projects. Post-2010 austerity left statutory bodies with almost no choice but to cut services for young people but, as these programmes demonstrate, public money is available as long as the initiatives so funded conform to a particular vision of volunteering. The government maintain that they continue to prioritise youth social action, although the responsible government department has a very broad brief, now encompassing culture, arts, media, sport, tourism and civil society. The pre-2024 government's 'national youth guarantee' embodied a commitment to give young people access to activities, trips away from home and volunteering opportunities (Gov.uk, 2022). Much of that was earmarked for NCS and further funding of #iwill and uniformed groups; how policy in this field will evolve under the new government remains to be seen.

Labour market policy

The evidence base for connections between volunteering and whether or not individuals obtain employment suggests that individuals generally *believe* that they have gained relevant experience and improved their skills. The evidence for a causal connection between volunteering and securing paid work is debatable (Chapter 8). But for over four decades, beginning with the large-scale programmes for the management of mass unemployment and urban decline in the early 1980s, initiatives have been set up to provide community benefits via the mobilisation of volunteers, offer work experience for disadvantaged young people and/or support the unemployed to carry out unpaid work in their communities.

The details of these schemes are covered by others (see Chapter 8; Kamerāde and Ellis Paine, 2014). The general policy issues concern the extent to which employability has been a primary goal of policy or whether it has been a subsidiary outcome of a more inclusive approach to promote volunteering for its own sake. The answer partly turns on economic conditions. When faced by mass unemployment, policy has tended to focus more narrowly on reintegrating the unemployed into the workforce; when economic conditions have been more propitious, governments have continued to mention the potential latent benefits of volunteering for employability but as part of a wider set of beneficial outcomes. Thus, towards the end of Labour's period in government, the financial crisis and the onset of recession prompted renewed investment in programmes that had the specific aim of using volunteering to enhance employability, for example by finding volunteering opportunities which would match the interests and skills of those who had been unemployed for some time.

The use of volunteering to promote employability means that policy will be addressed to the needs of people in receipt of benefits, raising the question of compulsion: at what point is engagement in unpaid work made a condition of receipt of benefits and what degree of coercion is involved? That became a reality in April 2014 when the government's Help to Work programme included compulsory six-month unpaid work placements called 'mandatory work activity' (MWA), including placements with voluntary organisations, for those who had been unemployed for more than two years. MWA was accompanied with benefit sanctions for non-compliance. A trial version of the scheme had shown no demonstrable beneficial outcomes, nor had individuals on the 'community work' strand of the programme been more likely to obtain work than those in other strands (Portes, 2013). The MWA initiative was strenuously opposed, including by leading voluntary sector figures, on the grounds that its compulsory nature compromised the freedom of choice inherent in voluntary action (Curley, 2014). In effect individuals were being coerced into reciprocal acts for the benefit of the community, with the glove of reciprocity disguising the iron fist of compulsion. This was work by any other name but, as legal scholars pointed out, those compelled to participate in it lacked employment rights, such as contracts of employment (Paz-Fuchs and Eleveld, 2016). The MWA scheme was eventually withdrawn some 18 months after it was first implemented, but there is a wider debate here about how legal systems recognise contributions of unpaid work to society (O'Brien, 2011; see also Chapter 1).

Nudging in the right direction

In terms of influencing the wider population, the Coalition was interested in behavioural change and the phenomenon of 'nudging' people (providing cues or information that prompt people to change their behaviour) to engage in volunteering and charitable giving (John et al., 2011). There was also much interest in innovative methods for giving money and time; for instance, the *Giving White Paper* (Cabinet Office, 2011) described various relatively small-scale and novel initiatives through which people could give more, or could give in different ways, such as 'slivers of time' through which people might engage in prosocial behaviours even while doing something else (the somewhat underwhelming notion that charity trustees could read committee papers while commuting was provided as one illustration).

Nudging of course implies relatively small-scale movement, and whether modifications to the choice architecture facing individuals can achieve substantial change in levels of engagement in prosocial behaviours has been questioned (Cotterill et al., 2012). The Coalition government supported projects on behavioural change which investigated the ways in which individuals could be prompted by receiving information which influences their own behaviour. An emerging literature considers the impacts of nudging on charitable giving, but there are few equivalent studies of volunteering; self-evidently there are differences between donations of money and the more sustained commitment implied by volunteering. But there are reasons to believe that social information might influence volunteering. First, we have few clear social norms or objective standards for levels of voluntary commitment. Second, peer group influences have been shown to be important – individuals are likely to take note of what they believe are typical levels of volunteering by their friends, parents and siblings. In this situation, field experiments offer an approach through which subsets of the population that are internally homogeneous can be divided randomly into groups, each of which is offered different levels of social information. Two British studies focused on subsets of the population – students and volunteers for a large national organisation concerned with the conservation of historic buildings and the environment – that could reasonably be regarded as homogeneous. In one study, individuals recorded the amount of volunteering they undertook for four weeks. They were then presented with four options: no information about volunteering by other study participants, and then information allowing them to compare the hours they had volunteered against the median hours volunteered by all study members, and by the most active 20 per cent and 10 per cent of participants respectively. They then continued to volunteer, and record their volunteering, for a further four weeks. Some effects were detectable for students but they were disappointingly negative: students volunteering *fewer* hours than the typical participant at the time they received information about volunteering actually *reduced* their level of engagement. This suggested that social information could be demotivating. For the group of generally older volunteers with the national conservation charity, social information had little visible effect on levels of engagement. Possible reasons were that this group was already highly engaged (and therefore had little available time for additional volunteering) and that they were relatively entrenched in their volunteering habits (Moseley et al., 2018). A second study presented different groups of students, selected from five universities, with two emails seeking volunteers. The students were divided into four groups, one being a control with the other three receiving endorsements of volunteering from politicians, celebrities and fellow students. The aim was to test whether these different types of endorsement resulted in differences in behaviour. In both that email and a subsequent reminder, students were given the opportunity to click links about volunteering opportunities and to pursue that by registering for volunteering opportunities, participate in volunteering and attend training or induction sessions for volunteering. The effects were limited, with no evidence that leader endorsements had any effect on becoming involved in volunteering among the target group (John et al., 2019).

These results contrast with those from other studies in which information about social norms has been used to prompt people to engage in behaviours such as registering as an organ donor or leaving a charitable bequest in their will (Farrell and O'Reilly, 2020). With this in mind, efforts were made to promote volunteering during the COVID-19 crisis by making suggestions about small and easily manageable tasks, reminding recipients about the numbers of people already engaged and including positive messages, fostering a sense of belonging, from those already engaged in volunteering (Farrell and O'Reilly, 2020). Clearly, seeking to use social information to influence behaviours that require significant expenditures of time and effort is more challenging than influencing one-off acts such as donations to charity. The field trials reported have not been rolled out more widely but the evidence from national social surveys suggests that the widespread COVID-19 messaging has not resulted in a detectable increase in volunteering rates (Chapters 2 and 12).

Cultivating and conserving the spirit of service

Alcoholic spirits mature, in controlled conditions, over long periods of time. Can that also be said in respect of policy frameworks for the spirit of service? Debates about long-run trends in voluntary action in Britain often look back to the Beveridge report on the subject (1948). Beveridge argued that there was a reserve of willingness to engage in voluntary action once people's immediate needs were met. He anticipated that the post-war welfare reforms would provide economic security to citizens, and that the UK could therefore expect its 'spirit of service' to be sustained. From comparative international research, we know that supportive welfare regimes can certainly play a role in providing the foundations from which individuals can play a part in their communities, whereas punitive or austere welfare policies may be inimical to engagement (Chapter 2). Recent policy in the UK has, for example, limited public support for housing costs, constraining the options available to individuals and forcing them to move. This limits the ability of people to commit to voluntary work, as do stringent tests of availability of work as a condition for claiming benefits.

What about public expenditure in general? The pace of shrinkage of public funding since 2010 has been dramatic, and the substantial cutbacks in local government funding have not brought forth a resurgence of voluntary action (Gibbon and Hilber, 2022). Financial pressures on public services have resulted in transfers of many services to voluntary groups, thereby increasing competition for available volunteers. Recent government policies have also stressed the opportunities available to citizens to take over public services and/or establish services for themselves. These have been presented as offering positive opportunities, though given their financial situation many public authorities have had little option but to hand over services to volunteer groups. Given that the proportion of the population engaged in volunteering has not increased, it seems at least plausible that such initiatives have drawn committed and skilled people away from other voluntary organisations in their communities, though there is little hard evidence on this.

Thus policy does not always seem well aligned with the desire to encourage voluntary action. Governments also need to consider their relationships with the voluntary sector and voluntary organisations. New Labour made strenuous efforts to develop good working relationships with the voluntary sector. Since 2010 these relationships have been by no means always harmonious. Consultative structures, infrastructural support provided by government, and partnership arrangements have been scaled back; criticism of voluntary organisations has regularly been voiced, by politicians and others, on the grounds of their allegedly politicised campaigning activities, their reliance on public funding, the high salaries paid to senior staff and the degree of political correctness in what voluntary organisations do. The legitimate activities of voluntary organisations have come under increased scrutiny and criticism. So, for all the supportive rhetoric since 2010, government support for voluntary action has not been unequivocal (Tibballs and Slocock, 2023: 15–20). In early 2024, Keir Starmer, the leader of the Labour Party, gave a high-profile speech praising the innumerable contributions of voluntary organisations, and indicating the ways in which – if elected – his government would seek more collaborative working relationships with the voluntary sector in delivering on their social and economic objectives. His speech was warmly welcomed by voluntary sector leaders as an antidote to the adversarial tactics evident from recent Conservative administrations. However, its focus was on the organisational base of the voluntary sector, with few direct references to volunteering by individuals or to how volunteering might be supported through public policy (Labour Party, 2024).

What would a different approach to policy look like? First, it is hard to deny that economic stability and individual financial security matter to volunteering, with the lessons of periods of recession as well as of austerity in mind (Chapter 11). This would point towards a more inclusive and broader conception of policy which ensures people have the resources to participate. One could, for example, envisage a public policy package which acknowledges that a number of different forms of work contribute to the functioning and stability of society (unpaid care and household work, informal neighbourliness and unpaid help to voluntary organisations, as well as paid work), and what is needed is a policy which supports them all.

What would it mean to attempt to universalise opportunities to volunteer? It is important to recognise that volunteering doesn't just happen spontaneously but needs an infrastructure to connect potential volunteers with opportunities to become involved. This requires investment in the support architecture for volunteering. There is awareness of this in recent conversations about 'left-behind' neighbourhoods and 'levelling up'. Concerns are expressed about community-level variations in levels of social capital (see Chapter 5) and about the importance of social infrastructure for communities. The latter term refers to spaces (e.g. community centres) in which individuals and groups can come together to pursue voluntary action and organisations concerned with the promotion of voluntarism (such as councils for voluntary service). There is widespread acknowledgement of the need to invest in such forms of support, so that volunteers can be mobilised in all communities. However, the recent general election saw almost no specific policy references to the provision of resources of this kind for the voluntary sector and volunteering, and it remains to be seen whether such support would be a priority in any likely future scenarios for public funding.

13

COVID-19 and voluntary action

Introduction

Since March 2020, the COVID-19 pandemic has had catastrophic health impacts on the UK, and the measures taken to contain it constituted a disruption of unprecedented magnitude to economic activity and social life (British Academy, 2021). It is not surprising that citizens would come forward to support their neighbours in such conditions of national emergency, nor that governments would seek to build on such expressions of support. But the conditions were exceptionally challenging, provoking changes in the character and extent of volunteering. The work of many volunteer-involving organisations was paused due to social distancing measures, while the delivery of their activities was reconfigured; at the same time, there was an apparent upsurge in mutual aid given directly to support individuals (British Academy, 2021). Despite dire, if not apocalyptic, warnings from the voluntary sector as to the imminent collapse of many voluntary organisations, in practice the organisational base of the sector remains largely intact, though it is now known that the immediate financial impacts of the pandemic were indeed exceptional by comparison with any recent period for which we have valid and reliable data (McDonnell et al., 2023; Clifford et al., 2023).

These far-reaching societal disruptions increased the demand for volunteers, but responses by government, individuals and institutions constrained the supply of them. Government-mandated requirements for social distancing restricted the routine activities of organisations (which were constrained to varying degrees depending on the type of activities undertaken and their settings), while individuals took various precautions to minimise infection risks. Aside from managing health risks, individuals may have reduced their commitments to volunteering because they perceived it to have limited social returns (e.g. the social benefits of interacting with their fellow volunteers were likely to be reduced in proportion to the numbers prepared to engage in person) and because the transition to online methods of volunteering reduced the attractiveness of volunteering in various domains (e.g. sports, culture, charity). Furthermore, the beginning of the pandemic caused an economic recession prompting unemployment and economic hardship, both of which are known to reduce voluntary engagement (Bundi and Freitag, 2020; Lim and Laurence, 2015). The restrictions not only affected the activities of engaged volunteers but also limited the opportunities for organisations to recruit new volunteers, which is particularly relevant given concerns about the increasingly sporadic and episodic patterns of volunteering (Hustinx et al., 2010).

For all these reasons, there was a conjunction of heightened demand for volunteers coupled with constraints on the availability of personnel and on the character of volunteering. At the same time, being confined to their homes and unable to access workplaces or take part in their usual leisure and social activities, and against the background of a national economic crisis, there is no doubt that many individuals were seeking a sense of purpose and therefore were searching for an outlet for their voluntary impulses. The combined consequences of all these developments for volunteering were likely to be difficult to predict. Moreover, the pandemic was experienced unequally: the extent to which an individual might change their behaviour would therefore differ depending on age, health status, gender, education and the presence of children in the household.

The initial stages of the pandemic were marked by an outpouring of expressions of prosocial intent, with some 750,000 individuals signing up for the NHS England Responder's scheme, mobilised through the GoodSam platform, and a further 76,000 on the corresponding platform in Scotland. While this was a demonstration of the willingness on the part of the British public to offer support, which prompted the then Prime Minister to declare that it showed there was such a thing as society, there was a disjuncture between the enthusiasm for and media celebration of the initiative and what actually happened on the ground. At four years' distance, what were the results? And how has the experience of the pandemic and the volunteering response to it influenced debate about the future of voluntary action? This chapter considers a range of evidence drawn partly from national social surveys that were running before the COVID-19 period as well as surveys administered during the pandemic itself.

Quantitative evidence: what actually happened to levels of volunteering?

The early stages of the pandemic were characterised by an apparently substantial mobilisation of the population, which was eagerly interpreted as evidence of a considerable latent potential to increase volunteering. However, what exactly happened in quantitative terms – how many volunteers were recruited, how many were new to volunteering and to what extent was the mobilisation sustained? And what changes were there in qualitative terms – what was done by those who came forward to volunteer, and was it different in character to existing voluntary activities? Assessing the impact of COVID-19 on volunteering returns us to the themes of the Introduction and Chapters 1–2, which showed how the questions asked in surveys of volunteering influence the answers given, but also points to another theme evident in this book, namely the tendency for stakeholders to invest excessive hopes in voluntary action, mistaking short-term responses for systemic shifts.

Of all the examples in the recent history of voluntary action in Britain – Major's active citizenship, Cameron's Big Society, the 'Gamesmakers' recruited for the 2012 London Olympics and potentially the efforts to boost volunteering as part of the celebrations of the Coronation – the voluntary response to COVID-19 appeared to be the largest and most widespread. Mobilisation was rapid and substantial, whether expressed through the rapid, large-scale signup for the NHS Responders scheme or the spontaneous establishment of local mutual aid groups. But producing an accurate picture of activity was challenging, since many different reports were competing for media attention. Less than two months into the pandemic, the media claimed that rates of volunteering were soaring, based on estimates which were actually substantially *lower* than those generated by routine robust national sources such as the Community Life Survey. Claims were repeated without challenge, such as the widespread statistic that three million people were engaged in mutual aid groups. With only some 4,000 groups of these in total, that implied an average size of over 700 members. Not only does this belie the small scale and local focus of such groups, which are held to be among their key advantages, it is over 10 times the mean number of volunteers reported for the 160,000 charities in England and Wales – a number

234 *Changing contexts*

which itself is heavily influenced by a small number of very large volunteer-involving charities.

How many people volunteered?

Aggregate data from the cross-sectional Community Life Survey indicated a slow but steady decline in volunteering in England for over a decade prior to 2020, a decline which continued, largely uninterrupted, through the COVID-19 years (Chapter 2). Quarterly survey data allow this to be explored in more detail. This survey captures over 2,000 survey responses in each quarter of the year and survey periods do not overlap. For the 2019–20 survey, the fieldwork for the first quarter of 2020 ended on 29 March, a week after the first national lockdown began. Thus the answers to the Community Life Survey for the first quarter of 2020 were for a period directly affected by lockdown restrictions for barely a week. Fieldwork for the second quarter of 2020 began in early April and continued until late June; national lockdown restrictions were therefore in place for the entirety of the fieldwork period. These restrictions would not have affected delivery of the survey (which was a combination of online and paper self-completion questionnaires). Thus the ability of the survey to measure voluntary action was not substantially affected by the pandemic and the measures taken to control it.

Tentatively we might argue that a downward trend for formal volunteering, and the converse for informal volunteering, were both evident from early 2020 and not just from the onset of COVID-19 (Figure 13.1). The downward change for monthly formal volunteering was visible in the first quarter of 2020 and continued through the subsequent five quarters before the level stabilised at around 16 per cent of the population. The first-quarter figures for monthly formal volunteering in 2020 were lower than, but statistically indistinguishable from, those for the second quarter. All the post-March 2020 figures for formal volunteering in 2020–1 were, statistically speaking, significantly lower than those for the corresponding quarter in 2019–20. For informal volunteering the reverse was true. Representing this graphically we see a clear divergence between the rates for formal and informal volunteering from early 2020. Lockdown restrictions were not in force at this point but one possibility is that some behavioural changes were already under way in January–March 2020, responding to growing awareness of the presence of COVID-19, which were picked up by the survey – for example, people taking steps to minimise risk by limiting their activities and therefore

COVID-19 and voluntary action 235

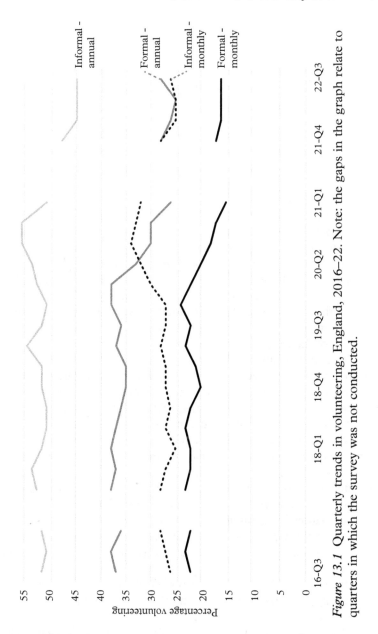

Figure 13.1 Quarterly trends in volunteering, England, 2016–22. Note: the gaps in the graph relate to quarters in which the survey was not conducted.

becoming less willing to turn out to volunteer in organisational settings.

The more recent data are also of interest and in some ways are of more concern. For informal volunteering, the initial boost to engagement – likely to be taking the form of mutual aid groups and informal, neighbourhood-based support – was sustained through to the end of 2020, but a decline was visible thereafter. The reduction in formal volunteering continued; indeed, monthly formal volunteering was at its lowest-ever recorded level in the first quarter of 2021, coinciding with the third national lockdown from January to March. Both kinds of volunteering appear to have settled around this lower level by the end of September 2022.

Were these people who were new to volunteering? Surveys claimed to discern a significant minority of individuals who said that they were volunteering for the first time. Dolan et al. (2021), surveying people who had signed up for the NHS Volunteer Responders Programme, found that four-fifths had previously volunteered. This is a higher estimate than the regular Community Life Surveys, which typically suggest that up to three-fifths of adults have volunteered in some capacity in the previous 12 months. Nevertheless, this still implies that one-fifth of the Responders were new to volunteering.

A further example is the widely publicised survey for British Future for their project Talk/together, which investigated perceptions of social divisions in the UK and the possibilities for overcoming such divisions in the aftermath of COVID-19 (British Future, 2021). Unlike the majority of national surveys, this explicitly made reference to (and therefore presumed some understanding of) the term 'volunteer'. It asked people whether they had 'offered their time as a volunteer' and whether that took the form of 'informal' volunteering (giving the example of 'shopping for a neighbour') or 'formal' volunteering (giving the example of 'volunteering for a local or national organisation'). Unlike national surveys, no additional prompts were offered as to the meaning of these terms, and the result was a relatively low estimate of volunteering (some 23 per cent of the population, compared to a typical figure for volunteering from the Community Life Survey in the order of 40–45 per cent; see Chapter 2). Of these, 9 per cent said they were volunteering for the first time.

Is this robust evidence of a desire for further involvement? The British Future (2021) survey asked further questions of the 9 per cent of first-time volunteers about whether they would be 'interested' in subsequent volunteering, to which 85 per cent replied in the affirmative. The survey results were subsequently cited as strong evidence of a latent desire to volunteer by a government minister (DCMS, 2021) and leaders of prominent volunteer-involving organisations (Third Sector, 2023) and were widely publicised in the media.

How much faith can we place in these results? It is not always recognised that the proportion of people who have *never* engaged in volunteering throughout their lives is actually small, and people may not accurately recall events that may have taken place many years previously (Chapter 6). Therefore, many of those represented as being 'new' to volunteering may, in the past, have had experience of it. It is also not surprising to find a strong expression of interest in future volunteering from a survey while significant lockdown restrictions were still in place and when the public mood was one in which people were likely to be predisposed to envisage a positive contribution they might make. But it is questionable whether this could reliably be taken as latent demand, based as it is on under 200 responses from people who would have been nudged towards a socially desirable response. If those figures had been accurate, that would have meant some four million additional volunteers – a figure of unprecedented magnitude, greater than any year-on-year change reported in volunteering in the UK. It is one which – as we now see from Figure 13.1 – did not come to pass (or at least has not done so yet; the survey report did refer to volunteering at some point 'in the future').

What was the effect on volunteering for organisations? The best data we have for this are from returns to the Charity Commission for England and Wales. There is always something of a time lag in obtaining some of these returns (charities have 10 months after the end of their financial year to submit returns and then there is a delay before data from the returns are publicly available). However, by July 2023, 44,060 charities with incomes greater than £25,000 had submitted returns for each of the three periods ending in the 12 months to March 2020 and the subsequent two 12-month periods, permitting an initial analysis of trends. In total these charities reported 5.25 million volunteers for 2019–20, 4.8 million for 2020–1 and 5.15 million for 2021–2. The initial decline is therefore approximately 9.2 per cent in the first full year after the onset of COVID-19, but the numbers had recovered to within 2 per cent of the pre-pandemic period by the time returns for 2021–2 were submitted. The figures relate to larger charities (those with incomes of greater than £25,000; if this seems a surprisingly low figure for the size of an organisation, the median income of a charity in England and Wales is around

£20,000).[1] The data therefore account for some two-thirds of larger charities, and their volunteers constitute a majority of volunteers engaged in the activities of English and Welsh charities. If the decline in the numbers reported by charities had been comparable with the reduction in formal volunteering as measured by the Community Life Survey over the same period, we would have expected a drop in numbers approaching 25 per cent and also no sign of a recovery in 2021–2. It is possible that the decline for smaller organisations was greater but since these do not account for many volunteers, that would not explain the whole picture. Other possibilities for the decline in formal volunteering visible in surveys of individuals could be reductions in voluntary activity in organisations that are not registered as charities. For example, we know that around one-third of volunteering takes place in public sector organisations (Low et al., 2007), and strict social distancing restrictions on these (such as schools) would have been applied to ensure that major sites for volunteering, such as education and health institutions, remained open. It is possible, but cannot be determined from these data, that there was a substantial reduction in volunteering in settings not captured by returns to the Charity Commission.

Reports from individual charities may help here, as they provide insights into the various ways in which organisations adapted to COVID-19. It is not inconceivable that the relatively limited decline visible in the Charity Commission data is consistent with the aggregate survey data. One possibility is that survey respondents were describing what they do in different ways. So, for instance, if a charity supporting ex-service personnel had moved all its services out of organisational settings (e.g. clubs of various kinds which brought people together) and instead moved its activities largely into one-to-one support, possibly online or telephone-based, how would volunteers for such an organisation respond to the prompts in the Community Life Survey? Could some of the apparent rise in 'informal' volunteering therefore be explicable because what formerly took place in an organisational context now in practice takes place in homes or online? A small-scale sample study I conducted of 120 charities, each of which reported at least 5,000 volunteers in the years

---

[1] There are extensive debates about what constitutes a 'typical' charity or, for that matter, a small or medium-sized one. The most widely quoted research on the topic converges on charities with incomes between £25,000 and £1.5 million which, in practice, includes approaching three-fifths of all charities.

prior to COVID-19, reveals no obvious patterns. Some reported a substantial decline, for example environmental organisations that were unable to mobilise during the summer of 2020 due to lockdown restrictions; this also applied to entities with substantial numbers of retail branches or visitor attractions. Other charities had moved substantial amounts of their activities online, including several very large national charities supporting elderly or isolated clients. Still others switched to mobilising people to carry out volunteering in their immediate neighbourhoods. The net effect – for this small sample – was that numbers were almost in balance from one year to the next.

So we have an aggregate picture of substantial decline, as measured by surveys of individuals, particularly if emphasis is placed on formal volunteering through organisations, though if the figures for informal and formal volunteering are combined, the net change is less substantial. This raises the question of whether or not the character of volunteering was changing.

The character of volunteering

Did people volunteer in different ways under pandemic conditions? Here I summarise a key study which posed a range of questions tailored to the specific circumstances obtaining in the spring of 2020, before summarising research evidence on patterns of mutual aid – an activity which was claimed to be one of the genuinely distinctive features of the pandemic.

Reports from the field first of all pointed to important differences in the character of voluntary action – some arising from the particular needs for support exposed by COVID-19, some enforced by restrictions on the activities of organisations and individuals. Researchers too were moving their activities online at an unprecedented pace and scale. The COVID-19 Social Study, developed at short notice once the pandemic began in March 2020, conducted monthly online surveys for over two years, each focusing on a particular impact. The study contained a well-stratified sample capable of being weighted so that the pattern of responses corresponded in terms of age, gender, ethnicity, level of education and country of residence to the characteristics of the UK population as a whole. Unlike the usual national surveys of voluntary action which divide their questions into formal and informal volunteering, respondents were presented with a list of 13 possible options, which included donating money, providing pro bono support to businesses (note that private businesses would not usually be regarded as a beneficiary in definitions of voluntary action), offering accommodation or food and providing entertainment. In this regard the survey was not directly comparable with the datasets typically used in the study of volunteering. On the other hand, it picked up distinctive features of the volunteering that *was* taking place in the very early stages of the pandemic (Mak and Fancourt, 2021).

Mak and Fancourt (2021) identified three broad patterns of volunteering using factor analysis. The first was termed 'formal volunteering', which included some specific examples of volunteering in support of NHS services, facilities and/or personnel, such as providing free accommodation. Approximately 12 per cent of the population were involved. The second, 'social action volunteering', encompassed donations of money and pro bono support to businesses or projects (some of this wouldn't normally be regarded as volunteering if in support of a commercial entity), providing entertainment (whether face to face or online) to boost morale and donating money to charities supporting COVID-19. Again, whether these actions would necessarily tick the 'social action' boxes recently introduced in government surveys is debatable. Given the wide range of activities, it is not surprising that they found that some 54 per cent of adults engaged in one or more such actions. Third, 'neighbourhood support' included volunteering with childcare, running errands and/or making meals for friends, relatives or neighbours. This component was closest to the definitions of informal volunteering deployed in household surveys and the proportion involved in it, at 41 per cent, was somewhat below the level that emerges from the Community Life Surveys for engaging in informal volunteering at least annually.[2] The important point about this study, though, is that the questions it deployed, and the responses to them, suggest a blurring of the divide between 'formal' and 'informal' actions, and thereby indicate that analyses ought to combine the two in providing an estimate of volunteering, especially in pandemic conditions when many organisations were off-limits.

Mutual aid

Going beyond a classification of types of actions carried out, the mobilisation of 'mutual aid' was regarded as a key feature of voluntary responses to the pandemic. Mutual aid is generally taken to refer to self-organising groups which bring people together to provide mutual

---

[2] Thanks to Karen Mak of the COVID-19 Social Study for providing these percentages.

support that enables them to address a shared health and social issue. As a practice, it eschews the hierarchies of charitable support and instead stresses equality in social interactions. It is widely acknowledged that these groups responded at speed, providing emergency support to those shielding or isolating across the UK. A widely quoted figure referred to some 4,000 organisations which involved three million people, although this implies a group size of 700 on average, and some studies found that that was the upper limit of the size distribution (Benton and Power, 2021). Mutual aid groups typically operated by offering support to those who they felt needed help among that segment of the population who were self-isolating or shielding, rather than relying on strict criteria to allocate resources.

These groups came about in diverse ways – some based on long-established community organisations, others emerging from WhatsApp exchanges, developing into lists of potential volunteers from residents of a small number of streets. The groups are generally thought of as having had a focus on immediate practical issues such as delivering food or prescriptions to those in need, or simply offering neighbourly support. Some concentrated on a single activity, for example providing a regular outdoor venue for meals or ensuring that basic everyday tasks such as shopping were taken care of; others, in some cases organised from community centres, provided a large range of services and activities.[3] As the pandemic continued, activities were developed that sought to combat social isolation, for instance through online social activities and telephone support. Subsequently, the scope became broader, to encompass a wide range of impacts of the pandemic in fields such as employment, mental health and homelessness (Mao et al., 2021: 1474).

An important theme in mutualist responses was place: the sense that groups were responding to local issues and providing support at the local scale. This motivated volunteers and generated trust (Alakeson and Brett, 2020: 19). But it also depended on the existing social infrastructure in communities. Studies interpreted that infrastructure widely, to encompass not just buildings or established organisations but also good working relationships between statutory and non-statutory bodies and also histories of community organising. There were also strong connections between the density of mutual aid

---

[3] For example, see descriptions of five groups exemplifying different levels of activity and approaches at: www.sussex.ac.uk/research/projects/groups-and-covid/community-support-and-mutual-aid/stories-mutual-aid-covid-solidarity.

groups and existing measures of socioeconomic advantage. Thus, to a degree, mutual aid may have built on and reinforced existing sociospatial divides (Mao et al., 2021; see also Tiratelli and Kaye, 2020). There was some duplication of effort – some groups were 'apparently surprised to discover a complexity of voluntary and charitable work already going on' (Tiratelli and Kaye, 2020: 13). It is hard to know what the overall impact was: studies suggest that some groups were dormant within months of the onset of the pandemic, once initial restrictions were lifted, and it's not known how many are still in existence.

The characteristics of individual volunteers: who were they and how did the behaviour of individuals change?

Some surveys have asked individuals whether they previously engaged in volunteering and, if so, whether they reduced or increased the amount of volunteering they did after the pandemic began. Mak and Fancourt (2021), studying volunteers of all ages (18+), found that 23 per cent decreased volunteering during the pandemic compared to their prior involvement, while 12 per cent increased their engagement and the rest reported about the same amount. Since this group had not been surveyed previously, this depends on subsequent recall, but other surveys have tracked individuals over time. In England, the Community Life Survey included a 'recontact' module, in which 2,812 individuals who had responded to the survey in 2018–19 and 2019–20 were traced and resurveyed in July 2020. The most interesting features concern changes at the individual level. For formal volunteering, three-fifths of respondents in July 2020 had the same formal volunteering status as when previously surveyed. This left 38 per cent who had done either more or less formal volunteering since the pandemic began. Of these, 23 per cent had done less formal volunteering compared to previous involvement while 15 per cent had increased their formal volunteering, including 9 per cent who had started volunteering during this period. Those who were most likely to have lapsed or paused formal volunteering were more likely to be women than men, young adults (16–24) and those with a limiting long-term illness or disability. Among those volunteering for the first time, those from non-white minority ethnic groups were more likely to do so than those characterising themselves as white. The survey found that two-fifths of respondents had done more informal volunteering – either by increasing their commitment to it or by doing so for the first time – compared to 22 per cent who had ceased to engage or were spending less time on this activity. The result was a net increase in the rate of informal volunteering, consistent with media and other reports. For both forms of volunteering, when the types of activity undertaken were considered, there were self-evidently reductions in activities that involved either going into other people's houses or working in groups; this would be an expected consequence of lockdown restrictions.[4]

Surveys such as the ELSA and the UKHLS also shed light on the behaviour of individuals. A study based on ELSA data compared pre-COVID-19 reports of volunteering by panel members with reports from after the pandemic began and found that 61 per cent of older volunteers were more likely to have decreased (18 per cent) or stopped (43 per cent) volunteering; fewer than one-tenth increased their involvement. Older workers were less likely to *stop* volunteering than non-working people, while being wealthier was associated with decreasing volunteer engagement. Older people having functional difficulties and those reporting COVID-19 symptoms were less likely to increase volunteer activities (Chatzi et al., 2020). A further study conducted on people aged over 70 years found that 17 per cent of older people continued with formal volunteering after the COVID-19 outbreak, 9 per cent stopped their engagement in voluntary work and 6 per cent started volunteering (Addario et al., 2022).

Dederichs's (2022) work using the UKHLS shows the extent to which individuals changed their behaviour from 2020 onwards. The narrow framing of this survey's questions on volunteering means that the proportion who volunteer is low by comparison with other studies. Dederichs shows that volunteer rates actually dropped by at least a third in the United Kingdom during the first lockdown in 2020, that is, from 14 per cent to 9 per cent. Until March 2021, when restrictions started to ease, the volunteer rate had declined even further (down to 8 per cent). As far as quitting volunteering is concerned, he shows that for the years prior to the pandemic, approximately two-fifths reporting volunteering at one wave of the survey did not do so (i.e. they quit volunteering) at the next wave. However, in 2020 the proportion who quit volunteering rose to two-thirds (representing an increase of over 50 per cent in the probability of quitting volunteering). At the same time, there was a substantial reduction in the proportion of people who had not volunteered at one wave of the survey but did so in the

---

[4] All figures drawn from the *Community Life Covid-19 Re-contact survey main report*: www.gov.uk/government/statistics/community-life-covid-19-re-contact-survey-2020-main-report.

next one. In 2019, 7 per cent of previous non-volunteers began to volunteer; in 2020 that figure was down to 5 per cent (a reduction of 29 per cent), while by 2021 it was only 3 per cent (a reduction of 57 per cent on the equivalent figure for 2019). Therefore, Dederichs argues that volunteering declined overall in the COVID-19 period because of a combination of more of the existing volunteers ceasing to do so while fewer individuals commenced volunteering for the first time. This is consistent with other evidence that the pandemic led to a significant reduction in volunteering over time, that prior volunteering experience was clearly associated with the likelihood of volunteering during COVID-19, and that there was little evidence of mobilisation of many people who were new to volunteering.

Socioeconomic background of volunteers

Conservative MP Danny Kruger celebrated the contribution of 'ordinary people stepping forward in substantial numbers' during the pandemic (Kruger, 2020), but in practice published research suggests that the socioeconomic background of COVID-19 volunteers shows various similarities with the volunteering population in general. Those volunteering during COVID-19 were more likely than non-volunteers to be female, live in a household with children, reside in rural or remote areas, possess higher educational qualifications and be part of households whose incomes were above average. There was some evidence that people with poorer physical and mental health were actually *more* likely to engage (a finding which contrasts with much previous work). The authors suggest that several of the activities included as prompts in their survey questions were capable of being conducted from home, which would have facilitated the participation of such groups (Mak and Fancourt, 2021).

If mutual aid was a new form of social action, did it involve people who were new to volunteering? One survey found that participants in mutual aid groups were middle class (with three-quarters being in managerial, administrative and professional occupations), highly educated (three-fifths had at least an undergraduate degree), female (84 per cent) and middle-aged (mean age 48 years) (O'Dwyer, 2020). On the face of it, this profile looks rather similar to the traditional population of volunteers. One reason for this is the government's furlough scheme, which meant that many relatively healthy people of working age were no longer spending time commuting to their workplaces, and therefore had the scope to become more directly engaged in the local community. Tiratelli and Kaye (2020) argue that this was the reason behind the emergence of entirely new mutual aid groups, as opposed to those based upon existing organisations.

Conclusions

Despite the initial upsurge in willingness to volunteer, we know now that no significant upward shift in volunteering has occurred to date. There was initially a switch in the balance between formal and informal volunteering, and some novel forms of voluntary action attained a very high profile, but those changes do not seem to have been sustained. Furthermore, the pandemic had little effect on the demographics of the volunteer population. The socio-demographic characteristics that were strongly associated with volunteering prior to the pandemic are also strongly associated with those volunteering in response to COVID-19. The subsequent trends in volunteering indicate an ongoing downward trend, albeit one which has levelled off, not levelled up.

It is important to emphasise these long-term trends, because an emphasis on what was novel during COVID-19, without paying attention to existing patterns of voluntary action, overstates the extent to which the voluntary spirit can easily be mobilised among groups or in communities in which it is less visibly evident. Put another way, if our analytical lens is trained solely on the immediate COVID-19 response, it provides a skewed picture.

The immediate responses to the pandemic from policymakers and stakeholders ranged from top-down centralised initiatives to a philosophy of creating the conditions in which local groups could act with relative freedom. Thus, national recruitment platforms were established quickly, but across the UK such initiatives soon encountered the problem of finding roles for all those who stepped forward. Some limited government funds were made available to support voluntary organisations – rather than simply bailing out entities that had lost income under COVID-19, the aim was to get money out quickly to organisations capable of responding to urgent pandemic-related needs. Mobilising volunteers was one – but only one – element of this process. Support was made available to the voluntary sector through the Voluntary and Community Sector Emergencies Partnership, which played a significant role in mobilising and coordinating national and local organisations in the response to pandemic exigencies. At a more local scale, various efforts were made through the local infrastructure bodies for the sector. Guidance was given to help sustain the growth of mutual aid organisations, but in practice these were left, by definition, to their own devices.

Within this there were differences in the policy context across the jurisdictions. In England, voluntary action tended to be characterised as a transactional activity that occurred in civil society, requiring little from the state beyond some fairly small-scale policy initiatives. Elsewhere in Scotland and Wales, commentators claim to have discerned a more collaborative approach and one which also pays more attention to inequalities in volunteering, though without much evidence that those approaches make a difference in terms of levels of volunteering (Hardill et al., 2022). Not all of these efforts have been or will be sustained, and it will be difficult to retain the best features of the pandemic response in a context of severe economic stress, enormous pressures on public finances, a cost-of-living crisis and international conflict.

Conclusions: Beveridge and the spirit of service

Influential commentators and politicians have frequently expressed confidence in the strength of voluntary action in the UK, epitomised by William Beveridge's statement that the 'spirit of service is in our people' (Beveridge, 1948: 151). We might interpret the meaning of 'spirit of service' in several ways. These could include: the importance of a spirit of service to national identity; the levels of the spirit of service – in other words, the extent of voluntary action by citizens, and whether that spirit can be internalised as a 'habit' of service; the extent to which we can place faith in the spirit, as something which is of value in healing society's ills (see Chapter 7), and the associated question of who believes in the spirit (and who is asked to believe in it or to receive it); and finally, whether the spirit of service, like its alcoholic equivalent, is something that requires careful distillation and preservation in controlled conditions, with associated ramifications for policy.

Voluntarism, politics and national identity

Beveridge seemed somewhat disappointed by the realisation that 'less than one third' of British adults gave 'any service outside their homes', but he also noted that those who were not engaged 'commonly feel that they should do so', making excuses of lack of time and resources. Research for Beveridge's inquiry, *Voluntary Action*, had concluded that there was a 'reserve of willingness [to volunteer] to be drawn upon if ways and means of dealing with people's more immediate material needs can be devised' (Beveridge, 1948: 151). His wider vision of the post-war welfare state was of the state taking responsibility for core services, which would provide adequate standards of living for all, and leave scope for individual voluntary initiative to supplement those services.

248 *Conclusions: Beveridge and the spirit of service*

Within five years the Nathan Committee concluded that as postwar prosperity had 'provided opportunities of voluntary service to the many which were before only available to the comparatively few', citizens ought to reciprocate: such voluntary action 'should come to be regarded as a normal part of citizenship' (Nathan Committee, 1952: para. 53). Optimistic views continued to be expressed as to the scope for greater voluntary action during the subsequent post-war decades (Chapter 12). A theme in the expression of such views has been the contribution that volunteering might make as part of a project of national renewal. Rhetoric includes nostalgia for an age of heroic (though decidedly non-political) volunteering, the belief that successful societies are judged by the strength of participation and the level of social capital, the need to reverse national decline in the social as well as the economic sphere and the importance of self-reliance and taking control of community affairs (Introduction and Chapter 12). These arguments all contain a sense that the 'spirit of service' is a component of British national identity and indeed that volunteering can play a central role in nation-building. It isn't surprising that major participatory events or national emergencies can evoke strong public support, but a sustained expansion of voluntary effort across the board requires a compelling narrative that doesn't just look backwards; nor can it just be based on sudden crisis, necessity or celebration. Short-lived boosts from such occasions as the 2012 Olympics did not translate into sustained increases, while the outpouring of voluntary effort in the initial stages of COVID-19 has faded (Chapter 13); volunteering rates have resumed their gentle decline (Chapter 2).

Levels of the spirit

To what extent has the spirit of service been absorbed by the public? There is a substantial bedrock of activity: significant proportions of the population engage in voluntary action, and the aggregate level of engagement is fairly stable over time. Whether this societal resource is a renewable one is a more complicated question.

First, whether people are indeed willing to engage depends on whether they have the resources to do so. Socioeconomic and demographic gaps and gradients in participation are large and persistent (Chapter 3). This means that the benefits of volunteering (Chapters 8–10) are not as widely distributed as they might be, and it also constrains the scope for expansion of volunteering. Effort is also concentrated (Chapter 4), with associated risks of heavy reliance on a small subset of the population – the 'civic core' – that carries out most of the volunteering. For those who speak of volunteering as a renewable resource, this dependence must imply the risk of resource exhaustion, in the form of burnout of volunteers, and resource depletion, namely the withdrawal of their contributions.

There are also substantial and persistent community-level variations in participation (Chapter 5). Despite the Wolfenden Committee's (1978: 58) observations about the comparative fertility of the soil for voluntary action in some communities, these are largely a function of variations in the mix of the population in different communities, and therefore they are not easily amenable to change. This is a general obstacle for any government wishing to place greater reliance on voluntary action to help deliver spatially targeted social policies.

However, there is little evidence of complete non-engagement: most people engage in voluntary action to some extent at some point in their lives, even if highly engaged long-term volunteering histories are less typical. Thus, there isn't a clearly identifiable 'periphery' to be contrasted with the 'civic core'. Longitudinal evidence on movements into and out of volunteering over time shows clearly that these trajectories are a function of the ways in which people manage combinations of family, work and caring activities (Chapter 6). For this reason, disengagement is not the result of a sudden absence of the voluntary spirit. When people give accounts of their routes into volunteering, the activities which they carry out and their motivations for engagement, we can see that it is not straightforward to assume that citizens in general can be drawn into greater levels of engagement (Chapter 6). The economic circumstances facing many young people in particular, and those on the margins of the job market in general, seem likely to continue to act as a brake on proposals to increase participation (Chapter 11).

The evidence on stratification in volunteering also raises questions about what we can reasonably expect of public policies predicated on mobilising voluntary action in communities. Decades ago Michael Ignatieff's (1989) response to John Major's policies of 'active citizenship' was that society was 'too riven by inequality to be sewn back together by rhetorical flannel'. Is it not contradictory to anticipate a contribution to social cohesion from a social phenomenon that is so stratified? There have been policy discussions that focus on the inculcation of habits of service – that is, investing in support for young people to have constructive opportunities to engage in volunteering, on the basis that a positive formative experience of volunteering will persuade them to engage in it habitually thereafter. There is evidence that once regular volunteering forms a regular part of someone's life, it is likely to be sustained (Chapter 6), although there is also evidence that economic adversity disrupts habitual patterns of behaviour, with long-term effects (Chapter 11). As a result, efforts to develop habits of service cannot necessarily overcome the challenges of the circumstances in which people (especially young people) make decisions about volunteering. Lambert and Rutherford (2020) place greater emphasis on circumstances than on habits. By this they mean the direct, tangible factors that can inhibit or enable participation, including not just short-term influences (time availability because of working patterns) but also longer-term influences on the resources that enable regular participation. Much evidence suggests that those who volunteer on a regular or committed basis are in relatively secure positions economically and possess high levels of social and cultural capital (Chapters 3 and 6); engendering habits among those with fewer resources will inevitably pose challenges.

Faith in the spirit

There are obvious direct benefits of voluntary action (Chapter 2), in terms of numbers of people involved or time spent engaging in voluntary activities. The latent or indirect benefits are much harder to identify; arguably there is something ineffable and intangible about them, and it sometimes seems as if they are matters of faith.

The latent benefits seem obvious at first sight. Those who volunteer have more resources and are healthier and more civically engaged, so surely it follows that volunteering is partly the cause of their better health, higher levels of engagement and greater success in the job market. And practitioners understandably would like to believe those claims: the court of experience of voluntary organisations tells them that their volunteers do get jobs, think that their health and well-being have improved, and so on. Such direct experiences need to be set against a more nuanced aggregate picture. The research evidence cautions us that the benefits of volunteering for employability and other outcomes are at best small and come with no guarantees (Chapters 8–10). Even so, there are occasional passionate expressions of faith in the spirit. As one example, it is not unusual for strong claims about employability to be made on the basis of reports by individual volunteers who state that they believe volunteering to have enhanced their skills in some way. Such self-reports are a limited basis on which to claim an impact (Chapter 7) to begin with, but it is a considerable extrapolation from here to assert that volunteering has the powers to help upward social mobility (presumably on the basis that it helped some people gain an advantage in the labour market through which they were placed on an upwards trajectory; Hogg and Smith, 2021).

For these reasons, while volunteering has been likened to a drug because of its various latent benefits (Chapter 7), if it were to be regulated and considered for licensing as a prescription drug, it would struggle to gain approval because of the difficulty of estimating its effects. There is considerable uncertainty about the extent and nature of the dose required to produce a given outcome; often it is almost impossible to say with certainty whether different outcomes between those in receipt of vitamin V result from the vitamin itself or other characteristics of the individuals involved.

Yet some people are still asked to believe in the spirit – young people, of course. Among the strategies available to them – which Streeck (2017: 41–6) has characterised as hoping, doping, coping and shopping – volunteering is one of the options that involve hope. If young people absorb and internalise the spirit, they are told, social success will follow (though note the comments in Chapter 8 about the 'fantasy of employability' of volunteering initiatives). Sometimes they are almost *required* to take it – the de facto compulsion of educational curricula for some, community payback orders requiring offenders to carry out unpaid work for others. Despite the lack of clarity about the impacts of volunteering, it is seen as normatively a good thing which easily gains support – hence the all-party consensus on volunteering initiatives for young people, for example, or the steady procession of reports proposing schemes for civic or national service (including in the recent general election campaign), without evidence of where the funding might come from or how their proposals might relate to existing efforts (Chapter 12). There's no obvious downside to an activity which is all about people giving their time unpaid – so why wouldn't it be attractive? But given the likely cost of similar international initiatives, such as the USA's Americorps or the more local City Year, a case would need to be made that rested on broader considerations than the uncertain latent benefits of voluntary service.

Conserving the spirit of service

Is there genuinely a reserve of willingness to volunteer which can be mobilised? When asked directly about our attitudes towards volunteering, we are likely to give a positive response to questions about whether we might engage in it in the future. In more general studies of people's attitudes and priorities, voluntary action comes some way down the list when ranked against other ways of spending time (Chapter 11). We therefore cannot take mobilisation of the public for granted; communities do not come when they are summoned (Clarke, 2014) and so the first point here is the basis on which appeals are made for volunteers. If the public mood is misjudged, it is possible that not only will there be no response but also that future appeals for volunteers will fail to excite potential participants.

Beveridge also argued that the spirit of service 'bloweth where it listeth' (1948: 152), implying that voluntary action cannot easily be channelled in accordance with policy priorities. Consequently, effecting changes in the distribution of the spirit is inherently challenging, which has ramifications for the belief that voluntary action, unevenly distributed as it is (Chapter 5), can be mobilised to help tackle spatially concentrated disadvantage. Communities do not provide the basis for social organisation that they once did (Ware, 2012); appeals for greater, locally focused voluntary action are likely to benefit rich, stable communities, not poorer communities characterised by considerable population turnover. What institutions and organisations exist around which voluntary efforts might be mobilised, and what can be done when they are not available? There is now active debate about this, sparked off by Klinenberg's (2018) study of social infrastructures: how do we enable participation in a context of urban sprawl, gentrification that is squeezing out spaces for participation, and the post-Covid reconfiguration of spatial relationships (notably, working from home and the 'dash for space' to the suburbs and rural areas). Conserving the spirit against the background of such changes requires relatively stable institutions and infrastructures; the negative effects of austerity on engagement (Gibbon and Hilber, 2022) imply that supportive public investment is also necessary.

Finally, the spirit is clearly not reaching all groups in society. If a norm of participation is to be established, all groups need to become more involved, although an increase could be achieved while not reducing gaps between socioeconomic groups. There are few demographic groups or geographical areas where, according to surveys, there is a majority of the population engaged in, for example, formal volunteering. Addressing gaps is also important – if the claims that volunteering provides other benefits to individuals are valid, the case can be made that opportunities should be available to all. What sort of policy framework might be required not only to raise levels of participation but to reduce inequalities in it?

Visions of the spirit: what sort of service and what sort of society?

Recent prominent publications have made the case for increasing levels of voluntary action, such as Kruger's (2020) report on levelling up, the high-profile think-tank Onward's view of the 'good life' (Stanley et al., 2022) and an inquiry into civil society (Law Family Commission, 2023). There is some acknowledgement in these of the constraints on expansion of volunteering. For instance, Stanley et al. (2022, 41) refer to the effects of contemporary employment practices on engagement, and Kruger (2020) accepts that the role of voluntary action cannot be to replace statutory provision but instead is to provide a 'spontaneous, organic and adaptive response' that complements statutory services. The main frame of reference, however, is an acceptance of the broad parameters that have informed policy since 2010, and consequently proposals for significant investment in voluntary action are limited. Nor is there consideration of the wider framework, such as the need for an alternative to poverty and precarity. Volunteering is treated as an unproblematic public good and the focus is then on how best to winkle out hitherto untapped reserves of potential volunteers, connect them to volunteering opportunities and boost the impact of volunteering.

Less attention is given to the nature of that volunteering, but it seems to be a mixture of direct support to individuals and public services (Kruger 2020) or specialist, skilled expertise to improve outcomes of charities (Law Family Commission, 2023). Almost absent are alternative visions of voluntarism – almost no mention of mutual aid, despite its prominence during the pandemic, and certainly no references to the role for voluntary action in activism and campaigning. Instead, Gramsci's 'cult of the volunteer' is visible here – the celebration of heroic and sustained actions by individuals, rather than raising questions about the need for these actions, and about the need for state action in response to public problems. The place of the volunteer is to respond to the superficial manifestations of social problems rather than work to address their causes (Bolton, 2014). Here, as Bolton observes, societies in which basic services are regarded as universal rights do not need them to be mediated by heroic acts of personal sacrifice or feelings of generosity or pity. In short, there is much more to volunteering than delivering services, and this raises important questions.

First, the voids in provision into which volunteers are expected to step are often those created by the substantial shrinkage of the state. What's not happening here is a conversation about where the boundaries *should* be drawn between the role of statutory and voluntary service provision, and therefore what communities *ought* to be expected to provide for themselves. Where in this era of austerity and local government bankruptcy is there a guarantee that essential services, such as libraries, will be available other than through voluntary effort? During that era, the role of volunteers in public services was to maintain them through unpaid labour, thereby maximising private profits (through contributing to keep the tax burden low) and minimising costs. Transfers of these services from public to voluntary agencies has taken place in an entirely ad hoc fashion, without clarity as to where the boundary should lie. Communities, and therefore potential volunteers, need to know where they stand and what they are being asked to do. Studies of public attitudes show clearly that potential volunteers wish to see a clear framework within which they can operate and not be asked to bail out the state (Chapter 11; see also Lindsey and Mohan, 2018).

Second, there are questions about a supportive framework within which individuals can engage. There is a general consensus that voluntary action is desirable and should be expanded. It is perceived as having numerous direct and latent benefits for both individuals and communities. So if voluntary action is a lynchpin to achieve future policy objectives, then first we need to create the economic circumstances to make engagement possible for everyone. People need to accommodate volunteering in contexts in which their livelihoods and lives are complex and challenging (Chapter 6). There are many initiatives in the voluntary sector that seek to do this – through efforts to tailor opportunities to the availability and circumstances of volunteers – but these cannot address questions of the overall supply of volunteers.

Unless individuals have a degree of control over their everyday lives, they are unlikely to engage in activities which cost them time or money. As Stella Creasy (now a Labour MP) put it, 'a time-poor public ... needs to be confident of the difference their contribution will make, but also to be given practical help to participate' (Creasy, 2007). She stressed that it ought not to be 'only those who can dictate their own work hours or pay and conditions who have the freedom to participate'. Written over 16 years ago, this seems an apt description of the current situation facing many people. The orderly careers (Chapters 6 and 11) that supported engagement during the economic boom times of the post-war years are a distant memory and are not coming back; without security through the welfare system, we can expect an erosion of volunteering.

There isn't anything in recent statements from government about how a policy framework might be put in place that addresses such issues. Instead, the emphasis is (as it has been since the Big Society policies from 2010 onwards) on the opportunities available to communities to take control of their own affairs. That won't address the lack of control that individuals experience in their own lives; nor will celebrations of voluntarism or attempts to measure it for the purposes of the national accounts. A more constructive approach to relationships between government and voluntary organisations, as indicated by the Labour Party leader in early 2024 (see Chapter 12) would be helpful here. But what about recognition of and support for voluntary action by individuals? Recognition of individual effort might take a more positive form. Frameworks could be constructed, as Sarah Harper has argued, that recognise and underwrite the range of contributions – paid work, caring, volunteering – that are made by individuals through the course of their lives. Harper proposes to replace the Department for Work and Pensions with a Department for Citizen Contribution (Harper, 2022), which would properly recognise the vital unpaid contributions of carers and volunteers; the ultimate goal would be to implement a Citizen Living Wage, providing national insurance credits to people involved in these activities. Harper suggests that this would embed a link between civic contribution and state support, thereby granting people the opportunity to make a positive choice to volunteer. Some initial thoughts along these lines were first put forward by Will Hutton (1996: 306–212), making recommendations for the greater uses of pension funds to enable individuals to balance careers with other commitments to caring and to community.

More inclusive and supportive arrangements for welfare provision might be part of a policy to promote voluntary action by responding to conditions of precarity, inequality and destitution. By doing so governments would give individuals and households greater control over vital aspects of their lives. Otherwise, talk of opening up opportunities for voluntarism and in the same breath expecting individuals to come forward, as if a hitherto untapped well of volunteers has been discovered, is naïve. An expanded discussion of policy frameworks to address the multidimensional nature of economic insecurity (Cooke, 2023) is relevant here – though it remains to be seen whether these discussions will influence policy formation. Security for individuals and families is not built solely on economic resources but also rests upon personal and community relationships that provide them with support, and upon supporting individuals to maximise the use of their capabilities to contribute to society. Among the foundations for security, Cooke recognises the importance of policy frameworks that enable voluntary action to mobilise the power of family, relationships and social networks, and facilitate the strengthening of communities. It is through the interaction between resources, relationships and capabilities that security confers a sense of control – and a route to dignity, opportunity and hope (Cooke, 2023). Without such thinking, policies which simply rely on maximising the scope for voluntary action without giving individuals and communities the resources to engage in it will reach their limits. Somewhere between the targetry of the New Labour era and the laissez-faire of the post-2010 governments, there is scope to recognise that voluntary action will develop better in a framework where people possess control and security that they currently lack in their daily lives.

Back where we began, the library's activities, and therefore those of the bookbinders, were inevitably disrupted substantially by COVID-19 and the associated restrictions. But the bookbinders returned in late 2021, new volunteers have joined the group and they now have a full roster. So the work, or the unpaid help, or whatever description best suits it, goes on. Individual organisations such as the library will mostly survive and adapt. That's actually true of the wider voluntary sector too. The larger societal question is about what sort of arrangements we want that will best sustain people in a way that enables them to engage in voluntary action, should they choose to do so.

References

Addario, G., Sivathasan, C. and Taylor, I. (2022) *Volunteering and Helping Out in the COVID-19 Outbreak*. London: Centre for Ageing Better, https://ageing-better.org.uk/sites/default/files/2022-03/Volunteering-and-helping-out-in-the-covid-19-outbreak.pdf.

Aiken, M. and Taylor, M. (2019) 'Civic action and volunteering: the changing space for popular engagement in England', *Voluntas*, 30(1): 15–28, https://doi.org/10.1007/s11266-019-00090-y.

Aksoy, O. and Wiertz, D. (2023) 'The impact of religious involvement on trust, volunteering, and perceived cooperativeness: evidence from two British panels', *European Sociological Review*, jcad024, https://doi.org/10.1093/esr/jcad024.

Alakeson, V. and Brett, W. (2020) 'Local heroes: how to sustain community spirit beyond Covid-19', London: Power to Change, www.powertochange.org.uk/blog/local-heroes-sustain-community-spirit-beyond-covid-19/.

Alcock, P. (2010) 'Building the Big Society: a new policy environment for the third sector in England', *Voluntary Sector Review*, 1(3): 379–89, https://doi.org/10.1332/204080510X538365.

Allen, M. (2018) *From Kindness* (video), https://vimeo.com/253931516/fae0cbafb1.

Alma Economics (2021) *Youth Social Action: Rapid Evidence Assessment*. Report prepared for DCMS, https://assets.publishing.service.gov.uk/government/uploads/system/uploads/attachment_data/file/1003521/DCMS_youth_social_action_REA_-_Alma_Economics_final_report__accessible_.pdf.

Andreoni, J. (1989) 'Giving with impure altruism: applications to charity and Ricardian equivalence', *The Journal of Political Economy*, 97(6): 1447–58, https://doi.org/10.1086/261662.

Andreoni, J. (1990) 'Impure altruism and donations to public goods: a theory of warm glow giving', *The Economic Journal*, 100: 464–77, https://doi.org/10.2307/2234133.

Baert, S. and Vujić, S. (2016) 'Immigrant volunteering: a way out of labour market discrimination?', *Economics Letters*, 146: 95–8, https://doi.org/10.1016/j.econlet.2016.07.035.

Baines, S. and Hardill, I. (2008) '"At least I can do something": the work of volunteering in a community beset by worklessness', *Social Policy and Society*, 7(3): 307–17, https://doi.org/10.1017/S1474746408004284.

BBC News (2000) 'Blair volunteers for community work', BBC News, 1 March, http://news.bbc.co.uk/1/hi/uk_politics/662692.stm.

BBC News (2004) David Blunkett quoted in 'Volunteer workers up by 1.3 million', BBC News, 10 February, http://news.bbc.co.uk/1/hi/uk/3477505.stm.

BBC News (2008) 'Blunkett urges mass volunteering', BBC News, 27 November, http://news.bbc.co.uk/1/hi/uk_politics/7751832.stm.

BBC News (2011) 'Statistics chief warns against axing Citizenship Survey', BBC News, 8 April, www.bbc.co.uk/news/uk-politics-13015705.

BBC Radio 4 (2011) Francis Maude interview with Eddie Mair: 'and what volunteering do you do?', www.youtube.com/watch?v=Ty3Tlf4Th8U.

Bekkers, R. and Verkaik, D. J. (2015) 'How to estimate what participation in third sector activities does for participants', Deliverable 3.2 of the project: Impact of the Third Sector as Social Innovation (ITSSOIN), European Commission – 7th Framework Programme, Brussels: European Commission, DG Research.

Bekkers, R., de Wit, A., Verkaik, D. and Ali, D. K. (2015) *Welfare Impacts of Participation*. Deliverable 3.3 of the project: 'Impact of the Third Sector as Social Innovation' (ITSSOIN), European Commission – 7th Framework Programme, Brussels: European Commission, DG Research, http://itssoin.eu/site/wp-content/uploads/2015/09/ITSSOIN_D3_3_The-Impact-of-Participation.pdf.

Bellah, R. N., Madsen, R., Sullivan, W. M., Swidler, A. and Tipton, S. M. (1985) *Habits of the Heart: Individualism and Commitment in American Life*. Berkeley: University of California Press.

Bennett, E., Coule, T., Damm, C., Dayson, C., Dean, J. and Macmillan, R. (2019) 'Civil Society Strategy: a policy review', *Voluntary Sector Review*, 10(2): 213–23, https://doi.org/10.1332/204080519X15617330887624.

Bennett, M. R. (2013) *Volunteering and Giving in England: A Multilevel Study of 313 Neighbourhoods*, www.sp2.upenn.edu/wp-content/uploads/2014/07/socialimpactfellows_Bennett.pdf.

Bennett, M. R. (2015) 'Religiosity and formal volunteering in global perspective', in L. Hustinx, J. von Essen, J. Haers and S. Mels (eds) *Religion and Volunteering: Complex, Contested and Ambiguous Relationships*. New York: Springer, pp. 77–120, https://doi.org/10.1007/978-3-319-04585-6_5.

Bennett, M. and Parameshwaran, M. (2013) 'What factors predict volunteering among youths in the UK?', TSRC Briefing Paper 102, Birmingham: Third Sector Research Centre, www.birmingham.ac.uk/documents/college-social-sciences/social-policy/tsrc/working-papers/briefing-paper-102.pdf.

Bennett, M., Bulloch, S. and Mohan, J. (2012) 'Age trends in civic engagement in the UK', Evidence to House of Lords Committee on Public Services and Demographic Change. London: House of Lords.

Benton, E. and Power A. (2021) 'Community responses to the Coronavirus pandemic: how mutual aid can help', *LSE Public Policy Review*, 1(3 – art. 4): 1–9, https://doi.org/10.31389/lseppr.21.

Beveridge, W. (1948) *Voluntary Action: A Report on Methods of Social Advance*. London: Allen and Unwin.

Binder, M. (2015) 'Volunteering and life satisfaction: a closer look at the hypothesis that volunteering more strongly benefits the unhappy', *Applied Economics Letters*, 22(11): 874–85, https://doi.org/10.1080/13504851.2014.985364.

Binder, M. (2021) 'Enhancing democracy: can civic engagement foster political participation?', *Social Science Quarterly*, 102(1): 47–68, https://doi.org/10.1111/ssqu.12882.

Binder, M. and Freytag, A. (2013) 'Volunteering, subjective well-being and public policy', *Journal of Economic Psychology*, 34(1): 97–119, https://doi.org/10.1016/j.joep.2012.11.008.

Birdwell, J., Scott, R. and Reynolds, J. (2020) *Service Nation*. London: DEMOS, http://demosuk.wpengine.com/wp-content/uploads/2015/09/ServiceNation2020.pdf.

Blair, T. (1999) *Speech to National Council for Voluntary Organisations*. Annual Conference, February.

Blond, P. (2010a) *Red Tory: How Left and Right Have Broken Britain and How We Can Fix It*. London: Faber and Faber.

Blond, P. (2010b) Letter on 'Cameron's "big society"', *Guardian*, 25 April, www.theguardian.com/theobserver/2010/apr/25/big-issue-big-society.

Blunkett, D. (2001) Speech to the National Council for Voluntary Organisations, Annual Conference, February.

Blunkett, D. (2008) *Mutual Action, Common Purpose: Empowering the Third Sector*. London: Fabian Society, https://image.guardian.co.uk/sys-files/Society/documents/2008/11/27/Blunkett-fabian.pdf.

Bolton, M. (2014) 'The cult of the volunteer', Curatess.RSSing.com, 12 March, www.newleftproject.org/index.php/site/article_comments/the_cult_of_the_volunteer.

Bolton, V. (2016) *Volunteering and Political Engagement: An Empirical Investigation*. Unpublished PhD thesis, University of Southampton.

Brady, H. E., Verba, S. and Schlozman, K. L. (1995) 'Beyond SES: a resource model of political participation', *The American Political Science Review*, 89(2): 271–94, https://doi.org/10.2307/2082425.

Brenton, M. (1985) *The Voluntary Sector in British Social Services*. Harlow: Longman.

British Academy (2021) *Shaping the COVID Decade: Addressing the Long-Term Society Impacts of COVID-19*. Report. London: British Academy, www.thebritishacademy.ac.uk/documents/3239/Shaping-COVID-decade-addressing-long-term-societal-impacts-COVID-19.pdf.

British Future (2021) *Our Chance to Reconnect*. Final report of the Talk/together project. March. London: British Future, www.britishfuture.org/wp-content/uploads/2021/02/Our-Chance-to-Reconnect.Final7MB.pdf.

Britton, T., Defriend, N., Michonski, K. et al. (2023) *Every One. Every Day 2023*. London: Every One Every Day, www.weareeveryone.org/.

Brodie, E., Hughes, T., Jochum, V. et al. (2011) *Pathways through Participation: What Creates and Sustains Active Citizenship?* London: NCVO, IVR, involve, and Big Lottery.

Brookfield, K., Parry, J. and Bolton, V. (2014) 'Fifty at fifty: long term patterns of participation and volunteering among the 1958 NCDS cohort at age 50', TSRC Working Paper 119, Southampton: Third Sector Research Centre, https://eprints.soton.ac.uk/395277/.

Brookfield, K., Parry, J. and Bolton, V. (2018a) 'Going solo: lifelong non-participation amongst the NCDS cohort', *Leisure Studies*, 37(5): 547–60, https://doi.org/10.1080/02614367.2018.1514527.

Brookfield, K., Parry, J. and Bolton, V. (2018b) 'Getting the measure of prosocial behaviours: a comparison of participation and volunteering data in the national child development study and the linked social participation and identity study', *Nonprofit and Voluntary Sector Quarterly*, 47(5): 1081–101, https://doi.org/10.1177/0899764018786470.

Brown, R. (2018) 'I promise that I will do my best', LRB blog, *London Review of Books*, www.lrb.co.uk/blog/2018/september/i-promise-that-i-will-do-my-best.

Bruno, B. and Fiorillo, D. (2016) 'Voluntary work and wages', *Annals of Public and Cooperative Economics*, 87(2): 175–202, https://doi.org/10.1111/apce.12090.

Bundi, P. and Freitag, M. (2020) 'Economic hardship and social capital in Europe: a comparative analysis of 27 democracies', *European Journal of Political Research*, 59(2): 290–311, https://doi.org/10.1111/1475-6765.12359.

Butrica, B. A., Johnson, R. W. and Zedlewski S. R. (2009) 'Volunteer dynamics of older Americans', *The Journals of Gerontology: Series B*, 64B(5): 644–55, https://doi.org/10.1093/geronb/gbn042.

Cabinet Office (2010) *Giving: Green Paper*. London: HMSO.
Cabinet Office (2011) *Giving: White Paper*. Cm 8084. London: HMSO.
Cabinet Office (2015) *Social action – harnessing the potential: a discussion paper*, www.gov.uk/government/uploads/system/uploads/attachment_data/file/439105/Social_Action_-_Harnessing_the_Potential_updated_June_2015.pdf.
Cabinet Office (2018) *Civil Society Strategy: Building a Future that Works for Everyone*. London: Cabinet Office.
Cameron, D. (2006) 'From state welfare to social welfare', speech to the National Council for Voluntary Organisations, 14 December.
Casiday, R., Kinsman, E., Fisher, C. and Bambra, C. (2008) *Volunteering and Health: What Impact does It Really Have?*. Final report. London: Volunteering England.
Chatzi, G., Di Gessa, G. and Nazroo, J. (2020) 'Changes in older people's experiences of providing care and of volunteering during the COVID-19 pandemic', in *ELSA COVID-19 Substudy*. London: English Longitudinal Study of Ageing (ELSA) Rapid Reports.
Child, P. (2020) 'Blacktown, Mass Observation, and the dynamics of voluntary action in mid-twentieth-century England', *The Historical Journal*, 63(3): 754–76, https://doi.org/10.1017/S0018246X19000268.
Civil Society Futures (2018) *Civil Society in England: Its Current State and Future Opportunity*. Report by the independent inquiry for Civil Society Futures, chaired by J. Unwin, https://civilsocietyfutures.org/wp-content/uploads/sites/6/2018/11/Civil-Society-Futures__Civil-Society-in-England__small-1.pdf.
Clark, T. and Heath, A. (2014) *Hard Times: The Divisive Toll of the Economic Slump*. New Haven, CT: Yale University Press.
Clarke, J. (2014) 'Community', in D. Nonini (ed.) *The Companion to Urban Anthropology*. Oxford: Wiley-Blackwell, pp. 45–64.
Clary, E., Snyder, M. and Stukas, A. (1996) 'Volunteers' motivations: findings from a national survey', *Nonprofit and Voluntary Sector Quarterly*, 25: 485–505, https://doi.org/10.1177/0899764096254006.
Clifford, D. (2012) 'Voluntary sector organisations working at the neighbourhood level in England: patterns by local area deprivation', *Environment and Planning A: Economy and Space*, 44(5): 1148–64, https://doi.org/10.1068/a44446.
Clifford, D. (2018) 'Neighborhood context and enduring differences in the density of charitable organizations: reinforcing dynamics of foundation and dissolution', *American Journal of Sociology*, 123(6): 1535–600, https://doi.org/10.1086/697895.
Clifford, D. (2020) 'Serving as a charitable trustee in England and Wales: trends in volunteering by birth cohort', *Sociology*, 55(2): 319–48, https://doi.org/10.1177/0038038520937596.

Clifford, D. (2023) 'Gender inequalities in unpaid public work: retention, stratification and segmentation in the volunteer leadership of charities in England and Wales', *British Journal of Sociology*, https://onlinelibrary.wiley.com/doi/10.1111/1468-4446.13070.

Clifford, D., Geyne Rajme, F. and Mohan, J. (2013) 'Variations between organisations and localities in government funding of third sector activity: evidence from the National Survey of Third Sector Organisations in England', *Urban Studies*, 50(5): 959–976.

Clifford, D., McDonnell, D. and Mohan, J. (2023) 'Charities' income during the COVID-19 pandemic: administrative evidence for England and Wales', *Journal of Social Policy*, https://doi.org/10.1017/S0047279422001015.

Clifford, D. and Mohan, J. (2016) 'The sources of income of English and Welsh charities: an organisation-level perspective', *Voluntas*, 27(1): 487–508.

Cnaan, R., Handy, F. and Wadsworth, M. (1996) 'Defining who is a volunteer: conceptual and methodological considerations', *Nonprofit and Voluntary Sector Quarterly*, 25: 364–83.

Committee of Public Accounts (2017) *46th Report, 2016–17: National Citizen Service*. House of Commons paper HC – 955, https://publications.parliament.uk/pa/cm201617/cmselect/cmpubacc/955/955.pdf.

Compion, S. and Janoski, T. (2020) 'The good, the bland, and the ugly: volunteering, civic associations, and participation in politics', in T. Janoski, C. de Leon, J. Misra and I. William Martin (eds) *The New Handbook of Political Sociology*. Cambridge: Cambridge University Press, pp. 681–714.

Cooke, G. (2023) *Economic Security: A Foundation for Dignity, Opportunity and Hope in an Age of Uncertainty*. York: Joseph Rowntree Foundation, www.jrf.org.uk/economic-security-a-foundation-for-dignity-opportunity-and-hope-in-an-age-of-uncertainty

Cotterill, S., Moseley, A. and Richardson, L. (2012) 'Can nudging create the Big Society? Experiments in civic behaviour and implications for the voluntary and public sectors', *Voluntary Sector Review*, 3(2): 265–74.

Creasy, S. (2007) *Participation Nation: Reconnecting Citizens to the Public Realm*. London: Involve.

Crick, B. (1998) *Education for Citizenship and the Teaching of Democracy in Schools*. Final report of the Advisory Group on Citizenship, led by B. Crick. London: Association for Citizenship Teaching (ACT).

CSJ (Centre for Social Justice) (2013) *Something's Got to Give: The State of Britain's Voluntary and Community Sector*. London: CSJ.

CSJ (Centre for Social Justice) (2014) *Social Solutions: Enabling Grassroots Charities to Tackle Poverty*. London: CSJ.

Curley, K. (2014) 'Community work placements are offensive – not to mention unworkable', *ThirdSector*, 20 May, www.thirdsector.co.uk/kevin-curley-community-work-placements-offensive-not-mention-unworkable/policy-and-politics/article/1294817.

Damian, E. (2019) 'Formal volunteering in Europe: evidence across nations and time', *Cross-cultural Research*, 53(4): 385–409, https://journals.sagepub.com/doi/10.1177/1069397118802228.

Davies, B. (2017) 'Youth volunteering: the new panacea?', *Youth and Policy*, 30 June, www.youthandpolicy.org/articles/youth-volunteering-the-new-panacea/.

Dawson, C., Baker, P. L. and Dowell, D. (2019) 'Getting into the "giving habit": the dynamics of volunteering in the UK', *Voluntas*, 30(5): 1006–21, https://doi.org/10.1007/s11266-019-00133-4.

Dayson, C., Baker, L. and Rees, J. (2018) *The Value of Small: In-depth Research into the Distinctive Contribution, Value and Experiences of Small and Medium-Sized Charities in England and Wales*. Report. Sheffield and London: Centre for Regional Economic and Social Research and Lloyds Bank Foundation.

DCLG (Department for Communities and Local Government) (2008) *National Indicators for Local Authorities and Local Authority Partnerships: Handbook of Definitions*. London: DCLG, http://webarchive.nationalarchives.gov.uk/20120920031457/www.communities.gov.uk/documents/localgovernment/pdf/735112.pdf.

DCMS (Department for Culture, Media and Sport) (2016) *2016 to 2017 Community Life Survey Questionnaire*. London: DCMS, www.gov.uk/government/publications/2016-to-2017-community-life-survey-questionnaire.

DCMS (Department for Culture, Media and Sport) (2021) 'Voluntary work'. Question for Department for Culture, Media and Sport. London: UK Parliament, https://questions-statements.parliament.uk/written-questions/detail/2021-06-17/17779.

DCMS (Department for Culture, Media and Sport) (2022) 'Government response to Danny Kruger MP's report: *Levelling Up Our Communities: Proposals for a New Social Covenant*', www.gov.uk/government/publications/government-response-to-danny-kruger-mps-report-levelling-up-our-communities-proposals-for-a-new-social-covenant.

De St Croix, T. (2017) 'Time to say goodbye to the National Citizen Service?', *Youth and Policy*, 30 June, www.youthandpolicy.org/articles/time-to-say-goodbye-ncs/.

De Tocqueville, A. (2000 [1835]) *Democracy in America*. H. C. Mansfield and D. Winthrop (trans. and eds). Chicago: University of Chicago Press.

De Wit, A., Qu, H. and Bekkers, R. (2022) 'The health advantage of volunteering is larger for older and less healthy volunteers in Europe:

a mega-analysis', *European Journal of Ageing*, 19: 1189–200, https://doi.org/10.1007/s10433-022-00691-5.

Deakin, N. (1999) 'Charity and philanthropy: towards a new perspective', in D. Campbell (ed.) *Promoting Participation: Law or Politics?* London: Cavendish, pp. 183–92.

Deakin, N. and Davis Smith, J. (2011) 'Labour, charity and voluntary action: the myth of hostility', in M. Hilton and J. McKay (eds) *The Ages of Voluntarism*. Oxford: Oxford University Press, pp. 65–94.

Dean, J. (2013) 'Manufacturing citizens: the dichotomy between policy and practice in youth volunteering in the UK', *Administrative Theory and Praxis*, 35(1): 46–62, https://doi.org/10.2753/ATP1084-1806350104.

Dean, J. (2014a) 'How structural factors promote instrumental motivations within youth volunteering: a qualitative analysis of volunteer brokerage', *Voluntary Sector Review*, 5(2): 231–47, http://doi.org/10.1332/204080514X14013591527611.

Dean, J. (2014b) 'Recruiting young volunteers in an area of selective education: a qualitative case study', *British Journal of Sociology of Education*, 37(4): 643–61, http://doi.org/10.1080/01425692.2014.973016.

Dean, J. (2016) 'Class diversity and youth volunteering in the United Kingdom: applying Bourdieu's habitus and cultural capital', *Nonprofit and Voluntary Sector Quarterly*, 45(1): 95S–113S, http://doi.org/10.1177/0899764015597781.

Dean, J. (2022) 'Informal volunteering, inequality, and illegitimacy', *Nonprofit and Voluntary Sector Quarterly*, 51(3): 527–44, http://doi.org/10.1177/08997640211034580.

Dean, J. and Verrier, D. (2022) 'Restudies, surveys and what counts as volunteering', in J. Dean and E. Hogg (eds) *Researching Voluntary Action: Innovations and Challenges*. Bristol: Policy Press, pp. 160–70.

Dean, M. (2013) 'UK philanthropy needs to up its game', *Guardian*, 15 October, www.theguardian.com/society/2013/oct/15/uk-philanthropy-up-game.

Dederichs, K. (2022) 'Volunteering in the United Kingdom during the COVID-19 pandemic: who started and who quit?', *Nonprofit and Voluntary Sector Quarterly*, https://doi.org/10.1177/08997640221122814.

Defty, A. (2011) 'The Conservatives, social policy and public opinion', in H. Bochel (ed.) *The Conservative Party and Social Policy*. Bristol: Policy Press, pp. 61–76.

Dekker, P. (2014) 'Tocqueville did not write about soccer clubs: participation in voluntary associations and political involvement', in M. Freise and T. Hallmann (eds) *Modernizing Democracy: Associations and Associating in the 21st Century*. New York: Springer, pp. 45–57.

DLUHC (Department for Levelling Up, Housing and Communities) (2022) *Levelling Up the United Kingdom: White Paper.* CP 604. London: HMSO.
Dolan, P., Krekel, C., Shreedhar, G., Lee, H., Marshall, C. and Smith, A. (2021) 'Happy to help: the welfare effects of a nationwide microvolunteering programme', IZA Discussion Paper 14431, http://dx.doi.org/10.2139/ssrn.3865456.
Doodeman, E., De Wit, A. and Mohan, J. (2023) 'Understanding volunteering intentions using topic modelling of a large textual corpus', presentation to ERNOP Conference, Zagreb.
Dowling, E. (2016) 'Valorised but not valued? Affective remuneration, social reproduction and feminist politics beyond the crisis', *British Politics*, 11(4): 452–68, https://doi.org/0.1057/s41293-016-0036-2.
Egerton, M. and Mullan, K. (2008) 'Being a pretty good citizen: an analysis and monetary valuation of formal and informal voluntary work by gender and educational attainment', *British Journal of Sociology*, 59(1): 145–64, https://doi.org/10.1111/j.1468-4446.2007.00186.x.
Eibich, P., Lorenti, A. and Mosca, I. (2022) 'Does retirement affect voluntary work provision? Evidence from Europe and the U.S.', *Labour Economics*, 76, https://doi.org/10.1016/j.labeco.2022.102185.
Eikenberry, A. and Nickel, P. (2016) 'Knowing and governing: the mapping of the nonprofit and voluntary sector as statecraft', *Voluntas*, 27(1): 392–408, https://doi.org/10.1007/s11266-015-9552-8.
Eimhjellen, I. (2023) 'Capital, inequality, and volunteering', *Voluntas*, 34(3): 654–69, https://doi.org/10.1007/s11266-022-00501-7.
Eliasoph, N. (1998) *Avoiding Politics: How Americans Produce Apathy in Everyday Life.* Cambridge: Cambridge University Press.
Eliasoph, N. (2013) *The Politics of Volunteering.* Cambridge: Polity Press.
Elliott, J., Miles, A., Parsons, S. and Savage, M. (2010) 'The design and content of the "Social participation" study: a qualitative sub-study conducted as part of the age 50 (2008) sweep of the National Child Development Study', CLS Working Paper 2010/3. London: Centre for Longitudinal Stuidies.
Ellis Paine, A. (2015) 'Telling tales of volunteering: community insights'. Research findings briefing paper. Leeds, Birmingham and London: Timescapes, TSRC and NCVO.
Ellis Paine, A., McKay, S. and Moro, D. (2013) 'Does volunteering improve employability? Insights from the British Household Panel Survey and beyond', *Voluntary Sector Review*, 4(3): 355–76, https://doi.org/10.1332/204080513X13807974909244.
Ellis Paine, A., Kamerāde, D., Mohan, J. and Davidson, D. (2019) 'Communities as "renewable energy" for healthcare services? A multimethods study into the form, scale and role of voluntary support

for community hospitals in England', *BMJ Open*, 9(10), https://bmjopen.bmj.com/content/9/10/e030243.
Enjolras, B. (2021) 'Explaining the varieties of volunteering in Europe: a capability approach', *Voluntas*, 32: 1187–212, https://doi.org/10.1007/s11266-021-00347-5.
Evans, S. (2020) *Forms of Distinction and Variations in Social Participation from Early Adulthood to Midlife: A Lifecourse Perspective using Longitudinal Data*. PhD thesis, School of Social Sciences, Cardiff University.
Farrell, A. and O'Reilly, F. (2020) 'Nudging to boost volunteer sign-ups during the coronavirus crisis', blog, 9 October, London: Behavioural Insights Team, www.bi.team/blogs/nudging-to-boost-volunteer-sign-ups-during-the-coronavirus-crisis/.
Ferguson, N. (2012) 'Civil and uncivil societies', BBC Reith Lecture, broadcast 10 July, www.bbc.co.uk/programmes/articles/1n02Kr5c1XCGkZbw8wvbv5s/niall-ferguson-civil-and-uncivil-societies.
Ferragina, E. and Arrigoni, A. (2016) 'The rise and fall of social capital: requiem for a theory', *Political Studies Review*, 15(3): 355–67, https://doi.org/10.1177/1478929915623968.
Filges, T., Siren, A., Fridberg, T. and Nielsen, B. C. V. (2020) 'Voluntary work for the physical and mental health of older volunteers', *Campbell Systematic Reviews*, 16(4), https://doi.org/10.1002/cl2.1124.
Fine, B. (2010) *Theories of Social Capital: Researchers Behaving Badly*. London: Pluto Press.
Finnegan, A. (2012) 'Promised and delivered? New Labour's support of volunteering', paper presented at the NCVO/VSSN Annual Voluntary Sector Research Conference, Birmingham.
Fisher, K. (2010) 'An overview of time in volunteering and adult care in the United Kingdom', Technical Paper 2010-02, Oxford: Centre for Time Use Research (CTUR), www.timeuse.org/sites/default/files/public/ctur_technical_paper/1476/CTUR_Technical_Paper_2010-02.pdf.
Forbes, K. F. and Zampelli, E. M. (2013) 'The impacts of religion, political ideology, and social capital on religious and secular giving: evidence from the 2006 Social Capital Community Survey', *Applied Economics*, 45(17): 2481–90, https://doi.org/10.1080/00036846.2012.667555.
Forrest, R. and Kearns, A. (2001) 'Social cohesion, social capital and the neighbourhood', *Urban Studies*, 38(12): 2125–43, https://doi.org/10.1080/00420980120087081.
Fox, S. (2023) 'Social action as the route to the ballot box: can youth volunteering reduce inequalities in turnout?', *European Journal of Political Research*, https://doi.org/10.1111/1475-6765.12586.
Fujiwara, D., Oroyemi, P. and McKinnon, E. (2018) 'Wellbeing and civil society: estimating the value of volunteering using subjective wellbeing data', Working Paper 112, London: Cabinet Office and DWP.

Fung, A. (2003) 'Associations and democracy: between theories, hopes, and realities', *Annual Review of Sociology*, 29: 515–39, https://doi.org/10.1146/annurev.soc.29.010202.100134.
Garlick, H. (2021) 'How to volunteer in 2021 and why it makes us feel so good', *Telegraph*, 10 November, www.telegraph.co.uk/family/life/best-volunteering-ideas-where-how-uk-christmas-festive-2021/.
Gay, P. (1998) 'Getting into work: volunteering for employability', *Voluntary Action*, 1(1): 55–67.
Gershuny, J. and Sullivan, O. (2019) *What We Really Do All Day: Insights from the Centre for Time Use Research*. London: Penguin.
Geyne-Rajme, F. and Smith, P. (2011) 'Modelling "volunteering types" in the UK', Southampton: TSRC Seminar paper, unpublished, www.birmingham.ac.uk/Documents/college-social-sciences/social-policy/tsrc/presentations/modelling-volunteering-types-uk.pdf.
Gibbon, S. and Hilber, C. (2022) 'Charity in the time of austerity: in search of the Big Society', discussion paper CEPDP1874, London: Centre for Economic Performance, https://cep.lse.ac.uk/_NEW/publications/abstract.asp?index=9616.
Glucksmann, M. (2005) 'Shifting boundaries and interconnections: extending the "total social organization of labour"', *The Sociological Review*, 53(2 suppl.): 19–36, https://doi.org/10.1111/j.1467-954X.2005.00570.x.
Goddard, E. (1994) *1992 General Household Survey: Voluntary Work*. Office of Population Censuses and Surveys (OPCS) publication, Series GHS 23A. London: OPCS.
Gov.uk (2010) 'National Citizen Service pilots announced', press release, London: Gov.uk, www.gov.uk/government/news/national-citizen-service-pilots-announced-2.
Gov.uk (2012–) *Community Life Survey*. London: Department for Culture, Media and Sport, www.gov.uk/government/collections/community-life-survey-2.
Gov.uk (2013) 'New official statistics show resurgence in volunteering as millions more give their time to help others', press release, London: Gov.uk, www.gov.uk/government/news/new-official-statistics-show-resurgence-in-volunteering-as-millions-more-give-their-time-to-help-others.
Gov.uk (2022) 'Government outlines ambitious plans to level up activities for young people', press release, London: Gov.uk, www.gov.uk/government/news/government-outlines-ambitious-plans-to-level-up-activities-for-young-people.
Granovetter, M. (1973) 'The strength of weak ties', *American Journal of Sociology*, 78(6): 1360–80.
Green, F., Anders, J., Henderson, M. and Henseke, G. (2020) 'Private benefits? External benefits? Outcomes of private schooling in 21st

century Britain', *Journal of Social Policy*, 49(4): 724–43, https://doi.org/10.1017/S0047279419000710.

Grice, A. (2013) 'Government's flagship work scheme in crisis after Poundland "slavery" case ruling', *Independent*, 12 February, www.independent.co.uk/news/uk/politics/government-s-flagship-work-scheme-in-crisis-after-poundland-slavery-case-ruling-8492346.html.

Hague, W. (2021) 'For the UK to survive, it needs a new identity', *The Times*, 4 May.

Haldane, A. (2014) 'In giving, how much do we receive? The social value of volunteering', speech, Pro Bono Economics lecture to the Society of Business Economists, 12 September, London.

Haldane, A. (2021) 'The power of charity', speech, Pilotlight event on the power of charity, 1 June, London: Pro Bono Economics, www.probonoeconomics.com/Handlers/Download.ashx?IDMF=5206e58c-0267-4117-9c36-2f24b3ceff04.

Halford, S., Leonard, P. and Bruce, K. (2015) 'Geographies of labour in the third sector: making hybrid workforces in place', *Environment and Planning A: Economy and Space*, 47(11): 2355–72, https://doi.org/10.1177/0308518X15599295.

Hall, P. (1999) 'Social capital in Britain', *British Journal of Political Science*, 29(3): 417–61, https://doi.org/10.1017/S0007123499000204.

Hardill, I. and Baines, S. (2011) *Enterprising Care? Unpaid Voluntary Action in the 21st Century*. Bristol: Policy Press.

Hardill, I., Grotz, J. and Crawford, L. (2022) *Mobilising Voluntary Action in the UK: Learning from the Pandemic*. Bristol: Policy Press.

Harflett, N. (2014) *For Ever, for Everyone*. PhD thesis, University of Southampton.

Harflett, N. (2015) '"Bringing them with personal interests": the role of cultural capital in explaining who volunteers', *Voluntary Sector Review*, 6(1): 3–19, https://doi.org/10.1332/204080515X14241616081344.

Harper, S. (2022) 'Establish a Department for Citizen Contribution in place of the DWP', *Prospect*, 8 December, www.prospectmagazine.co.uk/politics/60289/establish-a-department-for-citizen-contribution-in-place-of-the-dwp.

Harris, M. (1996) 'An inner group of willing people: volunteering in a religious context', *Social Policy & Administration*, 30(1): 54–68, https://doi.org/10.1111/j.1467-9515.1996.tb00481.x.

Haski-Leventhal, D., Meijs, L. C. P. M. and Hustinx, L. (2010) 'The third-party model: enhancing volunteering through governments, corporations and educational institutes', *Journal of Social Policy*, 39(1): 139–58, https://doi.org/10.1017/S0047279409990377.

Haski-Leventhal, D., Meijs, L. C. P. M., Lockstone-Binney, L., Holmes, K. and Oppenheimer, M. (2018) 'Measuring volunteerability and the capacity to volunteer among non-volunteers: implications for social policy', *Social Policy & Administration*, 52(5): 1139–67, https://doi.org/10.1111/spol.12342.

Hawksley, C. and Georgeou, N. (2019) 'Gramsci "makes a difference": volunteering, neoliberal "common sense", and the sustainable development goals', *Third Sector Review*, 25(2): 27–56.

Heley, J., Yarker, S. and Jones, L. (2022) 'Volunteering in the bath? The rise of microvolunteering and implications for policy', *Policy Studies*, 43(91): 76–89, https://doi.org/10.1080/01442872.2019.1645324.

Hietanen, H., Aartsen, M., Kiuru, N., Lyyra, T. and Read, S. (2016) 'Social engagement from childhood to middle age and the effect of childhood socio-economic status on middle age social engagement: results from the National Child Development study', *Ageing and Society*, 36(3): 482–507, https://doi.org/10.1017/S0144686X1400124X.

Hill, M. (2011) 'Volunteering and the recession', think piece, February, Norwich: Institute for Volunteering Research.

Hilton, M., Mouhot, J.-F., Crowson, N. and McKay, J. (2012) *A Historical Guide to NGOs in Britain: Charities, Civil Society and the Voluntary Sector since 1945*. Basingstoke: Palgrave.

HM Treasury (2002) *The 2002 Spending Review: Public Service Agreements*. London: HM Treasury.

Hogg, E. (2016) 'Constant, serial and trigger volunteers: volunteering across the lifecourse and into old age', *Voluntary Sector Review*, 7(2): 69–190, https://doi.org/10.1332/204080516X14650415652302.

Hogg, E. and Smith, A. (2021) *Social Mobility: Unleashing the Power of Volunteering*. Cardiff: Royal Voluntary Service.

Holmes, K. (2003) 'Volunteers in the heritage sector: a neglected audience?', *International Journal of Heritage Studies*, 9(4): 341–55, https://doi.org/10.1080/1352725022000155072.

Hooghe, M. (2011) *Contemporary Theoretical Perspectives on the Study of Social Cohesion and Social Capital*. Brussels: KVAB.

Hoskins, B., Leonard, P. and Wilde, R. (2020) 'How effective is youth volunteering as an employment strategy? A mixed methods study of England', *Sociology*, 54(4): 763–81, https://doi.org/10.1177/0038038520914840.

House of Lords (2013) Enquiry into Public Service and Demographic Change, Oral Evidence, Q. 155, www.parliament.uk/documents/lords-committees/Demographicchange/PublicServiceVol2.pdf.

House of Lords (2017) *Stronger Charities for a Stronger Society*. Select Committee on Charities. Report of Session 2016–17, 26 March, HL paper 133, London: House of Lords.

House of Lords (2018) *The Ties That Bind: Citizenship and Civic Engagement in the 21st Century*. Select Committee on Citizenship and Civic

Engagement. Report of Session 2017–19, 18 April, HL paper 118, London: House of Lords.

Hustinx, L. (2001) 'Individualisation and new styles of youth volunteering: an empirical investigation', *Voluntary Action*, 3(2), 47–55, http://hdl.handle.net/1854/LU-1114767.

Hustinx, L. and Lammertyn, F. (2003) 'Collective and reflexive styles of volunteering: a sociological modernization perspective', *Voluntas*, 14(2): 167–87, https://doi.org/10.1023/A:1023948027200.

Hustinx, L. and Meijs, L. C. P. M. (2011) 'Re-embedding volunteering: in search of a new collective ground', *Voluntary Sector Review*, 2(1): 5–21.

Hustinx, L., Cnaan, R. and Handy, F. (2010) 'Navigating theories of volunteering: a hybrid map for a complex phenomenon', *Journal for the Theory of Social Behaviour*, 40(4): 410–34, https://doi.org/10.1111/j.1468-5914.2010.00439.x.

Hutton W. (1996) *The State We're in*. London: Jonathan Cape.

Ignatieff, M. (1989) 'Caring just isn't enough', *New Statesman and Society*, 3 February.

ILO (International Labour Organization) (2011) *Manual on the Measurement of Volunteer Work*. Geneva: ILO.

Ipsos MORI (2014) *National Youth Social Action Survey 2014*. London: Ipsos MORI, www.ipsos.com/sites/default/files/publication/1970-01/sri-ecf-youth-social-action-in-the-uk-2014.pdf.

#iwill (2019) *The Power of Youth Social Action*. #iwill campaign Impact Report, May, London: #iwill, www.iwill.org.uk/wp-content/uploads/2019/05/iwill-impact-report.pdf.

#iwill (nd) 'What is youth social action?', London: #iwill, www.iwill.org.uk/about-us/youth-social-action#what.

Jackson, M. (2009) 'Volunteering "flourishing in recession"', BBC News, 21 April, http://news.bbc.co.uk/1/hi/uk/8008428.stm.

Jemal, J., Larkham, J., King, D. et al. (2022) 'Hands in the air like you just do care; an analysis of the VCSE Sector Barometer', in partnership with Nottingham Trent University VCSE Data and Insights Observatory, Nottingham: Pro Bono Economics and Nottingham Business School.

Jenkinson, C. E., Dickens, D., Jones, K., Thompson-Coon, J., Taylor, R. S., Rogers, M., Bambra, C., Lang, I. and Richards, S. H. (2013) 'Is volunteering a public health intervention? A systematic review and meta-analysis of the health and survival of volunteers', *BMC Public Health*, 13, https://doi.org/10.1186/1471-2458-13-773.

John, P., Cotterill, S., Richardson, L., Moseley, A. et al. (2011) *Nudge, Nudge, Think, Think: Experimenting with Ways to Change Civic Behaviour*. London: Bloomsbury.

John, P., James, O., Moseley, A., Ryan, M., Richardson, L. and Stoker, G. (2019) 'The impact of peer, politician, and celebrity endorsements on volunteering: a field experiment with English students', *Journal of Nonprofit and Public Sector Marketing*, 31(3): 328–46, https://doi.org/10.1080/10495142.2018.1526743.

Jump Projects (2019) *The ABC of BAME: New, Mixed Method Research into Black, Asian and Minority Ethnic Groups and Their Motivations and Barriers to Volunteering*. Report. Manchester and London: State of Life.

Jump Projects and Mime Consulting (2020) *In the Mix with NCS: Does a Summer of Mixing with People from Different Backgrounds Help to Build a more Engaged, Tolerant and Civic-Minded Group of Young People?* London: National Citizen Service Trust, https://wearencs.com/sites/default/files/2020-09/In%20The%20Mix%20with%20NCS-Sub-Group%20Analysis%20Report.pdf.

Kamerāde, D. (2013) 'Volunteering during unemployment: more skills but where is the job?', paper presented at the NCVO/VSSN Voluntary Sector and Volunteering Research Conference, http://blogs.ncvo.org.uk/wp-content/uploads/guest/volunteering_during_unemployment_kamerade.pdf.

Kamerāde, D. and Ellis Paine, A. (2014) 'Volunteering and employability: implications for policy and practice', *Voluntary Sector Review*, 5(2): 259–73, https://doi.org/10.1332/204080514X14013593888736.

Kamerāde, D., Mohan, J. and Sivesind, K.-H. (2015) 'Third sector impacts on human resources and community: a critical review', TSRC Working Paper 134, Seventh Framework Programme (grant agreement 613034), European Union. Brussels: Third Sector Impact, www.birmingham.ac.uk/Documents/college-social-sciences/social-policy/tsrc/working-papers/FP7-IMpact-review-TSRC-working-paperfor-website-20150915.pdf.

Kamerāde, D., Crotty, J. and Ljubownikow, S. (2016) 'Civil liberties and volunteering in six former Soviet Union countries', *Nonprofit and Voluntary Sector Quarterly*, 45(6): 1150–68, https://doi.org/10.1177/0899764016649689.

Kane, D. and Cohen, T. (2023) *Sector Infrastructure Funding Analysis*. London: 360 Giving.

Kanemura, R., McGarvey, A. and Farrow, A. (2023) *Time Well Spent 2023: A National Survey on the Volunteer Experience*. London: NCVO.

Kantar and London Economics (2020) *National Citizen Service 2018 Evaluation: Main Report*. London: Gov.uk.

Kelemen, M., Mangan, A. and Moffat, S. (2017) 'More than a "little act of kindness"? Towards a typology of volunteering as unpaid work', *Sociology*, 51(6): 1239–56, https://doi.org/10.1177/0038038517692512.

Kendall, J. (2009) 'The UK: ingredients in a hyperactive horizontal policy environment', in Kendall, J. (ed.) *Handbook on Third Sector Policy in Europe*. Cheltenham: Edward Elgar, pp. 67–94.

Kenyon, C. (2018) 'Charles Kenyon's country diary: pale, male and proud of our voluntary work', *ThirdSector*, 27 September, www.thirdsector.co.uk/charles-kenyons-country-diary-pale-male-proud-voluntary-work/governance/article/1494261.

Keohane, N., Parker, S. and Ebanks, D. (2011) *Realising Community Wealth: Local Government and the Big Society*. London: The New Local Government Network.

Klinenberg, E. (2018) *Palaces for the People*. New York: Crown.

Koolen-Maas, S. A., Meijs, L. C. P. M., Van Overbeeke, P. S. M. and Brudney, J. L. (2023) 'Rethinking volunteering as a natural resource: a conceptual typology', *Nonprofit and Voluntary Sector Quarterly*, 52(1S): 353S–377S, https://doi.org/10.1177/08997640221127.

Kruger, D. (2020) *Levelling Up Our Communities: Proposals for a New Social Covenant*. London: UK Government, www.dannykruger.org.uk/sites/www.dannykruger.org.uk/files/2020-09/Kruger%202.0%20Levelling%20Up%20Our%20Communities.pdf.

Kumlin, S. and Rothstein, B. (2005) 'Making and breaking social capital: the impact of welfare state institutions', *Comparative Political Studies*, 38(4): 339–65, https://doi.org/10.1177/0010414004273203.

Labour Party (2024) Keir Starmer's speech to Civil Society Summit, https://labour.org.uk/updates/press-releases/keir-starmers-speech-to-civil-society-summit/.

Lam, M. M., Grasse, N. J. and McDougle, L. M. (2022) 'Individual- and community-level factors associated with voluntary participation', *Nonprofit and Voluntary Sector Quarterly*, https://doi.org/10.1177/08997640221138764.

Lambert, P. and Rutherford, A. (2020) 'Occupational inequalities in volunteering participation: using detailed data on jobs to explore the influence of habits and circumstances', *British Journal of Sociology*, 71(4): 625–43, https://doi.org/10.1111/1468-4446.12756.

Lancee, B. and Radl, J. (2014) 'Volunteering over the life course', *Social Forces*, 93(2): 833–62, https://doi.org/10.1093/sf/sou090.

Lattimore, S., Wickenden, C. and Brailsford, S. (2015) 'Blood donors in England and North Wales: demography and patterns of donation', *Transfusion*, 55(1): 91–9, https://doi.org/10.1111/trf.12835.

Laurence, J. (2020) 'Cohesion through participation? Youth engagement, interethnic attitudes, and pathways of positive and negative intergroup contact among adolescents: a quasi-experimental study', *Journal of Ethnic and Migration Studies*, 46(13): 2700–22, https://doi.org/10.1080/1369183X.2019.1700787.

Laurence, J. and Lim, C. (2014) *'The Scars of Others Should Teach Us Caution': The Long-Term Effects of Job 'Displacement' on Civic Participation over the Lifecourse*. Manchester: Cathie Marsh Centre, University of Manchester.

Law Family Commission (2023) *Unleashing the Power of Civil Society*. London: Pro Bono Economics, https://civilsocietycommission.org/publication/unleashing-the-power-of-civil-society/.

Lawless, P., Foden, M., Wilson, I. and Beatty, C. (2010) 'Understanding area-based regeneration: the New Deal for Communities programme in England', *Urban Studies*, 47: 257–75, https://doi.org/10.1177/0042098009348324.

Lawton, R. and Watt, W. (2018) *A Bit Rich? Why Is Volunteering Biased towards Higher Socioeconomic Groups?* London: Jump Projects.

Lawton, R. N., Gramatki, I., Watt, W. and Fujiwara, D. (2021) 'Does volunteering make us happier, or are happier people more likely to volunteer? Addressing the problem of reverse causality when estimating the wellbeing impacts of volunteering', *Journal of Happiness Studies*, 22: 599–624, https://doi.org/10.1007/s10902-020-00242-8.

Lee, C. (2022) 'Which voluntary organizations function as schools of democracy? Civic engagement in voluntary organizations and political participation', *Voluntas*, 22: 242–55, https://doi.org/10.1007/s11266-020-00259-w.

Lee, S., Harris, B., Stickland, N. and Pesenti, S. (2017) *Taken on Trust: The Awareness and Effectiveness of Charity Trustees in England and Wales*. Report. Bootle and London: The Charity Commission, Cass Business School and Worshipful Company of Management Consultants.

Leonard, P. and Wilde, R. (2019) *Getting in and Getting on in the Youth Labour Market: Governing Young People's Employability in Regional Context*. Bristol: Policy Press.

Letwin, O. (2003) *The Neighbourly Society*. London: Centre for Policy Studies.

Li, Y. (2015) 'The flow of soul: a sociological study of generosity in England and Wales, 2001–2011', in Y. Li (ed.) *The Handbook of Research Methods and Applications on Social Capital*. Cheltenham: Edward Elgar, pp. 40–59.

Li, Y., Savage, M. and Pickles, A. (2003) 'Social capital and social exclusion in England and Wales (1972–1999)', *British Journal of Sociology*, 54(4): 497–526, https://doi.org/10.1080/0007131032000143564.

Lim, C. and Laurence, J. (2015) 'Doing good when times are bad: volunteering behaviour in economic hard times', *British Journal of Sociology*, 66(2): 319–44, https://doi.org/10.1111/1468-4446.12122.

Lindsey, R. (2013) 'Exploring local hotspots and deserts: investigating the local distribution of charitable resources', *Voluntary Sector Review*, 4(1): 95–116, https://doi.org/10.1332/204080513X661563.

Lindsey, R. and Bulloch, S. (2013) 'What the public think of the Big Society: Mass Observers' views on individual and community capacity for engagement', TSRC Working Paper 95, Birmingham:

Third Sector Research Centre, www.birmingham.ac.uk/generic/tsrc/documents/tsrc/working-papers/working-paper–95.pdf.

Lindsey, R. and Mohan, J. (2018) *Continuity and Change in Voluntary Action*. Bristol: Policy Press.

Low, N., Butt, S., Ellis Paine, A. and Davis Smith, J. (2007) *Helping Out: A National Survey of Volunteering and Charitable Giving*. London: Cabinet Office, Office of the Third Sector.

Lynn, P. (1994) 'Measuring voluntary activity', *Non-Profit Studies*, 1(2): 1–11.

Lynn, P. and Davis Smith, J. (1991) *The 1991 National Survey of Voluntary Activity in the UK*. Berkhamsted: Volunteer Centre.

Lyons, M., Wijkstrom, P. and Clary, G. (1998) 'Comparative studies of volunteering: what is being studied?', *Voluntary Action*, 1(1): 45–54.

Macduff, N. (2005) 'Societal changes and the rise of the episodic volunteer', in J. Brudney (ed.) *Emerging Areas of Volunteering: ARNOVA Occasional Paper Series 1(2)*. Indianapolis, IN: ARNOVA, pp. 49–61.

Macgillivray, A., Wadhams, C. and Conaty, P. (2001) *Low Flying Heroes: Micro-Social Enterprise below the Radar Screen*. London: New Economics Foundation.

Mackenzie, M., Skivington, K. and Fergie, G. (2020) '"The state they're in": unpicking *fantasy paradigms* of health improvement interventions as tools for addressing health inequalities', *Social Science and Medicine*, 256: 113047, https://doi.org/10.1016/j.socscimed.2020.113047.

Macmillan, R. (2013) 'Making sense of the Big Society: perspectives from the third sector', TSRC Working Paper 90, Birmingham: Third Sector Research Centre, www.birmingham.ac.uk/generic/tsrc/documents/tsrc/working-papers/working-paper–90.pdf.

Maddrell, A. (2000) '"You just can't get the staff these days": the challenges and opportunities of working with volunteers in the charity shop – an Oxford case study', *International Journal of Nonprofit and Voluntary Sector Marketing*, 5(2): 125–39, https://doi.org/10.1002/nvsm.105.

Mahony, N. and Northrop, F. (2020) 'This Participatory City ain't pretty', *Municipal Enquiry*, 26 July, www.municipal-enquiry.org/post/this-participatory-city-ain-t-pretty.

Mak, H.W. and Fancourt, D. (2021) 'Predictors of engaging in voluntary work during the COVID-19 pandemic', *Perspectives in Public Health*, 142(5), https://doi.org/10.1177/1757913921994146.

Maloney, W., van Deth, J.W. and Roßteutscher, S. (2008) 'Civic orientations: does associational type matter?', *Political Studies*, 56(2): 261–87, https://doi.org/10.1111/j.1467-9248.2007.00689.x.

Mao, G., Fernandes-Jesus, M., Ntontis, E. and Drury, J. (2021) 'What have we learned about COVID-19 volunteering in the UK? A rapid review of the literature', *BMC Public Health*, 21(1470), https://doi.org/10.1186/s12889-021-11390-8.

Marmot, M., Allen, J., Boyce, T., Goldblatt, P. and Morrison, J. (2020) *Health Equity in England: The Marmot Review 10 years on*. Report. London: Institute of Health Equity.

Marshall, T. H. (1950) *Citizenship and Social Class*. Cambridge: Cambridge University Press.

Martin, J. and Franklin, J. (2022) *Fuller Measures of Output, Input and Productivity in the Nonprofit Sector: A Proof of Concept*. Economic Statistics Centre of Excellence (ESCoE) discussion paper DP 22-4, London: ESCoE, https://escoe-website.s3.amazonaws.com/wp-content/uploads/2022/10/20170621/ESCoE-DP-2022-24.pdf.

May, T. (2017) 'The shared society: Prime Minister's speech at the Charity Commission annual meeting', 9 January, London: Gov.uk, www.gov.uk/government/speeches/the-shared-society-prime-ministers-speech-at-the-charity-commission-annual-meeting.

McCabe, A. and Phillimore, J. (eds) (2017) *Community Groups in Context: Local Activities and Actions*. Bristol: Policy Press.

McCulloch, A. (2011) 'Volunteering as unpaid work or unpaid help: differences in reports of voluntary activity', TSRC Working Paper, University of Southampton.

McCulloch, A. (2014) 'Cohort difference in voluntary association membership in the UK', *Sociology*, 48(1): 167–85, http://dx.doi.org/10.1177/0038038513481643.

McCulloch, A., Mohan, J. and Smith, P. (2012) 'Patterns of social capital, voluntary activity, and area deprivation in England', *Environment and Planning A*, 44(5): 1130–47, https://doi.org/10.1068/a44274.

McDonnell, D., Mohan, J. and Norman, P. (2020) 'Charity density and social need: a longitudinal perspective', *Nonprofit and Voluntary Sector Quarterly*, 49(5): 1082–104, https://doi.org/10.1177/0899764020911199.

McDonnell, D., Rutherford, A. and Mohan, J. (2023) 'The impact of COVID-19 on the formation and dissolution of charitable organisations', in J. Rees, R. Macmillan, C. Dayson, C. Damm and C. Bynner (eds) *COVID-19 and the Voluntary and Community Sector in the UK: Responses, Impacts and Adaptation*. Bristol: Policy Press, pp. 45–60.

McPherson, J. M. (1981) 'A dynamic model of voluntary affiliation', *Social Forces*, 59(3): 705–28, https://doi.org/10.2307/2578190.

Meier, S. and Stutzer, A. (2008) 'Is volunteering rewarding in itself?', *Economica*, 75(297): 39–59, https://doi.org/10.1111/j.1468-0335.2007.00597.x.

Meyer, M. and Rameder, P. (2022) 'Who is in charge? Social inequality in different fields of volunteering', *Voluntas*, 33(1): 18–32, https://doi.org/10.1007/s11266-020-00313-7.

Miliband, D. (2006) Keynote speech at NCVO annual conference 2006.

Mohan, J. and Bennett, M. (2019) 'Community-level impacts of the third sector: does the local distribution of voluntary organisations influence the likelihood of volunteering?', *EPA: Economy and Space*, 51(4): 950–79, https://doi.org/10.1177/0308518X19831703.

Mohan, J. and Bulloch, S. (2012) 'The idea of a "civic core": what are the overlaps between charitable giving, volunteering, and civic participation in England and Wales?', TSRC Working Paper 73, Birmingham: Third Sector Research Centre, www.tsrc.ac.uk/Research/QuantitativeAnalysis/Theideaofaciviccore/tabid/879/Default.aspx.

Mohan, J., Barnard, S., Jones, K. and Twigg. L. (2004) *Social Capital, Place and Health*. London: Health Development Agency.

Mohan, J., Twigg, L., Jones, K. and Barnard, S. (2006) 'Volunteering, geography and welfare: a multilevel investigation of geographical variations in voluntary action', in C. Milligan and D. Conradson (eds) *Landscapes of Voluntarism: New Spaces of Health, Welfare and Governance*. Bristol: Policy Press.

Moores, C. (2014) 'Society's volunteers', review essay, *History Workshop Journal*, 77(1): 326–30, https://doi.org/10.1093/hwj/dbu008.

Morgan Grenville, R. (2023) *Across a Waking Land*. London: Icon.

Morris, D. (1999) 'Volunteering: a nice little job for a woman?', in A. Morris and T. O'Donnell (eds) *Feminist Perspectives on Employment Law*. London: Cavendish, pp. 113–38.

Moseley, A., James, O., John, P., Richardson, L., Ryan, M. and Stoker, G. (2018) 'The effects of social information on volunteering: a field experiment', *Nonprofit and Voluntary Sector Quarterly*, 47(3): 583–603, https://doi.org/10.1177/0899764017753317.

Musick, M. and Wilson, J. (2008) *Volunteers: A Social Profile*. Bloomington: Indiana University Press.

Nash, V. (2002) 'Laying the ground: civic renewal and volunteering', in W. Paxton and V. Nash (eds) *Any Volunteers for the Good Society?* London: Institute for Public Policy Research, pp. 1–16.

Nathan Committee (1952) *Report of the Committee on the Law and Practice Relating to Charitable Trusts* (Chair: Lord Nathan). London: HMSO.

Natcen (National Centre for Social Research), IVR (Institute for Volunteering Research), University of Southampton, University of Birmingham and Public Zone (2011) *Formative Evaluation of v: The National Young Volunteers' Service*. London: NatCen.

NCVO (National Council for Voluntary Organisations) (annual) *Almanac of Civil Society in the UK*. London: NCVO.

Neil, R. and Sampson, R. J. (2021) 'The birth lottery of history: arrest over the life course of multiple cohorts coming of age, 1995–2018', *American Journal of Sociology*, 126(5): 1127–78, https://doi.org/10.1086/714062.

NHS England (2019) *Universal Personalised Care: Implementing the Comprehensive Model*, NHS Guidance. London: NHS England,

www.england.nhs.uk/wp-content/uploads/2019/01/universal-personalised-care.pdf.
Ní Bhrolcháin, M. and Dyson, T. (2007) 'On causation in demography: issues and illustrations', *Population and Development Review*, 33(1): 1–36, https://doi.org/10.1111/j.1728-4457.2007.00157.x.
Nichols, G. and Ralston, R. (2011) 'Social inclusion through volunteering: the legacy potential of the 2012 Olympic Games', *Sociology – the Journal of the British Sociological Association*, 45(5): 900–14, https://doi.org/10.1177/0038038511413413.
Nicol Economics (2019) *An Economic Estimate of theValue of People Power*. London: Nicol Economics, https://media.nesta.org.uk/documents/An_economic_analysis_of_the_value_of_people_power.pdf.
Norman, J. (2010) *The Big Society:The Anatomy of the New Politics*. Buckingham: University of Buckingham Press.
O'Brien, C. R. (2011) 'Drudges, dupes and do-gooders? Competing notions of "value" in the Union's approach to volunteers', *European Journal of Social Law*, 1(1): 49–75.
O'Dwyer, E. (2020) 'Covid-19 mutual aid groups have the potential to increase intergroup solidarity – but can they actually do so?', blog, *LSE British Politics and Policy*, London: LSE, https://blogs.lse.ac.uk/politicsandpolicy/covid19-mutual-aid-solidarity/.
O'Reilly, D., Rosato, M., Ferry, F. and Leavy, G. (2017a) 'Caregiving, volunteering or both? Comparing effects on health and mortality using census-based records from almost 250,000 people aged 65 and over', *Age and Ageing*, 46(5): 821–6, https://doi.org/10.1093/ageing/afx017.
O'Reilly, D., Rosato, M., Moriarty, J. and Leavey, G. (2017b) 'Volunteering and mortality risk: a partner-controlled quasi-experimental design', *International Journal of Epidemiology*, 46(4): 1295–302, https://doi.org/10.1093/ije/dyx037.
O'Toole, M. and Calvard, T. (2020) 'I've got your back: danger, volunteering and solidarity in lifeboat crews', *Work, Employment and Society*, 34(1): 73–90, https://doi.org/10.1177/0950017019862962.
O'Toole, M. and Grey, C. (2016) 'Beyond choice: "thick" volunteering and the case of the Royal National Lifeboat Institution', *Human Relations*, 69(1): 85–109, https://doi.org/10.1177/0018726715580156.
Ockenden, N. (ed.) (2007) *Volunteering Works: Volunteering and Social Policy*. Norwich: The Institute for Volunteering Research and Volunteering England.
Oesterle, S., Kirkpatrick Johnson, M. and Mortimer, J. T. (2004) 'Volunteerism during the transition to adulthood: a life course perspective', *Social Forces*, 82(3): 1123–49, https://doi.org/10.1353/sof.2004.0049.
ONS (Office for National Statistics) (2017) *Changes in the Value and Division of Unpaid Volunteering in the UK: 2000 to 2015*,

www.ons.gov.uk/economy/nationalaccounts/satelliteaccounts/articles/changesinthevalueanddivisionofunpaidcareworkintheuk/2015#valuation-of-unpaid-formal-volunteering.

Overgaard, C. (2019) 'Rethinking volunteering as a form of unpaid work', *Nonprofit and Voluntary Sector Quarterly*, 48(1): 128–45, https://doi.org/10.1177/08997640221127947.

Overgaard, C. and Kerlin, J. A. (2022) 'A legally-informed definition of volunteering in nonprofits and social enterprises: unpaid work meets profit motives', *Nonprofit Management and Leadership*, 32(3): 429–47, https://doi.org/10.1002/nml.21489.

Pahl, R. (1988) *On Work*. Oxford: Blackwell.

Parry, J., Brookfield, K. and Bolton, V. (2021) '"The long arm of the household": gendered struggles in combining paid work with social and civil participation over the lifecourse', *Gender, Work & Organization*, 28(1): 361–78, https://doi.org/10.1111/gwao.12569.

Pattie, C., Seyd, P. and Whiteley, P. (2004) *Citizenship in Britain: Values, Participation and Democracy*. Cambridge: Cambridge University Press.

Paz-Fuchs, A. and Eleveld, A. (2016) 'Workfare revisited', *Industrial Law Journal*, 45(1): 29–59, https://doi.org/10.1093/indlaw/dwv030.

Pearson, H. (2016) *The Life Project*. London: Allen Lane.

Penny, R. and Finnegan, A. (2019) 'Employability or self-respect? Justifying the use of volunteering to address unemployment', *Voluntary Sector Review*, 10(2): 151–65, https://doi.org/10.1332/204080519X15623206535256.

Petrillo, M. and Bennett, M. (2023) *Valuing Carers 2021: England and Wales*. London: Carers UK.

Petrovski, E., Dencker-Larsen, S. and Holm, A. (2017) 'The effect of volunteer work on employability: a study with Danish survey and administrative register data', *European Sociological Review*, 33(3): 349–67, https://doi.org/10.1093/esr/jcx050.

Plagnol, A. and Huppert, F. (2010) 'Happy to help? Exploring the factors associated with variations in rates of volunteering across Europe', *Social Indicators Research*, 97(2): 157–76, https://doi.org/10.1007/s11205-009-9494-x.

Portes, A. (1998) 'Social capital: its origins and applications in modern sociology', *Annual Review of Sociology*, 24: 1–24, https://doi.org/10.1146/annurev.soc.24.1.1.

Portes, J. (2013) 'The "Help to Work" pilots: success, failure or somewhere in between?', blog, London: National Institute of Economic and Social Research (NIESR), www.niesr.ac.uk/blog/help-work-pilots-success-failure-or-somewhere-between.

Power, C. and Elliott, J. (2006) 'Cohort profile: 1958 British birth cohort (National Child Development Study)', *International Journal of Epidemiology*, 35(1): 34–41, https://doi.org/10.1093/ije/dyi183.

Prime, D., Zimmeck, M. and Zurawan, A. (2002) *Active Communities: Initial Findings from the 2001 Home Office Citizenship Survey*. London: Home Office.

Purdam, K. and Tranmer, M. (2012) 'Helping values and civic engagement', *European Societies*, 14(3): 393–415, https://doi.org/10.1080/14616696.2012.691170.

Putnam, R. D. (2000) *Bowling Alone: The Collapse and Revival of American Community*. New York: Simon and Schuster.

Putnam, R. D., Leonardi, R. and Nanetti, R. (1993) *Making Democracy Work: Civic Traditions in Modern Italy*. Princeton, NJ: Princeton University Press.

Quintelier, E. (2008) 'Who is politically active: the athlete, the scout member or the environmental activist? Young people, voluntary engagement and political participation', *Acta Sociologica*, 51(4): 355–70, https://doi.org/10.1177/0001699308097378.

Qvist, H.-P.Y. and Munk, M. D. (2018) 'The individual economic returns to volunteering in work life', *European Sociological Review*, 34(2): 198–210, https://doi.org/10.1093/esr/jcy004.

Reed, P. and Selbee, K. (2001) 'The Civic Core in Canada: disproportionality in charitable giving, volunteering and civic participation', *Nonprofit and Voluntary Sector Quarterly*, 30(4): 761–80, https://doi.org/10.1177/0899764001304008.

Roberts, J. and Devine, F. (2004) 'Some everyday experiences of voluntarism: social capital, pleasure, and the contingency of participation', *Social Politics*, 11(2): 280–96, https://doi.org/10.1093/sp/jxh036.

Rochester, C. (2013) *Rediscovering Voluntary Action*. Basingstoke: Palgrave Macmillan.

Rochester, C., Ellis Paine, A., Howlett, S. and Zimmeck, M. (2010) *Volunteering in the 21st Century*. Basingstoke: Palgrave Macmillan.

Rooney, P., Steinberg, K. and Schervish, P. (2004) 'Methodology is destiny: the effects of survey prompts on reported levels of giving and volunteering', *Nonprofit and Voluntary Sector Quarterly*, 33(4): 628–54, https://doi.org/10.1177/0899764004269312.

Rotolo, T. (2000) 'A time to join, a time to quit: the influence of life cycle transitions on voluntary association membership', *Social Forces*, 78(3): 1133–61, https://doi.org/10.2307/3005944.

Rotolo, T. and Wilson, J. (2012) 'State-level differences in volunteerism in the United States: research based on demographic, institutional, and cultural macrolevel theories', *Nonprofit and Voluntary Sector Quarterly*, 41(3): 452–73, https://doi.org/10.1177/0899764011412383.

Royston, T. (2012) 'Treating volunteers as "members of an association" and the implications for English discrimination law', *International Journal of Discrimination and the Law*, 12(1): 5–26, https://doi.org/10.1177/1358229112446367.

Russell, I. M. (2005) *A National Framework for Youth Action and Engagement*. Report of the Russell Commission, March. London: HMSO.

Sacco, L., Corna, L., Price, D. and Glaser, K. (2021) 'Pathways of participation in paid and unpaid work in mid to later life in the United Kingdom', *Ageing and Society*, https://doi.org/10.1017/S0144686X21001537.

Salamon, L. M. and Sokolowski, S. W. (2003) *Institutional Roots of Volunteering*. New York: Springer.

Salamon L. M., Anheier, H. K., List, R., Toepler, S., Sokolowski, S. W. et al. (2004) *Global Civil Society: Dimensions of the Nonprofit Sector*. Bloomfield, CT: Kumarian Press.

Salamon, L. M., Sokolowski, W. and Haddock, S. (2011) 'Measuring the economic value of volunteer work globally: concepts, estimates and a roadmap to the future', *Annals of Public and Cooperative Economics*, 82(3): 217–52, https://doi.org/10.1111/j.1467-8292.2011.00437.x.

Sampson, R. (2012) *Great American City*. Chicago: University of Chicago Press.

Sampson, R. and Ash Smith, L. (2021) 'Rethinking criminal propensity and character: cohort inequalities and the power of social change', *Crime and Justice*, 50: 13–76, https://doi.org/10.1086/716005.

Sampson, R. J., McAdam, D., MacIndoe, H. and Weffer-Elizondo, S. (2005) 'Civil society reconsidered: the durable nature and community structure of collective civic action', *American Journal of Sociology*, 111(3): 673–714, http://dx.doi.org/10.1086/497351.

Sanghera, B. (2018) 'Contributive injustice and unequal division of labour in the voluntary sector', *Sociological Research Online*, 23(2): 308–27, https://doi.org/10.1177/1360780418754905.

Seddon, N. (2007) *Who Cares? How State Funding and Political Activism Change Charity*. London: Civitas.

Shachar, I.Y., von Essen, J. and Hustinx, L. (2019) 'Opening up the "black box" of "volunteering": on hybridization and purification in volunteering research and promotion', *Administrative Theory and Praxis*, 41(3): 245–65, https://doi.org/10.1080/10841806.2019.1621660.

Shaw, J. (2021) 'Levelling up – the case for social infrastructure: lessons from Barking and Dagenham', blog, 21 July. Cambridge: Bennett Institute for Public Policy, University of Cambridge, www.bennettinstitute.cam.ac.uk/blog/case-social-infrastructure-lessons-barking-and-dag.

Sheard, J. (1995) 'From "Lady Bountiful" to "Active Citizen": volunteering and the voluntary sector', in J. Davis-Smith, C. Rochester and R. Hedley (eds) *An Introduction to the Voluntary Sector*. London: Routledge, pp. 114–27.

Sherrott, R. (1983) 'Fifty volunteers', in S. Hatch (ed.) *Volunteers: Patterns, Meanings and Motives*. Berkhampsted: The Volunteer Centre, pp. 62–143.

Simpson, F. (2020) 'Social action: Step Up To Serve fails to reach most disadvantaged young people', *Children & Young People Now*, 24 November, www.cypnow.co.uk/analysis/article/social-action-step-up-to-serve-fails-to-reach-most-disadvantaged-young-people.

Slocock, C. (2019) *People Like Us: Margaret Thatcher and Me*. London: Biteback Publishing.

Smith, S. (2010) 'Social connectedness and retirement: evidence from the UK', CMPO Working Paper Series 10/255, Bristol: Centre for Market and Public Organisation, University of Bristol.

Smith, V. (2010) 'Enhancing employability: human, cultural, and social capital in an era of turbulent unpredictability', *Human Relations*, 63(2): 279–300, https://doi.org/10.1177/0018726709353639.

Snowden, C. (2012) *Sock Puppets: How the Government Lobbies Itself and Why*. London: Institute for Economic Affairs.

Sobieraj, S. and White, D. (2004) 'Taxing political life: reevaluating the relationship between voluntary association membership, political engagement, and the State', *The Sociological Quarterly*, 45(4): 739–64, https://doi.org/10.1525/tsq.2004.45.4.739.

Stadelmann-Steffen, I. (2011) 'Social volunteering in welfare states: where crowding out should occur', *Political Studies*, 59(1): 135–55, https://doi.org/10.1111/j.1467-9248.2010.00838.x.

Staetsky, L. and Mohan, J. (2011) 'Individual voluntary participation in the UK: a review of survey information', TSRC Working Paper 6, www.birmingham.ac.uk/generic/tsrc/documents/tsrc/working-papers/working-paper-6.pdf.

Stanley, L., Tanner, W. and Treadwell, J. (2022) *The Good Life: Resetting the Relationship between Citizens, Communities and the State*. London: Onward, www.ukonward.com/reports/the-good-life/.

Stebbins, R. (2007) *Serious Leisure: A Perspective for our Times*. New Brunswick: Transaction Books.

Steptoe, A. and Fancourt, D. (2019) 'Leading a meaningful life at older ages and its relationship with social engagement, prosperity, health, biology and time use', *Proceedings of the National Academy of Sciences (PNAS)*, 116(4): 1207–12, https://doi.org/10.1073/pnas.1814723116.

Steptoe, A. and Zaninetto, P. (2020) 'Lower socioeconomic status and the acceleration of ageing: an outcome-wide analysis', *Proceedings, National Academy of Sciences*, 117(26): 14911–17, https://doi.org/10.1073/pnas.1915741117.

Stevens, D. (2011) *International 'Volunteering League Tables': Their Value in Understanding Progress towards a 'Big Society'*. London: Institute for Volunteering Research.

Stewart, R. (2023) *Politics on the Edge: A Memoir from Within*. London: Jonathan Cape.

Stolle, D. and Hooghe, M. (2005) 'Inaccurate, exceptional, one-sided or irrelevant? The debate about the alleged decline of social capital and civic engagement in western societies', *British Journal of Political Science*, 35(1): 149–67, https://doi.org/10.1017/S0007123405000074.

Streeck, W. (2017) *How Will Capitalism End?* London: Verso.

Street-Porter, J. (2011) 'Big Society? For Cameron and co, it's a big cop-out', Mailonline, 21 February, www.dailymail.co.uk/femail/article-1358986/Big-Society-For-Cameron-Co-big-cop-out.html.

Stuart, J., Kamerāde, D., Connolly, S. et al. (2020) *The Impacts of Volunteering on the Subjective Wellbeing of Volunteers: A Rapid Evidence Assessment*. Technical report. London: What Works Centre for Wellbeing and Spirit of 2012.

Sundeen, R. A., Raskoff, S. A. and Garcia, M. C. (2007) 'Differences in perceived barriers to volunteering to formal organizations: lack of time versus lack of interest', *Nonprofit Management and Leadership*, 17(3): 279–300, https://doi.org/10.1002/nml.150.

Sutcliffe, R. and Holt, R. (2011) *Who Is Ready for the Big Society?* Research report. Birmingham: Consulting in Place, www.oneeastmidlands.org.uk/sites/default/files/library/Who%2520is%2520ready%2520for%2520the%2520Big%2520Society%2520v FINAL.pdf.

Tabassum, F., Mohan, J. and Smith, P. (2016) 'Association of volunteering with mental well-being: a lifecourse analysis of a national population-based longitudinal study in the UK', *BMJ Open*, 6(8), http://bmjopen.bmj.com/content/6/8/e011327.

Tarling, R. (2000) 'Statistics on the voluntary sector in the UK', *Journal of the Royal Statistical Society, Series A*, 163(3): 255–61, https://doi.org/10.1111/1467-985X.00169.

Taylor, R. F. (2004) 'Extending conceptual boundaries: work, voluntary work and employment', *Work, Employment and Society*, 18(1): 29–46, https://doi.org/10.1177/0950017004040761.

Taylor, R. F. (2005) 'Rethinking voluntary work', in L. Pettinger, J. Parry, R. F. Taylor and M. Glucksmann (eds) *A New Sociology of Work?* Chichester: Wiley.

Taylor-Collins, E. (2022) *Girlhoods and Social Action*. PhD thesis, University of Birmingham.

Taylor-Collins, E., Harrison, T., Thoma, S. J. and Moller, F. (2019) 'A habit of social action: understanding the factors associated with adolescents who have made a habit of helping others', *Voluntas*, 30: 98–114, https://doi.org/10.1007/s11266-018-00070-8.

Thatcher, M. (1981) 'Facing the new challenge', speech to Women's Royal Voluntary Service National Conference, London, Bloomsbury Centre, transcript. London: Thatcher Archive.

Theiss-Morse, E. and Hibbing, J. R. (2005) 'Citizenship and civic engagement', *Annual Review of Political Science*, 8(1): 227–49, https://doi.org/10.1146/annurev.polisci.8.082103.104829.

ThirdSector (2023) 'Are we on the brink of a volunteering boom?', podcast transcript, *ThirdSector*, 31 March, www.thirdsector.co.uk/podcast-transcript-brink-volunteering-boom/volunteering/article/1818335.

Thoits, P. A. and Hewitt, L. N. (2001) 'Volunteer work and well-being', *Journal of Health and Social Behavior*, 42(2): 115–31.

Tibballs, S. and Slocock, C. (2023) *Defending our Democratic Space: A Call to Action*. London: Sheila McKechnie Foundation.

Tiratelli, L. and Kaye, S. (2020) *Communities vs Coronavirus: The Rise of Mutual Aid*. London: New Local, www.newlocal.org.uk/publications/communities-vs-coronavirus-the-rise-of-mutual-aid/.

Titmuss, R. (1970) *The Gift Relationship: From Human Blood to Social Policy*. London: George Allen and Unwin.

Turk, A., Tierney, S., Wong, G., Todd, J., Chatterjee, H. J. and Mahtani, K. R. (2022) 'Self-growth, wellbeing and volunteering – implications for social prescribing: a qualitative study', *SSM – Qualitative Research in Health*, 2: 100061.

UN Volunteers (2022) *2022 State of the World's Volunteerism Report: Building Equal and Inclusive Societies*. Bonn: UN Volunteers.

Valentin, F. and Hawksbee, A. (2023) *Great British National Service*. London: Onward, www.ukonward.com/wp-content/uploads/2023/08/GreatBritishNationalService-Onward.pdf.

Van der Horst, M., Vickerstaff, S., Lain, D., Clark, C. and Baumberg Geiger, B. (2017) 'Pathways of paid work, care provision and volunteering in later careers: activity substitution or extension?', *Work, Ageing and Retirement*, 3(4): 343–65, https://doi.org/10.1093/workar/waw028.

Van der Meer, T. W. and Van Ingen, E. J. (2009) 'Schools of democracy? Disentangling the relationship between civic participation and political action in 17 European countries', *European Journal of Political Research*, 48(2): 281–308, https://doi.org/10.1111/j.1475-6765.2008.00836.x.

Van Ingen, E. and Van der Meer, T. (2011) 'Welfare state expenditure and inequalities in voluntary association participation', *Journal of European Social Policy*, 21(4): 1–21, https://doi.org/10.1177/0958928711412219.

Van Ingen, E. and Van der Meer, T. (2016) 'Schools or pools of democracy? A longitudinal test of the relation between civic participation and political socialization', *Political Behavior*, 38: 3–103, https://doi.org/10.1007/s11109-015-9307-7.

Van Overbeeke, P. S. M., Koolen-Maas, S. A., Meijs, L. C. P. M. and Brudney, J. L. (2022) 'You shall (not) pass: strategies for third-party

gatekeepers to enhance volunteer inclusion', *Voluntas*, 33: 33–45, https://doi.org/10.1007/s11266-021-00384-0.
Van Willigen, M. (2000) 'Differential benefits of volunteering across the life course', *The Journals of Gerontology B*, 55(5): S308–S318, https://doi.org/10.1093/geronb/55.5.s308.
Verba, S., Lehman Schlozman, K. and Brady, H. E. (1995) *Voice and Equality: Civic Voluntarism in American Politics*. Cambridge, MA: Harvard University Press.
Vision for Volunteering (n.d.) 'About the Vision for Volunteering', www.visionforvolunteering.org.uk/about-the-vision.
Ware, A. (2012) 'The Big Society and conservative politics: back to the future or forward to the past?', *Political Quarterly*, 82(S1): 82–97, https://doi.org/10.1111/j.1467-923X.2011.02335.x.
Weinberg, J. (2021) 'Who's listening to whom? The UK House of Lords and evidence-based policy-making on citizenship education', *Journal of Education Policy*, 36(4): 576–99, https://doi.org/10.1080/02680939.2019.1648877.
Weinberg, J. and Flinders, M. (2018) 'Learning for democracy: the politics and practice of citizenship education', *British Educational Research Journal*, 44(4): 573–92, https://doi.org/10.1002/berj.3446.
Wheatley, D. (with Hardill, I. and Bickerton, C.) (2017) *Time Well Spent: Subjective Well-being and the Organisation of Time*. New York: Rowman and Littlefield.
Wilensky, H. (1961) 'Orderly careers and social participation: the impact of work history on social integration in the middle mass', *American Sociological Review*, 26(4): 521–39, https://doi.org/10.2307/2090251.
Williams, C. (2003) 'Developing community involvement: contrasting local and regional participatory cultures in Britain and their implications for policy', *Regional Studies*, 37(5): 531–41, https://doi.org/10.1080/0034340032000089086.
Wilson, J. (2012) 'Volunteerism research: a review essay', *Nonprofit and Voluntary Sector Quarterly*, 41(2): 176–212, https://doi.org/10.1177/0899764011434558.
Wilson, J. (2000) 'Volunteering', *Annual Review of Sociology*, 26(1): 215–40, https://doi.org/10.1146/annurev.soc.26.1.215.
Wilson, J. and Musick, M. (1997) 'Who cares? Toward an integrated theory of volunteer work', *American Sociological Review*, 62: 694–713, https://doi.org/10.2307/2657355.
Wilson, M. and Leach, M. (2011) *Civic Limits: How Much More Involved Can People Get?*. London: ResPublica.
Wolch, J. (1990) *The Shadow State: Government and Voluntary Sector in Transition*. New York: Foundation Center.
Wolfenden Committee (1978) *The Future of Voluntary Organisations*. Report. London: Croom Helm.

Wollebaek, D. and Selle, P. (2002) 'Does participation in voluntary associations contribute to social capital? The impact of intensity, scope, and type', *Nonprofit and Voluntary Sector Quarterly*, 31(1): 32–61, https://doi.org/10.1177/0899764002311002.

Index

Bold page numbers indicate tables, *italic* numbers indicate figures.

age
  core volunteering 80, **80**, 82
  diversity in volunteering 62
  mental health benefits of volunteering 169–71, *170*
  minority groups 63
  non-engagement in volunteering 85, *86*
  roles in organisations and 71, **72**
  socioeconomic disadvantage, older people and 118–19
  trajectories into engagement/non-engagement 125
alternative visions of voluntarism 253–6
appeals for volunteers 251–2
Asian ethnic groups 62, 63
association membership, changes in 207
attitudes towards volunteering 199, 200–5, 214

Bekkers, R. 139, 143, 144, 149, 178
benefits of volunteering 10, 133–4
  bookbinding example 1–2, 10, 15
  functions of volunteering 23
  inequalities in volunteering and 56
  for society 35
  spirit of service 250–1
  see also impacts of voluntary action
Bennett, M.R. 62, 63
Beveridge, W. 5, 11, 53, 110, 176, 198, 228, 247, 252
BHPS (British Household Panel Study) *see* British Household Panel Study (BHPS)
Big Society 6, 7, 39, 43, 94–5, 199, 205, 210–14, 215, 218–19
Binder, M. 167, 184–8, **187**
Black ethnic groups 62–3
Blair, T. 177
Blair government 94, 149, 218
Blond, P. 7, 200
blood donation rates 99–100
Blunkett, D. xii, 1, 5, 177
Bolton, V. 118, 182–8, *183*, **187**, 253
bookbinding example 1–2, 10, 15, 256
British Future's survey 236–7
British Household Panel Study (BHPS) 19, 36, 37, 114, 118, 141, 169–70, *170*, 185, 202
British Social Attitudes Survey (BSAS) 201

Brookfield, K. 87, 88–9, 90, 122
Brown government, employability as impact of volunteering and 149
BSAS (British Social Attitudes Survey) *see* British Social Attitudes Survey (BSAS)
burnout, volunteer 127

Cameron, D. 6, 94
capital, economic, cultural, social and symbolic 28–9, 73–4
non-engagement in volunteering 88
see also cultural capital; social capital
caring responsibilities 119–20
cessation of volunteering and 127
roles in organisations and 72
volunteering and 59, 60, **61**, 62
CELS (Citizenship Education Longitudinal Study) *see* Citizenship Education Longitudinal Study (CELS)
charities
core giving 76–7, 78, **79**, 80
public funding of 47–8
volunteering in 46
children in households 60, **61**, 62, **72**
circumstances
caring responsibilities 119–20
family/household 112
influence on participation 58, 250
life-course transitions 112, 119–24, 130
longitudinal studies on 112–17
persistence in volunteering 117–19
reasons for moves to non-engagement/engagement 124–8, 129–30

retirement, effect on volunteering 119–21, 130
socioeconomic 112, 117–19
citizenship education 223–5
Citizenship Education Longitudinal Study (CELS) 153–4
Citizenship Survey 6, 18–19, 36, 37, 41, 60, 100, 105
City Year initiative, USA 177–8
civic core 75
see also core volunteering
civic engagement
democracy, volunteering and 178–9
early adulthood, volunteering in 182–4, *183*
group membership **187**
interest in politics 184–8
longitudinal studies **87**, 181–8, *183*
measurement issues 180–1
National Citizen Service (NCS) programme 188–9
political party support 186, 188
type of volunteering and 180
volunteering as promoting 176–8, 189–91
civic voluntarism model 75–6
civil society paradigm 21–2
class 57–8, 65, 118, *183*, 183–4
see also socioeconomic status
Coalition government 94–5, 177
Big Society 199, 210–14
employability as impact of volunteering 148
goals and targets 222
National Citizen Service (NCS) programme 224
nudging 226–8
volunteering and 5
commencement of volunteering 125, 129
communities, Big Society and 213–15

community-based groups, volunteering in 47
community-level variations in volunteering
 blood donation 99–100
 census data on Northern Ireland 99, *100*
 compositional influence 96
 contextual factors 96–7
 data sources 97
 deprivation and 100–1, *102*, *103*, 104, 106, 107, 108
 distribution of voluntary organisations 106, 107–8
 ethnic heterogeneity 106
 government policy and 94–5, 110
 individual-level variations 104–5
 multi-level effects 104–8
 Place Survey 2008 97–9
 regional patterns 100–1
 residential stability 106, 107
 social mix of communities 95–6
 spirit of service and 249
 time, patterns over 100–1
 urban/rural areas 107, 108
Community Life Survey 6, 18–19, 20, 36, 37, 39–40, 41, 60, 70, 76, 100, 234, 236
community punishment orders (CPOs) 157
community service, mandated 17
compulsion 17–18, 31, 225–6
Conservative governments
 COVID-19 response 219–20
 employability as impact of volunteering 147
 rhetoric used to endorse volunteering 217–20
 volunteering and 6, 39
constant, serial, trigger typology 122

Cooke, G. 255, 256
core volunteering
 age 80, **80**, 82
 defined 76
 education 80, 81, **81**, 82
 ethnicity 80, **80**
 expanding 91–2
 gender 80, **80**, 82
 geographical areas and 81–3, 92
 informal volunteering 76
 measuring 76–9, **79**
 primary 77–8
 secondary 77–8
 socioeconomic status 80, **81**, 83
 as stable feature of voluntary action 83
corporate actors 220
corporate social responsibility initiatives 31
corporate volunteering 133–4
country-level comparisons 41–3, 49
COVID-19 pandemic 6
 character of volunteering during 239–42
 COVID-19 Social Study 239–40
 England - Scotland/Wales comparison 246
 first-time volunteers 236–7, 242
 formal/informal volunteering 40, 234, 235, 236–9, 240, 242–3
 impact on volunteering 231
 individual volunteers, characteristics of 242–5
 Johnson government's response to 219–20
 levels of volunteering 233–9, 235
 long-term trends following 245
 mutual aid groups 22, 240–2, 244–5

NHS England Responder's scheme 232, 236
number of people volunteering 234–9, *235*
organisational volunteering 237–9
policy responses to 245–6
reduction in volunteering during 243–4
socioeconomic background of volunteers 244–5
trends in volunteering 39–40
volunteering during 168, 231–2
CPOs (community punishment orders) *see* community punishment orders (CPOs)
Crick Commission on Citizenship 223
cultural capital 28, 29, 88
cultural orientations with occupations 58

Dean, J. 16–17, 28, 30, 155–7, 159, 223
definition of volunteering 15–16
democracy, volunteering and 178–9
demographics, increased longevity 198–9
Department for Citizen Contribution, proposal for 255
deprivation 100–1, *102*, *103*, 104, 106, 107, 108
depth of engagement 20
De Tocqueville, A. 178
De Wit, A. 165, 166
direct benefits of volunteering 10
disability, engagement/non-engagement and 127–8
distribution of voluntary organisations 106, 107–8
diversity in volunteering
  age 62, **72**
  caring responsibilities 59
  concerns over 55–6
  dominant status model 56–7
  educational qualifications 57, 63–4, **72**
  ethnicity 58–9, **61**, 62–3, 74
  formal/informal volunteering 59
  health status 63
  household income 65, 71
  importance of 74
  lack of attention to from policymakers 74
  occupation 64–5
  of organisations 66–8
  religiosity 59, **61**, 63, **72**
  resource theory 56–7
  roles within organisations 68–73, *70*, **72**, 73
  socioeconomic status 57–8, **61**, 64–5, 69–70, **72**, 73–4
  stereotypes about volunteers 55
  temporal changes 65
  trustees 69–70
dominant paradigm 21, 22
dominant status model 27–8, 56–7

East/West Germany, reunification of 166
economic capital 28
economic circumstances 199, 205, 207–10, 214–15, 254–6
economic returns on voluntary work 43–5, 49, 153
education
  attitudes towards volunteering on retirement 202–4
  benefits of volunteering during 155–7
  compulsion, volunteering and 17–18
  core volunteering 80, 81, **81**, *82*
  diversity in volunteering 63–4, **72**
  non-engagement in volunteering 85, *86*

education (cont.)
  as predictor of volunteering 57
  school curricula, volunteering in 155–7, 223–5
  trustees 69
Ellis Paine, A. 67, 152, 153
ELSA (English Longitudinal Survey of Ageing) *see* English Longitudinal Survey of Ageing (ELSA)
employability
  employers, value of volunteering for 158–9
  engagement with initiatives by people/organisations 155–9
  frequency of engagement and 152, 153
  government policy and 146
  as impact of volunteering 225–6, 250–1
  limitations of 159–60
  longitudinal analyses 151–5
  policies and programmes 147–9
  prior qualification levels 151
  progression within the labour market 153
  reasons for unemployment 152–3
  school curricula, volunteering in 155–7
  self-reports by individuals 150–1, 159
  self-respect as benefit 161
  signalling function 146
  skills and experience acquisition 145
  social network expansion 145–6
  stratification of volunteering and 159
employers, corporate volunteering and 31, 133–4
engagement in volunteering
  core 76–83, **79**, **80–1**, *82*
  disproportionality 91
  expanding 91–2
  geography and 81–3, 92
  non-engagement 83–5, *86*, 87–90
  spirit of service and 249
English Longitudinal Survey of Ageing (ELSA) 119, 168, 243
enjoyment of volunteering 204–5, *206*
episodic volunteering 20
ethnicity
  core volunteering 80, **80**
  diversity in volunteering 58–9, **61**, 62–3, 74
  heterogeneity, community-level variations in volunteering and 106
  roles in organisations and **72**
extent of volunteering 3, 4–5

Fair Labor Standards legislation (US) 26
family expectations, gendered 127
family/household circumstances 112, 119–20
Fancourt, D. 168, 240
Finnegan, A. 147, 148, 160, 161
fish analogy 32
formal/informal volunteering 19, 29–30
  age and 62
  children in households 60, 62
  class gradient 65
  volunteering 76, **79**
  COVID-19 pandemic 40, 234, *235*, 236–9, 240, 242–3
  deprivation *102*, *103*, 104
  diversity in volunteering 59
  economic value of voluntary action 44–5
  educational qualifications 57, 63–4

household income 65
resource theory 56–7
trends in volunteering 36, 38
frequency of engagement 37, 39, 117
employability as impact of volunteering 152, 153
health benefits of volunteering 174
mental health benefits of volunteering 169, *170*
future for volunteering 11, 195, 196, 253–6

gender
core volunteering 80, **80**, *82*
engagement in voluntary action 60, **61**
family expectations and 127
minority groups 63
roles in organisations 69–70, *70*, **72**, 73
trustees 69–70, *70*
General Health Questionnaire (GHQ) 166, 169–70, *170*
General Household Survey (GHS) 36, 37, 60, 104
geographical areas, core volunteering and 81–3, 92
Gershuny, J. 205, *206*
GHQ (General Health Questionnaire) *see* General Health Questionnaire (GHQ)
GHS (General Household Survey) *see* General Household Survey (GHS)
Gini coefficient 42
goals and targets, government 221–2
governance roles 70, 220
government(s)
alternative approaches to policy 230
community-level variations in volunteering 94–5, 110
employability as impact of volunteering 146, 147, 148, 225–6
goals and targets 221–2
Help to Work programme 226
labour market policies 225–6
nudging 226–8
policy measures to encourage volunteering 216–17
relationships with voluntary sector 229
rhetoric used to endorse volunteering 216
spirit of service 228–9
support architecture for volunteering 230
volunteering and 5–9, 39
welfare systems 216
young people 223–5
gross domestic product (GDP) 42

habits 58, 111, 130
Hague, W. 220–1
Haldane, A. 4, 32, 45
Harflett, N. 24, 66–7
Harper, S. 255
health benefits of volunteering
activity undertaken and 163
COVID-19, volunteering during 168
engagement/non-engagement 127–8
frequency of engagement 169, 174
interest in 162
life satisfaction 166–8
longitudinal surveys 165, 166–8
mechanisms and analytical challenges 163–5
mental health 168–71, *170*
mortality, reduced risk of 171–3
as overstated 165
physical/cognitive 164

292 Index

health benefits of volunteering (cont.)
  psychological 164
  purpose in life 167–8
  reduction of health inequalities and 175
  reverse causation 165
  selection bias 165
  social prescribing 173–4
  status of, diversity in volunteering and 63
Help to Work programme 226
Hogg, E. 122
Holmes, K. 67
Hoskins, B. 153–4, 157
household circumstances 112
household divisions of labour 59
household income, diversity in volunteering and 65, 71
Hunting of the Snark (Carroll) 33
Hutton, W. 255
hybridisation of volunteering 31

identification of voluntary actions 18–20
Ignatieff, M. 249
impacts of voluntary action
  amount and length of volunteering 139–40
  intensity of activity 140
  measurement and analysis issues 140–4
  mechanisms affecting 137–40
  nature of voluntary activity 138–9
  organisational types and 137–8
  paradigms of voluntary action 138
  realism and 144
  reverse causation 141–2
  selection bias 141
  self-respect as benefit 161
  social capital as 139
  spirit of service 250–1
  see also employability

incentive schemes 17–18, 31
Index of Material Deprivation (IMD) 82, 100–1
indirect benefits of volunteering 10, 11
inequalities in volunteering
  age 62, **72**
  benefits of volunteering and 56
  caring responsibilities 59
  concerns over 55–6
  dominant status model 56–7
  educational qualifications 57, 63–4, **72**
  ethnicity 58–9, **61**, 62–3, 74
  health status 63
  household income 65, 71
  importance of 74
  lack of attention to from policymakers 74
  occupation 64–5
  organisations, diversity of 66–8
  religiosity 59, **61**, 63, **72**
  representation of population 56
  resource theory 56–7
  roles within organisations 68–73, **70**, **72**, 73
  socioeconomic status 57–8, **61**, 64–5, 69–70, **72**, 73–4
  temporal changes 65
  trustees 69–70
informal/formal volunteering *see* formal/informal volunteering
infrastructure for volunteering 252
(in)security, economic 255–6
International Labour Organization (ILO) 10, 15
#iwill campaign 222

job displacement, effects on engagement 209–10, 214
journeys into volunteering *see* trajectories into engagement/non-engagement
Jubilee Centre 111

Kruger report 219, 220, 244, 253

labour, volunteering and social organisation of 25–7
Labour governments
  employability as impact of volunteering 147
  goals and targets 221–2
  relationships with voluntary sector 229
  rhetoric used to endorse volunteering 218
  volunteering and 5, 7, 39
labour market 128, 207, 209, 225–6
  see also employability
Lambert, P. 58, 64, 250
language used by government 217–21
latent benefits of volunteering 10, 11
Lawton, R.N. 134, 167
Lee, S. 69, *70*
Letwin, O. 198
Li, Y. 58, 60, 62, 63, 64
life-course transitions 112, 119–24, 130
life satisfaction 45, 166–8
lifetime engagement 111
lifetimes, contributions made during 114
Lindsey, R. 22, 36, 87, 122, 213
local demographics 67–8
longevity, increased 198–9

McCulloch, A. 207, 208
Maddrell, A. 67
Mak, H.W. 240
'mandatory work activity' (MWA) 226
Marshall, T.H. 8
Mass Observation Project (MOP) 113, 121–2, 176, 177, 210–14, 215

May, T. 6
measurement of volunteering 3, 4–5, 18–20
  see also trends in volunteering
men *see* gender
mental health, benefits of volunteering and 168–71, *170*
Meyer, M. 66, 68
micro volunteering 20
Miliband, D. 5
minority groups, diversity in volunteering and 62–3
Mohan, J. 22, 36, 62, 63, 87, 99
monetary value of volunteering 43–5, 49
MOP (Mass Observation Project) *see* Mass Observation Project (MOP)
Morgan Grenville, R. xii, 3
mortality, reduced risk of 171–3
motivation for volunteering 1–2, 3, 21–2, 23–4
Musick, M. 26, 27, 58, 59, 96
mutual aid 21–2, 240–2
MWA ('mandatory work activity') *see* 'mandatory work activity' (MWA)

Nathan Committee 248
National Child Development Study (NCDS) 85, 87, 118, 182–4, 202–3
National Citizen Service (NCS) programme 111, 148, 177, 188–9, 224
national identity, spirit of service and 247–8
National Statistics Socioeconomic Classification 57
National Survey of Volunteering (NSV) 16–17, 36, 37, 201
National Trust volunteers 55, 66–7

294 Index

National Youth Social Action
  Survey 20
natural resources analogy 32
NCDS (National Child
  Development Study) see
  National Child Development
  Study (NCDS)
NCS (National Citizen Service)
  programme see National
  Citizen Service (NCS)
  programme
Neuberger, J. 10
New Deal for Young People 148
NHS England Responder's
  scheme 168, 232, 236
non-engagement in volunteering
  age 85, *86*
  barriers to volunteering 88–9,
    91
  characteristics of
    nonparticipants 88–9, 91
  community participation 90
  education 85, *86*
  extent of 84–5, *86*, 87–9
  geography and 81–3, 92
  health and 89
  lifelong 85, 87, 88–9
  reasons given for 89–90
  resource theory 88
  spirit of service and 249
norms, social, giving information
  on 226–8
Northern Ireland 99, *100*, 172–3
NSV (National Survey of
  Volunteering) see National
  Survey of Volunteering
  (NSV)
nudging 226–8

occupation, diversity in
  volunteering and 57–8, 64–5
one-off voluntary acts 20
online volunteering 20
operational roles 70
O'Reilly, D. 120

organisations
  diversity of 66–8
  roles within, diversity of 68–73,
    70, *72*
Overgaard, C. 26, 56
owner occupation 65

Pahl, R. 2
paid/unpaid work, volunteering
  and 25–7
paradigms of voluntary action
  as broad categories 23–4
  civil society paradigm 21–2
  dominant paradigm 21, 22
  functions of volunteering 23
  impacts of voluntary action 138
  serious leisure paradigm 22
parental influences on
  engagement/non-engagement
  125
parenthood, engagement/non-
  engagement and 125–6
participation in volunteering
  core 76–83, **79**, **80–1**, *82*
  disproportionality 91
  expanding 91–2
  geography and 81–3, 92
  non-participation 83–5, *86*,
    87–90
patterns of volunteering 27–9
Penny, R. 147, 160, 161
periphery see non-engagement in
  volunteering
persistence in volunteering
  117–19
personal connections 126
Place Survey 2008 97–9, *98*
political participation
  concerns over low levels 176
  democracy, volunteering and
    178–9
  early adulthood, volunteering in
    182–4, *183*
  group membership **187**
  interest in politics 184–8

longitudinal studies **87**, 181–8, *183*
measurement issues 180–1
National Citizen Service (NCS) programme 188–9
party support 186, 188
resource model and 179
social capital 179
type of volunteering and 180
volunteering as promoting 176–8, 189–91
population turnover 106, 107
Portes, A. 136
primary core 75
see also core volunteering
private initiatives to encourage volunteering 220
private sector, volunteering in 46
psychological benefits of volunteering 164
public funding of voluntary sector 21, 22
public services
boundaries with voluntary service 254
financial pressure on 229
volunteering as supporting 21, 22, 45
purity of actions 17–18
Putnam, R. 35, 90, 136, 162

qualitative/quantitative research, use of 54

Rameder, P. 66, 68
recession, effects on engagement 208–10
recognition of individual effort 255
Reed, P. 75, 76, 78
religiosity 29, 42
 diversity in volunteering 59, **61**, 63, **72**
 'visiting people' activity 71
renewable societal resource, volunteering as 31–3

replacement cost 44–5
requests to volunteer 126, 199
residential stability 106, 107
resource theory
 diversity in volunteering and 56–7
 non-engagement in volunteering 88
 spirit of service and 248–9
 trajectories into engagement/non-engagement 112
 of volunteering 27–9
responsibilities, rights and 8
retirement, effect on volunteering 119–21, 126–7, 130, 199, 202–4
reverse causation 141, 165
rewards, defining volunteering and 17–18
rights and responsibilities 8
Roberts, J. 126, 129
Rochester, C. 21
role substitution/extension 119, 120, 121
roles within organisations 68–73, *70*, **72**
Royal National Lifeboat Institution (RNLI) rescue volunteers 67
rural/urban areas 107, 108
Rutherford, A. 58, 64, 250

Sacco, L. 118, 120
Salamon, L.M. 32, 33, 35
Sampson, R. 20, 215
school curricula, volunteering in 155–7, 223–5
security, economic 255–6
Selbee, K. 75, 76, 78
selection bias 141, 165
self-employment 128
self-help as motivation for volunteering 21–2
self-respect as benefit of volunteering 161

serious leisure paradigm 22
Shachar, I.Y. 31, 32, 220
Shapps, G. 133, 134
short-term voluntary acts 20
Smith, D.H. 27
Smith, S. 119
social attitudes towards volunteering 199, 200–5, 214
social capital 28–9
  as benefit of volunteering 35
  bookbinding example 2
  employability as impact of volunteering 145–6
  impact of volunteering and 136, 139
  non-engagement in volunteering 88
  political participation and 179
social deprivation *see* deprivation
social discipline and control 8
social infrastructure for volunteering 252
social mix of communities 95–6
social networks 126, 129, 145–6, 164
social norms, giving information on 226–8
social organisation of labour, volunteering as part of 121
Social Participation and Identity Study (SPIS) 87
social prescribing 173–4
social return on investment 45
sociocultural context 42
socioeconomic changes, future of volunteering and 11
socioeconomic status
  core volunteering 80, **81**, 83
  COVID-19 pandemic 244–5
  diversity in volunteering 57–8, **61**, 64–5, 73–4
  early adulthood, volunteering during *183*, 183–4
  longitudinal patterns of volunteering and 112
  mutual aid and 244–5
  persistence in volunteering and 117–19
  roles in organisations 69–70, **72**
  spirit of service and 249–50
spirit of service
  activation of 198
  benefits of voluntary action 250–1
  community-level variations 249
  conserving 251–2
  cultivating and conserving 228–30
  different demographic groups and 252
  effects of 134
  faith in 250–1
  future visions of 253–6
  infrastructure for volunteering 252
  levels of 248–50
  meaning of 197, 247
  national identity and 247–8
  presence of as continuing 5
  proportion of population imbued with 53
  resource theory and 248–9
  rhetoric of governments 217
  security, level of 110
  stratification in volunteering 249–50
  'vitamin V' 139
SPIS (Social Participation and Identity Study) *see* Social Participation and Identity Study (SPIS)
'spurious' state dependence 117
stability in rates of engagement 34
Starmer, K. 229
start of volunteering 125, 129
state
  interventions by, attitudes towards 201–2, 213–14
  shrinkage of 253–4

state-level comparisons 41–3, 49
Steptoe, A. 118, 168
stereotypes about volunteers 55
stratification in volunteering *see* inequalities in volunteering
Streeck, W. 251
Sullivan, O. 205, *206*
Sundeen, R.A. 88
support architecture for volunteering 230
support roles 70
symbolic capital 28, 57

Tabassum, F. 118, 169–70, *170*, 174
Taylor, R. 16, 24, 25, 27, 30, 121, 146
Taylor-Collins, E. 111, 156, 200
terminology used by volunteers 2–3, 18–20
Thatcher, M. 34, 198, 201, 217
third-party initiatives 31
time spent volunteering 43–4
Time Use Surveys 204–5
Titmuss, R. 23, 34
total social organisation of labour 25
trajectories into engagement/non-engagement
  age and 125
  caring responsibilities 119–20, 127
  civic core 116
  constant, serial, trigger typology 122
  disability and 127–8
  disruptions, impact of 130
  frequency of engagement 117
  health and 127–8
  labour market, changes in 128
  life-course transitions 112, 119–24, 130
  lifetimes, contributions made during 114
  longitudinal studies on circumstances 112–17, *116*, 128
  natural switchers (moves between commitments) 123
  parental influences 125
  persistence in volunteering 117–19
  pragmatic switchers (life events determining commitment) 123
  qualitative analyses 121–4
  reasons for moves to non-engagement/engagement 124–8, 129–30
  requests to volunteer 126
  resources and 112
  retirement, effect on volunteering 119–21, 126–7, 130
  short-term, episodic commitment 123–4
  social networks 126, 129
  socioeconomic circumstances 112
  start of volunteering 125, 129
  stickers (continuous commitment) 122
  stop-starters (short-term, episodic commitment) 123–4
  transitions in volunteering status 114–15
  typologies of 122–4
  variety of 115–16, *116*
trends in volunteering 2001–2023 *38*
  country-level comparisons 41–3, 49
  COVID-19 pandemic 39–40
  decline in rates 36, 41
  difficulties identifying 34–5
  economic value of voluntary action 43–5, 49
  formal volunteering 36

trends in volunteering (cont.)
 frequency of engagement 37
 importance of identifying 35
 post-recession 37, 39
 stability over time 37, 40–1, 49
 survey data 36–7, *38*, 39–41
 time spent volunteering 43–4
 variations in estimates 36–7
 voluntary sector, volunteering in 46–8
'true' state dependence 117
trust, political participation and 179
trustees 69–70, 207–8

UKHLS (UK Household Longitudinal Survey) 19, 36, 37, 114, 151, 189, 190, 202, 204, 243
under-represented groups, volunteering by 7–8
Understanding Society 36, 63, 114, 115, 142
 see also UKHLS
unemployed people, volunteering by 7–8
unemployment-related support for volunteering (URSV) 147
 see also employability
unpaid/paid work, volunteering and 25–7
urban/rural areas 107, 108

Verkaik, D.J. 139, 143, 144, 149, 178
Verrier, D. 16–17
Vision for Volunteering 220
'vitamin V' 11, 139, 141, 152, 154, 170, 173, 251

voluntary sector
 changes in, volunteer numbers and 49–50
 future for 48
 public funding of 47–8
 transfer of large organisations to 47
 volunteering in 46–8
volunteerability 31–2
Volunteer Functions Inventory 23
volunteering
 definition 15–16
 expansion of, constraints on 253
 public's understanding of 16–18
voting *see* political participation
v youth charity 148, 150, 223–4

wage rates, effect of voluntary work on 153
welfare provision
 expenditure on, volunteering and 42–3, 228–9
 inclusive and supportive arrangements 255–6
well-being 45, 162, 167–71, *170*
 see also health benefits of volunteering
West/East Germany, reunification of 166
Wheatley, D. 60, 119–20
Williams, C. 64
Wilson, J. 26, 27, 58, 59, 68, 96
Wollebaeck, D. 138
women *see* gender
work, volunteering and 25–7
 see also employability
Work Together 148

young people 7–8, 20, 251

Printed in the USA
CPSIA information can be obtained
at www.ICGtesting.com
JSHW011728181124
73831JS00004B/13